Understanding Melville's Short Fiction

Herman Melville in 1885, three years before he began writing "Billy Budd." Gansevoort-Lansing Collection, Manuscripts and Archives Division, the New York Public Library, Astor, Lenox, and Tilden Foundations.

Understanding
Melville's Short
Fiction

A STUDENT CASEBOOK TO
ISSUES, SOURCES, AND
HISTORICAL DOCUMENTS

Claudia Durst Johnson

The Greenwood Press
"Literature in Context" Series
Claudia Durst Johnson, Series Editor

GREENWOOD PRESS
Westport, Connecticut • London

Library of Congress Cataloging-in-Publication Data

Johnson, Claudia D.

Understanding Melville's short fiction : a student casebook to issues, sources, and historical documents / Claudia Durst Johnson.

p. cm.—(The Greenwood Press "literature in context" series)

Includes bibliographical references and index.

ISBN 0–313–33129–4 (alk. paper)

1. Melville, Herman, 1819–1891—Criticism and interpretation—Handbooks, manuals, etc. 2. Short story—Handbooks, manuals, etc. I. Title. II. Series.

PS2387.J64 2005

813'.3—dc22   2004028488

British Library Cataloguing in Publication Data is available.

Library of Congress Catalog Card Number: 2004028488

ISBN: 0–313–33129–4

ISSN: 1074–598X

First published in 2005

Greenwood Press, 88 Post Road West, Westport, CT 06881

An imprint of Greenwood Publishing Group, Inc.

www.greenwood.com

Printed in the United States of America

The paper used in this book complies with the Permanent Paper Standard issued by the National Information Standards Organization (Z39.48–1984).

10 9 8 7 6 5 4 3 2 1

Copyright Acknowledgment

Jeff Eckhoff and Mark Seibert; "Des Moines Activists Ordered to Testify in US Court by Jeff Eckhoff and Mark Seibert," *The Des Moines Register* (Iowa), February 5, 2004, p. 1. Copyright 2004, reprinted with permission of *The Des Moines Register*.

Contents

Contents

Introduction

Herman Melville is best known for *Moby Dick,* a novel that has long been regarded as the first grand American epic. But most students approach Melville for the first time by reading two of his most famous short novels: "Bartleby the Scrivener" and "Billy Budd." Since the rediscovery of Melville in the second decade of the twentieth century, the canon of American literature has altered remarkably, as some writers have fallen from favor and others have been rediscovered, but the importance of these two works has not diminished, and anthologies of American literature and American fiction inevitably include them.

The timidly defiant Bartleby is an instantly recognizable icon of American culture, and his line—"I prefer not to"—is a phrase universally applied to the eternal revolt against dehumanization. In the arena of "Billy Budd," readers have seen played out the individual's continuing relationship to authority and the law—both human and divine.

Without ignoring a traditional literary approach to fiction, Greenwood's series "Literature in Context" has nevertheless candidly stressed the historical contexts and enduring issues of the works it presents. These are not only literary studies but examinations of the times out of which the literature came. "Bartleby the Scrivener" and "Billy Budd" lend themselves to such study because they are striking lessons in history—a history of the abuse of power and the struggle of the common man that is often lost or distorted. Bartleby's story is played out on Wall Street in New York City, at a time when rampant, unregulated capitalism resulted in the dehumanization of workers. And "Billy Budd" resonates with the class struggles that followed the French Revolution.

These nineteenth-century works are astonishingly pertinent to such burning issues in the twenty-first century as homelessness, money and power, working conditions, war, and civil liberties.

The study of each work begins with a traditional literary analysis of structure, characterizations, conflicts, themes, and issues. Subsequent chapters place the works in context and explore their pertinence to contemporary issues. The study of "Bartleby" includes

- Wall Street and the pursuit of wealth in both the nineteenth and the twenty-first centuries
- the office worker in the nineteenth and twenty-first centuries
- worker resistance
- religious justification of Wall Street values in the nineteenth century
- homelessness in the nineteenth and twenty-first centuries
- agoraphobia

Following a literary analysis of "Billy Budd" are chapters on

- the French Revolution
- the mutinies at the Spithead and the Nore
- the *Somers*
- the Patriot Act

Excerpts from a wide variety of documents are provided to enlarge the student's understanding of these two works of fiction. The documents provided in the "Literature in Context" series are generally materials to which the student would not have ready access in the school library. Among those used in this study of Melville are

- the last will and testament of John Jacob Astor
- an address by educator Horace Mann
- recent articles from the *New York Times*
- portraits from Charles Dickens
- poems in honor of Fitz-Greene Halleck, Astor's business manager
- sermons in praise of the pursuit of wealth
- official reports on church tenements
- an interview with an administrator working with the homeless
- an essay by Voltaire
- a list of grievances presented to the monarchy on the eve of the French Revolution
- a letter sent by the Nore mutineers to the public
- poems and songs in praise of rebellious sailors
- a chapter on the *Somers* by Thurlow Weed
- excerpts from the Patriot Act

In addition to the documents, chapters include introductory essays, possible questions and projects, and a list of further readings.

1 ───────────────────────────────

"Bartleby the Scrivener: A Story of Wall Street"

"Bartleby the Scrivener," the first short story Herman Melville published and the fourth one he wrote, appeared in the November and December 1853 issues of *Putnam's Monthly Magazine*. It is one of Melville's most important works, having generated hundreds of scholarly articles and books devoted to this one story alone. So universal and compelling is its meaning that literary critics have convincingly identified the title character and the narrator with such diverse figures as Don Quixote, Nathaniel Hawthorne, Ralph Waldo Emerson, Henry David Thoreau, Edgar Allan Poe, Charles Dickens, Melville himself, and Jesus Christ. In the tale, an elderly lawyer, whose chambers are located near the stock exchange and are solely devoted to business transactions, oversees an office of three copyists (or *scriveners*) and an office boy. His expressed intention is to write character sketches of the eccentric men, chiefly Bartleby, who have worked in his office as copiers of documents. In the process he unintentionally reveals a great deal about his own character.

SETTING

The subtitle of "Bartleby the Scrivener" is "A Story of Wall Street," reference to an area in lower Manhattan Island that was then, and is now, the heart of the nation's finances, encompassing the New York Stock Exchange, brokerage houses, commodity exchanges, mortgage houses, banks, and offices, like the narrator's, that handled the legal affairs of these financial institutions. West of the stock exchange, also located on Wall Street, is the Episcopal Trinity Church, which the narrator attends occasionally. North of the immediate area around Wall Street are located public buildings in which the city's business is conducted: city hall, courthouses (where one of the clerks sometimes does business), and the combined courthouse and prison known as the Tombs, where Bartleby ends his life. The action of the story remains in this area. Though the narrator makes reference to his "dwelling," nothing domestic, no wives or children or extended family or homes, are involved in the story we are told. When the narrator wants to escape the embarrassment of Bartleby's remaining in his vacated chambers, he does not go home, but drives around the area—the "upper part of town," Manhattanville and Astoria, and across the river to Jersey City and Hoboken in New Jersey.

The business of the office where most of the story occurs is to conduct title searches and the drawing up of business documents: bonds, mortgages, and deeds.

STRUCTURE

The tale that unfolds against the background of lower Manhattan is loosely organized into several parts, beginning with the narrator's statement of intent—to tell the story of some of the copyists he has hired in his many years in business. The irony is that his intentions go awry. Despite his aim, the story ends up being primarily about himself. Bartleby, the title character, does not appear until nine pages into the short story.

Following the narrator's statement of intent is his introduction of himself to his reader: he cites his life philosophy and the peculiar nature of his law practice. He boasts gently of his reputation; drops the name of John Jacob Astor, for whom he has done business; mentions his brief position as a Master in Chancery; and gives a physical description of his office.

Three characterizations of his employees follow his introduction of himself: of his oldest copier, Turkey; of his second copier, Nippers; and of his office boy, Ginger Nut. Most of his attention is directed to Bartleby, the third scrivener to join the chambers.

The initiating circumstance or irritant that upsets the orderly business of the office and interrupts the flow of the narrator's life is Bartleby's refusal to perform a chore, correcting copy, expected of all scriveners. The action rises from this event, incorporating the dual, intertwined strands of Bartleby's increasing resistance and the narrator's heightened rationalization of his own refusal to act decisively. The story ends in Bartleby's death.

The culmination of the story of Bartleby and the narrator is the final paragraph of rumor about Bartleby's past, which throws light on their behavior and the human condition in general.

THE IRONIC NARRATOR

While Bartleby is the title character as well as the most memorable, even classic, character, immortalized with his phrase "I prefer not to," this is chiefly the tale of the unnamed ironic narrator. For it is he who, within the frame of the narrative, is met with a life-changing challenge. Bartleby is crucial to the story as an agent, a test of the narrator's potential, as old as he is, to leave his self-protective cocoon, to rise above ego, and to join life in the performance of a supremely humane act. The reading at hand argues that, while the narrator's humanity is stirred by Bartleby, he fails the test.

An ironic narrator is one whose own words reveal to the reader more than the narrator realizes himself. A first grader in show-and-tell may reveal far more to the teacher, in a story about a family event, than the child understands him- or herself. So it is with the narrator of "Bartleby," whose descriptions of himself and others disclose attitudes, values, and rationalizations that lead the reader to conclusions lost on the person telling the tale.

In this, "A Story of Wall Street," Wall Street and the narrator are synonymous. Its life is his life. Its work is his work. Its values are his values. Their world is ruled by the accumulation of capital by a few. All other humane instincts are secondary to that single-minded pursuit. Passion, sympathy, emotion, and creativity are merely hindrances.

The narrator's initial self-portrait is of a Wall Street man who, though elderly, has never issued out into the realm of the living. This he reveals in what he sees as the key to his character: "Imprimis: [legalese for "in the first place"] I am a man who, from his youth upwards, has been filled with a profound conviction that the easiest way of life is best" (McCall, *Melville's Short Novels*, 4). While other lawyers may deal with life-and-death measures, some even fighting for justice in a "turbulent" arena, the narrator allows "nothing of that sort to invade my peace" (4). The words he chooses suggest that, metaphorically, he has never issued out of the womb: "cool tranquillity," "snug retreat," "safe," "prudence" (4). This safety is what he sees as serving the best interests of his own pocketbook and those of his Wall Street clients.

Like the particular society he serves, he values above all else money and the reputation that brings in money. His icon is not Jesus Christ but John Jacob Astor, the fur-trade and real estate multimillionaire who most surely represented the corruption and greed of unchecked nineteenth-century capitalism. The narrator repeats Astor's name like a mantra because, he says, "it rings like unto bullion" (4).

The narrator reveals volumes about himself in his mention of the Master in Chancery. This old sinecure, bestowed as a political favor, paid handsomely but required very little work: "It was not a very arduous office, but very pleasantly remunerative" (4). The narrator was honored with the position shortly before Bartleby came to work for him, but after only a few years, the office of Master in Chancery was abolished, depriving him of the handsome funds he had received and expected he could depend on for the rest of his life. What the narrator has to say about this is self-revealing. He reiterates that he is a calm, safe man who rarely loses his temper, one especially, he says, who never "indulge[s] in dangerous indignation at wrongs and outrages" (4). So, he makes clear, injustice doesn't anger him, but losing a salary for which he didn't have to work infuriated him.

His law office is symbolic of his existence. It is, as he writes, "deficient in what landscape painters call 'life' " (5). The window looks out at a tall, black wall, built within 10 feet of the window, giving one the impression of looking out at a "cistern" or grave (5).

Later, after Bartleby has become ensconced in the narrator's office, we and even the narrator see the cold, mechanical character of Wall Street. It comes to the narrator that murder, like the one committed by John C. Colt, was far more likely to occur in a solitary office on Wall Street that lacks "humanizing domestic associations" (34) than in a neighborhood made up of friends and family.

TURKEY AND NIPPERS

The narrator, in the process of describing his reaction to his employees, exposes aspects of his character of which he seems to be oblivious. To know these men, it is essential to know their work and their times. They toiled in the narrator's office in the days before typewriters, copying machines, and computers. It was work that had to be handwritten with a pen dipped in ink. For six days a week they worked making four copies each of 500-page documents, "closely written in a crimpy hand" (12), which they were then required to proofread for errors. For their work, they were paid four cents for 100 words of finished correct copy. They were not paid by the hour. Nor were they paid for pages on which spilled ink or made errors. Such pages had to be rewritten. Notice that the narrator says of Turkey's frequent blots on the page that most of his money went for "red ink" (9). Nor were they paid for the arduous, deadly process of proofreading four copies of their 500-page documents.

Both the narrator's scriveners—Turkey, the elderly man of long tenure, and Nippers, the 25-year-old man of hopeless aspirations—obviously suffer from intense poverty. Turkey's clothes are ragged and filthy. Nippers moonlights for extra money but necessarily labors under debts. Mysterious men, probably bill collectors, come to the narrator's office in search of him. While Turkey's economic tragedy is his poverty in old age, Nippers's tragedy is facing an economic dead end even in his youth. Turkey is a constant reminder to Nippers that life will probably never improve. As the narrator observes upon Nippers's displeasure with the height of his writing table, "if he wanted anything, it was to be rid of a scrivener's table altogether" (8).

On top of the intense poverty and hopelessness, Turkey and Nippers suffer from very real physical infirmities. Turkey is, without a doubt, an alcoholic. He functions well in the mornings, but in the afternoons, after he has been out for his lunch, his face turns bright red, he begins to make mistakes on every page, and he becomes noisy, even unruly. Obliquely referring to Turkey's outlay for liquor, the narrator speculates that "a man with so small an income could not afford to sport such a lustrous face and a lustrous coat at one and the same time" (9). Nippers's physical disorder, like Turkey's alcoholism, is likely a byproduct of his poverty. He is doubtless plagued by stomach ulcers. Opposite of Turkey, Nippers is irritable and in intense discomfort in the mornings, before he has put food in his stomach. After lunch, he is calm and productive.

Yet the narrator describes the poverty, illness, and despair of his two scriveners as if it were a comic opera. Moreover, he complains of Turkey's appearance and then his insolence, comparing Turkey's pride in having been given the narrator's hand-me-down coat to a horse who has been given too much oats.

Two incidents in this description of Turkey and Nippers shed light on the narrator's character and predict his later behavior toward Bartleby. First is his handling of Turkey's inability to perform in the afternoons under the influence of alcohol. When the employer suggests that the old man only come to work in the mornings, Turkey flatly refuses. The narrator, believing that "the easiest way of life is best," lets the matter drop.

The second key story in the characterizations introduces the idea of charity that will arise again in the narrator's rationalization of his treatment of Bartleby. It is essential here to examine motive. The narrator extends his charity to Turkey by providing him with a hand-me-down coat—not because Turkey might be cold and miserable and ashamed in his filthy coat, but because the coat reflects poorly on his employer's chambers, embarrassing the narrator in front of his business associates and thus damaging his reputation. His so-called charity toward Turkey comes not from concern for Turkey, but from concern about himself.

THE CHALLENGE OF BARTLEBY

The narrator's every action shows him wrapped in the lifeless, loveless grave of self, taking not the right way but the easiest way, to spare himself discomfort, rationalize his inaction, and protect his income and good name.

Into the smooth nonlife of the narrator comes the vexation called Bartleby to challenge him, to dare him to give up some small part of his materialistic comfort, to call forth his humanity.

Bartleby disrupts the Wall Street office and the Wall Street man with his *preferences*. The word is key, for any slave, including a Wall Street slave, does not have the luxury of preferences. But Bartleby *prefers* not to—will not—correct copy, that most deadly part of the scrivener's job, then prefers not to copy at all, then prefers not to leave the chambers at all. Bartleby is a puzzle, but the reaction of the narrator to the challenge that Bartleby throws in his path is equally puzzling until we remember what he has said of himself in the second paragraph: "Imprimis: I am a man who, from his youth upwards, has been filled with a profound conviction that the easiest way of life is best." Just as he refused to act, to spare himself a scene, by not pressing Turkey to leave work in his drunken afternoons, the narrator now meets the challenge of Bartleby's passive resistance with his own passive inaction.

The plight of Bartleby distinctly touches the narrator, awakening humane feelings that he has never experienced. Finding Bartleby alone in the office on a Sunday, he writes,

> For the first time in my life a feeling of over-powering stinging melancholy seized me. Before, I had never experienced ought but a not unpleasing sadness. The bond of a common humanity now drew me irresistibly to gloom. A fraternal melancholy! For both I and Bartleby were sons of Adam. (23)

At times he even convinces himself that the new purpose of his whole life is to shield Bartleby. But the real test is not whether latent feelings have been aroused, but whether he is willing to give up something he values for someone else.

RATIONALIZATIONS OF INACTION

It is important for the narrator that he rationalize what he knows is "impossible to be solved by his judgment" (17), to claim humane motives in retaining in his employ a scrivener who refuses to work. But what he really seems afraid of is a confrontation, creating a "scene," like the one Turkey threatened. His rationalization betrays the same overriding egotism and self-interest that he displayed in giving Turkey a coat. A self-referential conclusion undercuts each expression of concern for Bartleby's welfare. He argues with himself that he will keep Bartleby on because the strange man will suffer seriously if he is kicked out. But this altruistic impulse is undercut with his further observation that Bartleby won't do him any harm, and he even says, "He is useful to *me*" (17; italics mine). His choice of words betray that, in true Wall Street fashion, he puts his relationship with Bartleby in business terms, attempting, as his religious contemporaries did, to combine capitalism and theology. He will "buy" goodness for himself, but buy it "cheaply" and even "save" up the goodness from his kind acts, presumably to offset later bad behavior (17):

> Yes, here I can cheaply purchase a delicious self-approval. To befriend Bartleby, to humor him in his strange willfulness, will cost me little or nothing, while I lay up in my soul what will eventually prove a sweet morsel for my conscience. (17)

CHRISTIAN LOVE

The narrator even broaches the subject of love and charity, quoting an admonition of Jesus: "A new commandment give I unto you, that ye love one another" (34). But any hope remaining that he will be changed by love is dashed with his interpretation of the scripture. He entirely misses the point of love's selflessness. Instead, he is warmed by the prospect that "love" works to the advantage of the one who loves:

> Yes, this it was that saved *me*. Aside from higher considerations, charity often operates as a vastly wise and prudent principle—a great safeguard to its possessor.... Mere *self* interest, then, if no better motive can be enlisted, should, especially with high-tempered men, prompt all beings to charity and philanthropy. (34; italics mine)

The charity of the narrator reminds one of the wealthy philanthropist who endows a hospital or museum, certainly wishing to do some good, but also— dare one say equally?—to perpetuate his reputation and enjoy a useful tax break. But love is the extreme opposite of ego and self. One gives up something of one's self for love. One does not profit from it.

So the narrator uses, or misuses, Christian doctrine to justify his actions with regard to Bartleby. He also latches onto certain theological theories to comfort himself for failing to act. The books that "induced a salutary feeling" are *Edwards on the Will* and *Priestley on Necessity.* Both the American clergyman Jonathan Edwards and the scientist and English clergyman Joseph Priestley argued that God had predetermined everything that happened in this world before the beginning of time; therefore, human beings have scant free will. As the narrator puts it:

> Under the circumstances, those books induced a salutary feeling. Gradually I slid into the persuasion that these troubles of mine, touching the scrivener, had been all predestined from eternity. (35)

He is, in short, relieved of responsibility, because if everything is already determined, nothing he does will change anything.

FAILING THE TEST

Despite the narrator's self-congratulatory sufferance of Bartleby, he knows full well that there are limits beyond which his tolerance will not go: "So true it is, and so terrible, too, that up to a certain point the thought or sight of misery enlists our best affections; but, in certain special cases, beyond that point it does not" (24). As long as he can cheaply purchase self-approval by allowing Bartleby to remain in his office, he is taking the easiest way out of the situation, and the easiest way is supremely important to him. But what happens when he is called upon to sacrifice something that really matters to him? When the price is no longer cheap but expensive? When his goodwill toward Bartleby costs him something he values greatly? That moment does inevitably arrive. And not to the reader's great surprise, the narrator capitulates. For Bartleby's bizarre presence in his chambers begins to threaten his reputation and his ability to do business.

> I believe that this wise and blessed frame of mind would have continued with me, had it not been for the unsolicited and uncharitable remarks obtruded upon me by my professional friends who visited the rooms. But thus it often is, that the constant friction of illiberal minds wears out at last the best resolves of the more generous. (35)

In a supremely passive action, when Bartleby refuses to leave the office peaceably, the narrator moves out himself, leaving his strange employee behind. The narrator, Bartleby, and the reader realize that the invitation to Bartleby to "come home with me now" is too little offered too late (41). On his part, Bartleby's supreme act of passive resistance is to starve himself to death.

SCRIPTURAL REFERENCES

The narrator refers to his attendance at Trinity Church, which lies at the head of Wall Street, and to the commandment of Jesus that we love one another. There are further indirect but unmistakable biblical references that suggest that the narrator fails to sustain genuine, loving, selfless humanity. One reference is to Matthew 25. Here, Jesus says in effect that how one treats one's fellow human beings, especially the lowliest among us (like Bartleby), is how one treats Jesus himself. Jesus says,

> For I was an hungred and ye gave me meat: I was thirsty, and ye gave me drink: I was a stranger, and ye took me in: Naked, and ye clothed me: I was sick, and ye visited me: I was in prison, and ye came unto me. (King James Version, 25: 35–36; all subsequent quotations are also from this version)

Jesus' hearers then ask him,

> Lord, when saw we thee an hungred, and fed thee? or thirsty, and gave thee drink? (25:37)

Jesus answers them,

> Verily I say unto you, Inasmuch as ye have done it unto one of the least of these my brethren, ye have done it unto me. (25:45)

The narrator, ironically, has clothed Turkey and now visits Bartleby in prison and tries to feed him, but his own reputation and comfort have always been foremost in his mind, and he has essentially abandoned Bartleby in his old office.

Another obvious biblical reference leads the reader to compare the narrator's denial of Bartleby to Peter's denial of Jesus. After the narrator has moved his office, the new tenants accost him, accusing him of being responsible for Bartleby—which, of course, he is, in a philosophical sense. But the narrator denies all association with Bartleby. " 'I am very sorry, sir,' said I, with assumed tranquillity, but an inward tremor, 'but, really, the man you allude to is nothing to me—he is no relation or apprentice of mine, that you should hold me responsible for him' " (38). The scene is a direct reference to Peter, Jesus' disciple, denying all knowledge of his friend and mentor after Jesus has been arrested. On the night of Jesus' arrest, a woman who recognizes Peter approaches him and asks him if he isn't the friend of Jesus. Then, according to the Gospel of Mark, "he denied, saying, 'I know not, neither understand I what thou sayest'.... And he denied it again.... But he began to curse and to swear, saying, 'I know not this man of whom ye speak' " (14:68–71).

DEAD LETTERS

In the final paragraph, the narrator states that he believes he has discovered something of Bartleby's past. In the rumor that he had worked as a clerk in the Dead Letter Office in Washington, D.C., much of the meaning of the dead scrivener and the other characters begins to unfold. The narrator explains that Bartleby's job there was to burn letters that were undeliverable. The dreadful significance of this can only be understood if one has a full grasp of the critical importance of the mail at a time when it provided the only means of long-distance communication. Consider that one is living at this time and has to communicate something of import to someone several states away or even across state. There are no cars to leap into to carry the message in person, few trains (none transcontinental), no airplanes that would allow someone to quickly reach a friend or relative in distress. There were no telephones, and certainly no e-mails. Telegraph service was a fledgling technology not readily available to the general public. The postal service bore the full burden of long-distance communication.

It was Bartleby's job to burn undeliverable letters, many of which would have saved lives and lifted people out of desperation:

> For by the cart-load they are annually burned. Sometimes from out the folded paper the pale clerk takes a ring—the finger it was meant for, perhaps molders in the grave; a bank-note sent in swiftest charity—he whom it would relieve, nor eats nor hungers any more; pardon for those who died despairing; hope for those who died unhoping, good tidings for those who died stifled by unrelieved calamities. (46)

Bartleby's job in the Dead Letter Office is a commentary on several different planes. First is its social significance, second is the story of the plight of the artist in particular, and third is the broader consideration of the human condition as it has existed since the beginning of time. The key to the paragraph's meanings lies in two statements, separated by the description of the burning of the letters:

> Dead letters! Does it not sound like dead men?...
>   On errands of life, these letters speed to death. (46)

On the social plane, these words describe what the Wall Street world has inflicted on the vast army of poverty-stricken workers who serve it—not just scriveners, but factory workers, slaves, and poor farmers. Human beings "on errands of life" are born with the capacity to hope, aspire, make decisions and choices, communicate, and create. Yet Wall Street values in a society of unbridled capitalism condemn them to poverty (as in the case of Turkey), blast their hopes for a good life (as in the case of Nippers), and turn them into robots, ciphers, drones, working at soul-deadening jobs. The copyists might well be compared with the later assembly-line workers for Henry Ford. They were born on errands of life, but this society takes away their human beingness and "speeds them to death"—long before their literal deaths.

The job of copyist is a particularly appropriate figure of the dehumanization caused by the financial world, for, though they are dealing with words, they have no words themselves. Those things that make them human have been taken away. They do not make choices in their work; they don't communicate; they are not creative.

Wall Street is an appropriate name for the setting of the story, because each of the workers has run up against a blank wall. It stops them from climbing out of poverty and debasement. Things can never be any better for the vast majority of such workers throughout the country. Notice the wall pushed up against the window of the narrator's office that Bartleby stares at, and finally the wall that he faces in the Tombs.

Another suspicion about the narrator's story of the Dead Letter Office must also be broached here. Is his insistence (that Bartleby has been emotionally crippled by his work in the Dead Letter Office) merely a way of absolving himself from his own guilt as an employee in a system that kills those on whose backs Wall Street fortunes are made?

The dead-letter lines also refer specifically to the artist/writer and are thus Melville's statement of his own condition at a time when his reading public seemed to have deserted him. Somewhat like Bartleby, Melville had sequestered himself in his room in Arrowhead, his house in western Massachusetts, even having his meals left outside his door. His family and friends, including his brother, a Wall Street lawyer, became concerned that he was mentally disturbed and tried to lure him out of his solitude to travel and perhaps take on a consulship. The Wall Street world scorned the creative writer, originally on an errand of life. For such artists were not perceived as contributing to the national economy. If writers were to achieve even a limited degree of success, they were expected to turn aside their creativity and become little more than copyists, pandering to the tastes of the reading public for literary pap. Melville, who wanted to capture a popular audience, had just tried valiantly to give the public what it wanted with his novel *Pierre*. But the communication had failed, and he had ended up with a parodic masterpiece that infuriated the public and his family as well. He had been virtually driven from the literary arena. Like the letters consigned to the flames, writers and their work, capable of healing, clarifying, and uplifting, were lost, communication rendered essentially impossible.

The lines about dead letters sounding like dead men also speak to the human condition in general, implied in the narrator's lament in his last lines, "Ah, Bartleby! Ah, humanity." Note how excruciating, how emotionally painful the narrator perceives Bartleby's job at the Dead Letter Office to be—so agonizing as to psychological cripple Bartleby for the rest of his life. "Conceive a man by nature and misfortune prone to a pallid hopelessness, can any business seem more fitted to heighten it than that of continually handling these dead letters, and assorting them for the flames?" (46). The significance for all humans is that we are all born on errands of life—to feel, to sympathize, to empathize— leaving ourselves alive and open to grievous pain. One reading the dead letters, for example, feels the pain of one dying of hunger, never having received the caring letter and money to help. Declarations of love and letters of forgiveness never reach those who so desperately need the letters. Those for whom the letters are intended labor under the conviction that no one cares enough to send help, that they haven't been forgiven or that a true love has abandoned them. The pain of human sympathy, the story argues, leads us to refuse to expose ourselves to hurt again, to deaden our feelings, cut ourselves off from others, and so relinquish our humanity.

Bartleby's story also leads us to reflect on the narrator's character. He has already inadvertently shown us parallels between himself and Bartleby. Like the narrator, Bartleby is neat and orderly, passive and careful. In a symbolic move when Bartleby first appears, the narrator even places his new employee's desk in a corner of his own large office, separated from him only by a screen.

Both the narrator and Bartleby are outside the give and take of human existence. But while the narrator supposes Bartleby has begun to "speed toward death" after his work in the Dead Letter Office, the narrator appears, from the beginning, to have sensed the potential for pain in human involvement, choosing always the snug, safe, easy life. So, though we are all on errands of life, fear of the inevitable pain of loving and caring leads us to choose death.

Unexpectedly, in this tale of routine, order, inactivity, passivity, and determinism, one finds one of America's classic rebels. Bartleby's is not the only rebellion in the narrative. His story is prefaced by the small rebellions of Nippers and Turkey. Turkey throws his pens on the floor, slaps a ginger cookie instead of a seal on a document, dares to be "insolent," and flatly refuses to have his hours cut to half a day. And Nippers dares to moonlight as a solicitor, curses over his work, and madly adjusts and readjusts the height of his writing table.

Bartleby, of course, is the classic rebel, refusing to take any orders whatsoever, in effect removing himself from the system. Even his use of the word *prefer* is a subversive act. And though on the surface Turkey and Nippers despise him for his refusal to work, they are infected with his rebellion as they also come under his influence and use the word *prefer.*

Most people of nineteenth-century America (or of any time, for that matter) seem to plod on day to day with scant objection or question, but Bartleby was, as the narrator points out, a "passive resister," like Melville's contemporary Henry David Thoreau. Given the abasement inflicted upon him by a Wall Street world and the inevitable pain of human interaction, he simply but firmly refused, starved, preferred not to.

QUESTIONS AND PROJECTS

1. To better understand ironic narration, write an episode using the voice of someone who conveys more about themselves than they understand.

2.   Write an essay on the use of the word *prefer* in the story.

3.   Examine the name the narrator uses for the three men. What is implied in the narrator's attitude by the names he calls his employees? What is the effect of his failing to provide his own name?

4.   Write your own extended definition of love, perhaps using a prime example from your own observation.

5.   Write an essay on the word *wall,* reflected in the title and used throughout the story. Consider other walls and their meanings.

6.   From the facts we are given in the story about the pay for scriveners, estimate about how much a scrivener made a week. About how much did Turkey make a week?

7.   Stage a debate about the narrator. What words best describe him? Egotistical? Weak? Sensitive? Sympathetic?

8.   As a class project, provide a copy of "Bartleby" to a psychologist and arrange for him or her to address the class on the nature of the disorder afflicting Bartleby and other characters in the story.

9.   What conclusions do you reach regarding the psychological nature of the scriveners' ailments?

10.   Write an essay on the subject of "communication" in the novel.

11.   The novel presents contrasting reactions to personal freedom and responsibility. Examine the contrasting reactions of the scriveners to being able to make decisions (even symbolic ones) and the narrator's comfort in not acting and being told that he has no free will.

12.   The narrator writes that his encounter with Bartleby in his office on Sunday morning "disqualified [him] for the time from church-going" (25). Have a discussion of why he feels "disqualified."

FURTHER READING

Ayo, Nicholas. "Bartleby's Lawyer on Trial." *Arizona Quarterly* 28 (1972): 27–38.

Barnett, Louise K. "Bartleby as Alienated Worker." *Studies in Short Fiction* 11 (1974): 379–85.

Berthoff, Warner, ed. *Great Short Works of Herman Melville,* edition 69. New York: Harper and Row, 1969.

Campbell, Marie A. "A Quiet Crusade: Melville's Tales of the Fifties." *American Transcendental Quarterly* 7 (1970): 8–12.

Cohen, Hennig. "Bartleby's Dead Letter Office." *Melville Society Abstracts* 10 (1972): 5–6.

D'Avanzo, Mario L. "Melville's 'Bartleby' and John Jacob Astor." *New England Quarterly* 41 (1968): 259–64.

Dillingham, William B. *Melville's Short Fiction.* Athens: University of Georgia Press, 1977.

Fisher, Marvin. *Going Under: Melville's Short Fiction and the American 1850s*. Baton Rouge: Louisiana State University Press, 1977.

Fogle, Richard Harter. *Melville's Shorter Tales*. Norman: University of Oklahoma Press, 1977.

Hardwick, Elizabeth. "Bartleby and Manhattan." *New York Review of Books*, July 16, 1981, 27–31.

Inge, M. Thomas, ed. *Bartleby the Inscrutable: A Collection of Commentary on Herman Melville's Tale "Bartleby the Scrivener."* Hamden, Conn.: Archon Books, 1979.

Jehlen, Myra, ed. *Herman Melville: A Collection of Critical Essays*. Englewood Cliffs, N.J.: Prentice-Hall, 1994.

McCall, Dan. *The Silence of Bartleby*. Ithaca, N.Y.: Cornell University Press, 1989.

————, ed. *Melville's Short Novels*. New York: W. W. Norton, 2001.

Newman, Lea Bartani Vozar. *A Reader's Guide to the Short Stories of Herman Melville*. Boston: G. K. Hall, 1986.

Randall, John H., III. "Bartleby vs Wall Street: New York in the 1850s." *Bulletin of the New York Public Library* 78 (1975): 138–44.

Rogin, Michael Paul. *Subversive Genealogy*. New York: Knopf, 1983.

Thomas, Brook. "The Legal Fictions of Herman Melville and Lemuel Shaw." *Critical Inquiry* 11 (1984): 24–51,

Vincent, Howard P., ed. *"Bartleby the Scrivener": A Symposium*. Kent, Ohio: Kent State University Press, 1966.

2

Wall Street and the Pursuit of Wealth

I am one of those unambitious lawyers who...do a snug business among rich men's bonds, and mortgages, and title-deeds. (4)

The importance of the business world context for "Bartleby" impresses itself upon the reader from the first, in the subtitle, "A Story of Wall Street." The story rarely moves from its setting on Wall Street and the narrator's Wall Street office, which is often "full of lawyers and witnesses, and business driving fast" (36). Its characters know each other only as business associates. The narrator, who served as a Master in Chancery, designed to bring equity to financial arrangements, does a "snug business among rich men's bonds, and mortgages, and title-deeds" (4). The god of the Wall Street world is John Jacob Astor, with whom the narrator has done business and whom he admires. Accumulating money and maintaining a reputation as a safe and solid business professional are uppermost among the narrator's ambitions. John Jacob Astor and the narrator are typical of the American Wall Street type of the 1840s and 1850s, for whom acquiring capital was the noblest of aims, never realizing the detrimental effect it was having on the American spirit.

On March 8, 1848, five years before the publication of "Bartleby," an event occurred that set off a heated discussion, continuing well into the 1850s. "Bartleby" was a part of that discussion. The event was the death of John Jacob Astor, prominently mentioned in Melville's story. The discussion, brought into open debate by Astor's death and will, was about America's veneration of wealth and the wealthy man, a figure represented by Astor in the 1840s.

THE GROWTH OF COMMERCE

So exactly what was the course of affairs that led to the accumulation of great wealth in the United States? In the eighteenth century, the chief areas of American commerce included the acquisition of land, trade in furs, and investment in ships, used largely to import European goods into the United States. Agriculture and the home industries exemplified what was essentially a rural society. By the end of the eighteenth century, however, new technology and an increase in population, with a subsequent increase in the demand for goods, caused urban factories and the building of railroads to develop at the expense of home industry. By the 1820s, the growing amount of goods made in the United States cut into the importation of foreign goods. And men with means changed their investments in ocean commerce to investments in such things as railroads, insurance, textile mills, and the development of the seemingly limitless raw materials in the West.

In the 1830s and 1840s, cities began to achieve far greater populations and importance than they had had before, and New York City assumed an ascendancy that once had belonged to Boston and Philadelphia. It was the building of the Erie Canal in 1825 that opened the floodgates of enterprise in New York City. By the late 1830s, massive amounts of goods were exported or imported through New York Harbor. Commercial houses sprang up in the wake of increased technology and trade, many concentrating on a single line of goods like textiles, metals, or real estate and depending on colossal warehouses to store commodities. Within a year of the canal's completion, 39 new banks were established in the city.

The Democratic presidencies of Andrew Jackson and then Martin Van Buren—from 1829 to 1840—generated discussion about how much power banks and the private businessmen of the country should exercise and to what extent legislation should limit the power of big business. In the 1820s and 1830s, power in both parties was held by the well-to-do: bankers, owners of large tracts of land, lawyers, merchants, industrialists. Thus, legislation was skewed to favor monopolies and the protection of and aid for businessmen. But with the term of Jackson in 1829, businessmen, especially bankers, began to feel more constrained than they had before. Banks and businesses fell victim to the Democratic Party's insistence on regulation. Calvin Colton, a probusiness Whig, described the federal government between 1829 and 1841 as ringing a message throughout the land of "Down with the Banks! Down with the Manufactories! Down with Corporations! Down with Capitalists!" (Colton, 357). In his first message to Congress, Jackson questioned the constitutionality of the Bank of the United States. In 1832, he refused to renew the bank's charter, hoping eventually for a national bank. This angered the community of finance and big business. In 1833, Jackson submitted to Congress a plan for removing government funds from the private Bank of the United States. By 1834, Northern industrialists and Southern planters had joined forces with the new Whig party against Jackson. Other of his policies were regarded as working to the detriment of financial institutions. For instance, to counter monopolies, the Supreme Court ruled against the Charles River Bridge Company, which wanted sole rights over transportation routes. Jackson left office in March of 1837 with a speech condemning monopolies and speculation. The policies of Jackson and Congress created a financial crisis shortly after he left office and Democrat Martin Van Buren became president, causing a run on banks, bank closings, high rents, and unemployment. In 1841, the presidency was in the hands of Whigs, and power again resided with the bankers and business entrepreneurs.

Despite shifts in presidential philosophies, the 20 years between the two major economic panics of the century—in 1837 and 1857—were decades of tremendous business growth. For an enterprising man of means, practices were developed to facilitate investing in promising businesses, even those far away out west. During those years, corporate stocks and bonds, investment banking houses and new securities in railroad construction, textile factories, iron factories, shipbuilding, banks, and insurance companies soared, with the cooperation of government. Political parties and the government after 1841 favored big business over all other segments of American society. Railroads, for example, provided congressmen with stock in exchange for free government land. Railroad interests received 25 million acres of public land between 1850 and 1857 without paying a penny for it.

In 1829, four percent of the population owned half the country's wealth. Four percent of the population in New York City owned 90 percent of New York's personal property. By 1845, one percent of the wealthiest New Yorkers owned 50 percent of the city's wealth. The richest four percent of the city's population owned 80 percent of the city's wealth.

By 1850, investments in American factories had risen in 20 short years from $50 million to $250 million. Fortunes continued to be made in land speculation and transportation in the North and cotton in the South. Between 1851 and 1853, 27 new banks—both savings banks and investment banks—were established in New York City alone. During this period, trading in stocks and bonds also began serious development. Stocks in the Erie Canal, railroads, banks, and coal mines were especially prominent issues. Hundreds of brokerage houses appeared in the 1850s. The whole financial community expanded into credit businesses, law offices, and a variety of insurance companies, all in the service of the stock exchange.

Among the wealthiest professions in New York were attorneys who had inherited wealth and used their law degrees primarily to manage their own vast
holdings in stocks, bonds, and real estate. Others, like the narrator of Bartleby,
were able, chiefly through family connections, to maintain thriving Wall Street
businesses, doing legal work for rich men, as the narrator says. Edward Pessen,
in *Riches, Class, and Power before the Civil War,* describes, from extensive research, a truth that emerges about the lawyer-narrator of "Bartleby":

> Even in the great cities, rich men usually classified as lawyers appear to have de-
> rived most of their wealth from fields other than the law. During the second
> quarter of the nineteenth century, lawyer-capitalists may have been attorneys in
> terms of their identifiable occupations. As wealthholders however they were pri-
> marily merchants, investors, corporate officers, and real estate owners—in ad-
> dition to being sons and sons-in-law to the rich. (58)

All this growth created the need for more capital. The emphasis now
changed from wealth in land to wealth in paper property—stocks and bonds,
mortgages, and paper currency. Most of this burgeoning investment was man-
aged by institutions, particularly the New York Stock Exchange, in collabora-
tion with banks, mortgage companies, and law offices specializing in financial
matters.

The forerunner of the New York Stock Exchange actually began in 1792 as
informal, outdoor meetings of businessmen engaged in the buying and selling of stocks, bonds, and mortgages. In 1794, the group moved to a coffee-
house on Wall Street. The area, concentrated on Wall Street and Broad Street,
became the first district in the world devoted to financial transactions. In 1817
the stock exchange moved again, formalized regulations, and took the name
of the New York Stock and Exchange Board. In the late 1830s, with New York
having become the country's leading money-market city and the center of railroad financing, the board saw the construction of a gigantic building called
the Merchants' Exchange, which could house thousands of traders. America,
from its seventeenth-century beginning, had, of course, been founded on enterprise and exploitation—the Spanish looking for gold in the South and English companies formed to make money in Virginia and Massachusetts—but
now a new tone emerged in the country, as the pursuit of profit became a defin-
ing characteristic of American life.

Thomas C. Cochran and William Miller, in *The Age of Enterprise: A Social
History of Industrial America,* describe the tenor of nineteenth-century society
in terms of business:

> In the United States each year after 1800 more and more men spent their days
> in factories and mines, on canals and railroads, tending machines, locomotives,

and steamboats, keeping account, selling commodities, digging coal, copper, lead, and iron, drilling oil and natural gas. As time passed they spent their profits, wages, and commissions on goods announced for sale in newspapers supported by business advertisements and friendly to business objectives. Their literature was issued by publishers engaged in business enterprises. Their amusements were not spontaneous street dances but spectacles staged for profit. Their colleges, founded in many areas to prepare young men for the ministry of God, became devoted to science, and their scientists became servants of business. Their public architecture concerned itself with banks, insurance offices, grand hotels for commercial travelers. Their mature philosophy discarded metaphysics—or so its practitioners claimed, describing their speculation felicitously for our pecuniary culture as the quest for the "cash value" of ideas. (1)

The business attitudes in the 1840s and 1850s paved the way for the notorious inequities of post–Civil War America. During the war, rich men could buy their way out of the war with $300, and many of the nation's barons did this: J. P. Morgan (banking), John D. Rockefeller (oil), Andrew Carnegie (steel), Philip Armour (meat-packing), and Jay Gould (railroads). The collaboration of big business and government can be seen in the notorious fraud during the war. In one case, the government paid Drexel, Morgan and Company $5 million to sell bonds, which the government could have sold directly to buyers and saved the taxpayers the huge commission.

Howard Zinn, in *The People's History of the United States*, writes of "an economic system not rationally planned for human need, but developing fitfully, chaotically out of the profit motive" (214).

JOHN JACOB ASTOR

> I was not unemployed in my profession by the late John Jacob Astor; a name which, I admit, I love to repeat; for it hath a rounded and orbicular sound to it, and rings like unto bullion. (4)

Astor probably also had contact with the narrator through his position for a time as Master in Chancery, because Astor repeatedly took legal cases to that court to foreclose on mortgages and collect debts. From the narrator's comments, we can pinpoint the time of the telling of the story to between 1848 and 1853, because he refers to Astor's having already died. The death of Astor in 1848, five years before the publication of Melville's story of Wall Street, was reported respectfully in the conservative, business-friendly press immediately after the event. But when, in April 1849, news of Astor's will surfaced, a fury of criticism hit the newsstands and other public forums. The immediate opprobrium was sparked by the conditions of his will. In the first place, Astor, easily the richest man in the United States, worth between $20 and $30 million, had left only a small fraction, some $400,000, for the public good.

In the second place, he had left pittances to his poor relations, and to Fitz-Greene Halleck, for 16 years the principal manager of Astor's monetary and business affairs, he left the grand total of $200 a year. Halleck was a beloved character and a poet in New York City, and the public, knowing full well the devotion and insight Halleck had brought to enrich Astor, was furious at Astor's ingratitude. A Wall Street lawyer named George Templeton Strong seemed to blame Astor's lawyer, Daniel Lord, for a botched document. In his diary of October 16, 1850, he writes, "Up late every night trying to understand the Astor will, a document of which Lord must be ashamed. Few papers of importance have I ever seen so full of ambiguities and so bunglingly put together" (vol. 2, 23). Halleck became, in the minds of many in the New York community, a symbol of the artist who had been silenced and betrayed by Wall Street values.

The will opened the floodgates of resentment, not only of Astor himself, but of a society where the pursuit of money was the principal value. Astor was held up as the worst example of greedy, unscrupulous behavior. To make his first fortune in the fur trade, he had ordered or allowed his agents to give and sell watered-down liquor to the Native Americans so that he could get the best possible deals in buying furs from them. Some writers declared that Astor alone was responsible for debasing the whole Native American culture. Furthermore, Astor had been a shameless profiteer during the War of 1812. He had been without morals or conscience in his pursuit of bonds and bank investments on Wall Street. He had greedily amassed tremendous amounts of land in New York City and New Jersey, enough to earn his son the title of "the landlord of New York." He was a ruthless landlord, throwing his long-term tenants out after they had made valuable improvements to his property, foreclosing on mortgages in hard economic times, and refusing to cut tenants any slack in paying their rent. He had made constant use of the city's fire brigades to protect his vast holdings in New York real estate and then had given them nothing in return. He had not been above bribing public officials in his quest for more and more power and property. Matthew Hale Smith, who knew and admired him, reported in *Sunshine and Shadow* that at the end of Astor's life, he declared, "Could I begin life again, knowing what I now know, and had money to invest, I would buy every foot of land on the Island of Manhattan" (115).

The will of John Jacob Astor was very much on Melville's mind as he approached the writing of "Bartleby." The subject of the will was discussed by those in New York City, among them Melville's family and friends, who laughed at the old man's endless codicils to his will in which he continually reduced or entirely subtracted the amount of money he had originally intended leaving to poor relations. Melville was so impressed by the will that he included a parody of it in his novel *Mardi,* a hilarious piece that he recited for the amusement of friends.

This Wall Street world, shaped by and perpetuated by the worship of money above all else, was one in which Bartleby preferred not to participate. And in Wall Street, the seat of power and influence in the country, a man like John Jacob Astor became an icon, not only to the narrator, but to many others. The reference to the narrator's being Master in Chancery sets up an interesting connection with Astor: in this court, which heard cases involving contract violations, debts, and real estate, John Jacob Astor had appeared repeatedly to foreclose on mortgages and collect debts.

The excerpts that follow demonstrate the values and the objection to those values in the mid-nineteenth century, the setting of Melville's story. An excerpt from reporter George G. Foster's 1849 book *Fifteen Minutes around New York* illustrates that some ordinary citizenry found the quest for capital on the part of a few wealthy men to be obscene and ridiculous.

An excerpt from John Jacob Astor's will, showing the many codicils and outlining his contributions to charity and to a library, indicate the sum total of his immense fortune that went to entities other than his immediate family and friends. Following Astor's will is an excerpt from Melville's parody of it, which appeared in *Mardi.* James Gordon Bennett's writings on Astor in the April 5, 1849, edition of the *New York Herald* reflect the disgust that many of the nation's citizens felt with what Astor represented. It is a view more delicately put by Horace Mann, the country's leading educator at the time, in *A Few Thoughts for a Young Man,* a speech delivered in 1849, the year after Astor's death.

A GLIMPSE OF WALL STREET BY REPORTER GEORGE G.
FOSTER

Foster minces no words in his portrait of Wall Street, zeroing in on the "no mistake magnates of our financial and commercial aristocracy," the "misshapen images" created by the "demon of snob democracy." He stresses the inordinate power of these men, whose smallest decision can immediately change the lives of millions of common people. They are those who have bought their positions with money. Underneath the elegant and artistic social lives, he writes, may lie an ugly truth, but no one dares question them. Those with the power to question them are like them and approve of them. And those without the power would be crushed by them. Their implied preoccupation with the reputation they can purchase reminds us of Melville's narrator, as does Foster's final paragraph of what would happen if one of the wealthy man's "victims" were to ask him for a handout.

FROM GEORGE G. FOSTER, *FIFTEEN MINUTES AROUND NEW YORK* (NEW YORK: DEWITT AND DAVENPORT, 1849), 222–26

Here, at this hour, daily congregate the real, bona fide, no-mistake magnates of our financial and commercial aristocracy. Having taken their two shilling dinner at Brown's, or their cut of pie and coffee (or perhaps even something stronger), at the Verandah, they meet here to discuss the commercial news of the day—the prices of exchange, money and produce—and to play the great game of gambling, which leads to respectability and success, or to disaster, bankruptcy and ruin.

Treason is ne'er successful; what's the reason?

When 'tis successful, 'tis no longer treason.

Hudibras, nor any other satirist of human nature, ever wrote anything truer than that; and it applies with especial force to the Merchants' Exchange of New York. The hours devoted to the brokers and avowed speculators are a different affair. But at this particular hour of the day—this "High Change," as it is called par excellence—the millionaires and magnates of the city—those men whose slightest remarks uttered on Change are greedily recorded by the commercial reporters and trumpeted forth the next morning as if the Delphian oracle had spoken, meet here, and in whispers, shrugs and inuendoes, decide prices, fortunes and destinies, which ramify through every rank of society, and effect, for good or evil, the whole movement and life of the community. It is they who get up or suppress panics—who cause money to be "light" or "easy"—and whose decisions, formed upon their own personal and private gambling interests, settle the question whether the country is to be prosperous or unfortunate.

...

But we must not quit this important and interesting quarter of New York without some grave and profitable reflections. Who, then, are these favored and powerful individuals who exert this immense control over society and the world? What they were, we will say nothing about: as to who and what they are, go to Jullien's or Ole Bull's, or Sontag's, and you will see. They are the patrons of the Opera—the hope of Art in this country and this age: and the beauty of it is, that they know as much of painting, of statuary, of architecture, and the belles lettres, as of music. They are quite as familiar with Shakespeare and Milton, Shelley and Tennyson, Byron and Coleridge, as with Rossini and Meyerbeer. There is no conceivable subject of poetry, art or literature, upon which they will not pronounce a judgment with the authority of a critic and the prolixity of an amateur. They have that which is so much better than knowledge, or study, or experience, or brains, or in fact, than anything but money—they have position; and that position they have obtained and can only keep because of their money. No one cares to dispute with them their claims to fashion and exclusiveness. No one dares to exhibit the ludicrous mockery of their pretensions to elegance and social eminence. No one dares lay bare the lie upon which they live, nor to hold them up for what they are. No one dares question them, as they stride insolently through the temple of fashion and good society, or march disdainfully and with flying colors to their velvet-cushioned pew in Grace Church. While all know the truth, yet they pass unquestioned. Why is this? Because the great majority of their neighbors are as bad as themselves, and dare not for their lives agitate the question of an investigation into the title deeds of those who hold within their grasp the lordly domains of aristocracy and fashion. The few who might safely challenge these vulgar pretenders, shrink with instinctive disgust from the thankless task; while of the great struggling, fighting, straining world below them, each hopes to receive, at some remote period, the favor of a smile of recognition from these misshapen images that the demon of snob democracy sets up in the niches of the beautiful and the great.

Let us return from our long and interesting detour to Wall street and the purlieus of the Exchange. Let us watch the process by which the fortunes are accumulated that enable their possessors thus to lord it over the world, and climb to these places of eminence and distinction which should be reserved alone to the wise, the brilliant and the good. We will not descend to the particulars of the various transactions which go to make up the sum of that profession known as trade. Suffice it to say, that the foundation of it all, the secret of success, the key to wealth and power, is the cautious overreaching of the neighbor. So long as the merchant or the speculator maintains untarnished that conventional honor which thieves find it absolutely necessary to enforce in the division of their plunder; so long as his bank account is good and his credit untainted in "the street," no matter how savagely he may oppress the poor man within his power—no matter how many hearts he may have wrung with anguish, how many lips may turn white with hunger, how many desperate souls driven to crime, how many milk white virgin bosoms be given to the polluting touch of lust, for money to buy bread—how many fellow beings may be wholly crushed and made forever desperate by the iron grasp of this man, he is still respectable, "one of the most respectable of our citizens." And should one of his beggared victims cross his path on his way to church, or entreat but a solitary penny to stave off the pangs of hunger, he would assume the indignant air of a martyr, suffering under the persecutions of an insolent and ungrateful world.

JOHN JACOB ASTOR'S CHARITY: THE WILL

The subject of charity is central to the story of Bartleby, as we see that the narrator is willing to be charitable to Bartleby only in so far as it will "cost him little or nothing" (17). The remark is appropriate to the will of his hero, John Jacob Astor, whose sense of charity had been very much in the news only four years earlier. The amount Astor left various charities was only a minuscule percentage of his vast fortune of between $20 and 30 million. Furthermore, in various codicils to his will, he even decreased the amounts he had originally designated to some charities.

FROM "THE LAST WILL AND TESTIMONY OF JOHN JACOB ASTOR," *NEW YORK HERALD,* 5 APRIL 1849

In the name of God, Amen.

I, John Jacob Astor, of the City of New-York, dispose of all the real and personal Estate to which I may be entitled at the time of my decease, [interlineated: in the manner hereinafter expressed] do make this my last Will and Testament.

. . .

Eighth. [Revoked by codicil.] To each of the *four daughters* of my deceased brother, George Astor, I give twenty thousand Dollars; to his son Joseph, I give *twenty five thousand dollars;* to his son William H. Astor, I give *ten thousand dollars;* to George Astor, Jr., I give *three thousand dollars;* to the widow of my said brother George, I give *two hundred pounds sterling,* yearly for her life, commencing the first payment one year after my death, the same to be estimated here at the current rate of exchange. To my niece Sophia Astor, of Nieuwid in Germany, I give *five thousand dollars.* To my Sister Catherine wife of Michael Miller, I give *one thousand dollars;* to the *children of her daughter,* Maria Moore, I give five thousand dollars, to be equally divided among them and to be paid to their mother for their use.

. . .

To the Trustees of Columbia College [revoked by codicil] in the City of New York I give *twenty five thousand dollars,* upon condition that they do, within a reasonable and convenient time, establish a professorship of the German language and literature, and do appoint and continue a professor therein of competent learning, who shall give proper lectures and instruction in the said language and literature.

. . .

To the German Reformed Congregation [revoked by codicil], in the City of New York, of which I am a member, I give *two thousand Dollars.*

Tenth. All the rest, residue, and remainder of my real and personal estate [changed by codicil], I give and devise to my sonWilliam B. Astor; to have and to hold the said real estate to him him [*sic*] for his life.

· · ·

A Codicil to the Will of John Jacob Astor.
[January 19, 1838]
In order to render some provisions of my Will more plain, to make some alterations therein, and to consolidate sundry codicils thereto, (which codicils I hereby revoke,) I make this codicil to my will bearing date the fourth day of July Eighteen hundred and thirty six; and do declare the said Will and this codicil to contain my last Will.

· · ·

Seventh. The service of plate excepted from the gift to Mrs. Langdon in my will, and therein mentioned as my new service of plate, and given for the use of William B. Astor for life, I describe more particularly as my service of French plate, at this time in his possession. And in case he shall not leave any appointment of it among his children, I give the same, on his death, to his eldest surviving son.

· · ·

To Mrs. Sarah Oxenham [modified in codicil of March 3, 1841], daughter of my late brother, George Astor, I give *thirty thousand dollars*; to his son, Joseph Astor [modified Oct. 24, 1839], I give *fifty thousand Dollars*; provided however, that my executors if they think fit, may retain the same in whole or in part, and apply the same, and the income thereof, to his use, and the maintenance of him and his family during his life; and any balance is to be given to his children, or next of kin. *To each of, the other daughters* [modified as to Mrs. Reynell, March 3, 1841] *of my said brother George*, surviving me, I give *twenty thousand dollars.* To William Henry Astor; son of my said brother George, I give the *annual sum of five hundred dollars* during his life,

· · ·

Ninth. I reduce the legacy to the German Society of New York, from *thirty thousand dollars to twenty five thousand dollars. I I* [*sic*] *have given* to the Association for the Relief of Respectable Aged Indigent Females, in the City of New York, *five thousand dollars,* which is to be deducted from the legacy of twenty five thousand dollars given in my will. To the Institution for the Blind, in the City of New York, I give *five thousand Dollars.* To To [*sic*] the Society for the relief of Half Orphans and Destitute Children in the City of New York, I give Five thousand dollars. To the New York Lying-In Asylum I give *Two Thousand Dollars.* And in case of any of these three legacies failing to go into effect, I give the same to my executors, confiding in their honor alone to make such dispositions of such sums as they shall deem most analogous to the objects of the said charities.

· · ·

Eleventh. In case any devises, bequests or legacies, trusts, powers, conditions, limitations or other dispositions or clauses in *my said will or in this codicil, or in any subsequent codicil should for any reason be deemed invalid* (having intended, however in all things to make them conformable to the law) then it is my will, that in all events the said Will and codicils shall stand valid as to all other parts and provisions; and that no failure of any clause of my will, or the codicils thereto, shall defeat or render void any other parts thereof; and in case of the invalidity of any devises or legacy, or other provision, I direct that the property or subject of such invalid disposition, shall be given to the persons for whose benefit the same appears by the expressions of such defeated clause; as to which property or subject I authorize my executors to appoint the same to said person or persons, in such estates, manner and proportions as they shall judge conformable to my will, and as shall be lawful. And inasmuch as I make advancements or beneficial provisions for persons or purposes provided for in my will and codicils, it is my direction that such advancements, if charged in my books of account, shall be deemed so much on account of the provision in my will or codicils in favor of such person or purposes.

· · ·

Item. I give to my niece Sophia Astor, of Nieuwid in Germany, in addition to her legacy, an annuity of *three hundred dollars per annum,* to commence from my decease, and paid up to the time of her death, payable yearly.

· · ·

[Third Codicil, August 22, 1839]
I, John Jacob Astor, do make this additional codicil to my last Will, bearing date the fourth day of July in the year of our Lord Eighteen hundred and thirty six.

Desiring to render a public benefit to the City of New York, and to contribute to the advancement of useful knowledge and the general good of society, I do by this codicil, appropriate *four hundred thousand dollars* out of my residuary estate to the establishment of a *Public Library* in the City of New York.

For this purpose, *I give to my executors four hundred thousand dollars,* to be taken from my personal estate, or raised by a sale of parts of my real estate to be made by my executors, with the assent of my son William B. Astor, upon condition, and to the intent, that the said amount be settled, applied and disposed of as follows,

· · ·

[Fourth Codicil, October 24, 1839]
A further codicil to the will of John Jacob Astor, bearing date the fourth day of July A.D. 1836.

First. I *revoke* and annul *the legacy* of fifty thousand dollars given *to Joseph Astor* and his children, or next of kin, contained in the eighth item of the codicil to my Will, which codicil bears date the nineteenth day of January A.D. 1838; and *I give* to the said Joseph Astor for his life, an annuity of *three hundred pounds sterling* per annum, to commence from my decease, and to be paid half yearly, and up to his decease, provided that my executors, if they think fit, may retain the same, or any payment thereof, and apply the same to the use of him or his family, as they may judge most beneficial to him.

Second. I *revoke* and annul the legacy of *Twenty five Thousand Dollars* given in my will to *the Trustees of Columbia College,* in the City of New York.

...

[Fifth Codicil, March 3, 1841]
A further codicil to the Will of John Jacob Astor, bearing date the fourth day of July in the year of our Lord eighteen hundred and thirty six.

Having before me the said will and the four several codicils thereto, bearing date January 19, 1838, January 9 August 22 and October 24, 1839, I do make this additional codicil, that is to say:

First. I *revoke* so much of the codicil dated in January eighteen hundred and thirty eight, as gives to my daughter, Mrs. Langdon, for her life, the lot on Lafayette Place, given in my will to Charles Bristed, for life; so that the estate of Charles Bristed in the said lot shall not be subject to any estate of my daughter therein. And in relation to the plan of the lots on the West side of Lafayette Place, by which a gangway is established as is mentioned in the second item of the said codicil, I hereby revoke so much of the said codicil, as relates to the establishment or enjoyment of the *gangway* therein mentioned; and I abolish and annul the said gangway, and impose it as a condition on my daughter and grandchildren holding lands adjacent to it that such gangway be wholly abandoned.

Second. I *revoke the legacy* of two thousand dollars given in my will to *the German Reformed Congregation* in the City of New York, intending during my life, to apply that amount to the religious and moral welfare of Germans in some other mode.

Fifth. I give to my friend Fitz Greene Halleck, *an annuity of two hundred dollars,* commencing at my decease, and payable half yearly for his life; to be secured by setting apart so much of my personal estate as may be necessary; which I intend as a mark of my regard for Mr. Halleck.

...

Seventh. I reduce the legacy bequeathed to the German Society of New York, from *twenty five thousand dollars* to *twenty thousand dollars,* of which I have already advanced them fifteen thousand [dollars—stricken through] six hundred and ninety seven dollars [and—stricken through] fifty cents, to be deducted, therefore, from the said last mentioned sum. Also I *reduce* the legacy which my niece, Mrs. Mary Reynell, wife of George Reynell, would have taken, under the first codicil to my will, to *fifteen thousand dollars.* I *reduce the legacy* of my niece, Sarah Oxenham, given in the said codicil, from thirty thousand to *twenty thousand dollars.*

...

[Sixth Codicil, June 3, 1841]
A further Codicil to the Will of John Jacob Astor, dated July 4, 1836.

. . .

Third. As to the two legacies of twenty five thousand dollars each, and the share of water-stock, to which the said Louisa would have been entitled under my will and a codicil thereto, I revoke the two legacies entirely; I give the income of her share of stock to my daughter Dorothea for life and on her death I give the capital to her other children, and their issue, in case of their decease.

Fourth. As to the lot on the Westerly side of Lafayette Place, given to the said Louisa in a codicil to my will, I give the same to Cecilia Langdon, to be had and holden as if her name had been written in the devise thereof, instead of Louisa, with every advantage, power and benefit, and subject to every condition power and limitation therein contained.

Fifth. I expressly authorize my daughter, Dorothea Langdon by deed or will, to appoint and give to the said Louisa and her issue, or to her or their use, any part not exceeding in value one half of the real or personal estate by this codicil taken from Louisa and given to others.

Sixth. I direct and devise that Charles Bristed be one of the Trustees of the devise and legacy for a public library, provided for in former codicils to my will, and I give him the same estate, interest and power, as if he were originally named in such devise and legacy.

Seventh. Considering the advantages which Mr. Vincent Rumpff has received from the marriage Settlement of my daughter, I revoke the devise to him for his life of my estate near Geneva. But if an accounting shall take place between us, touching the property in the said settlement, after this date, and within two years, and the balance of that account shall be paid, then I renew such devise to him for life, of the estate near Geneva.

. . .

Last. I publish this as a codicil to my will, and as altering and revoking the same, and the codicils thereto, so far as a different disposition is made by the present codicil.

In Witness whereof, I have hereunto set my hand and seal this third day of June, in the year of our Lord one thousand eight hundred and forty one.

. . .

[Seventh Codicil, December 15, 1842]
I, John Jacob Astor, of the City of New York, do make this additional codicil to my last Will, bearing date July 4th 1836.

. . .

[Eighth Codicil, December 22, 1843]
A further codicil to the Will of John Jacob Astor, bearing date July 4, 1836.

MELVILLE ON JOHN JACOB ASTOR'S CHARITY

When John Jacob Astor's will appeared in the *Herald,* Melville, along with many people who had connections on Wall Street, was both amused and disgusted by it. The document was a ridiculous example of the worst of legal jargon. It was appended by many codicils in which Astor changed his mind about what he wanted done with his money. Each time he altered his original will with a codicil, it was to leave less money to his poor relations and various charities. And then there was the insult to Halleck, who was left a comparative pittance, as, Astor wrote, a sign of his regard for him.

Melville, who used his novel *Mardi* to parody a number of people and aspects of his culture, made fun of Astor's will in chapter 177, where a pagan character named Bardianna has made provision for his earthly belongings, like his breadfruit orchards, his vegetable pills, his lotions, his gargles, and, especially, his teeth, using the fanciest legal jargon. Note Melville's use of the word *imprimis,* which appears on the first page of "Bartleby."

FROM HERMAN MELVILLE, *MARDI* (CHICAGO: NORTHWESTERN UNIVERSITY PRESS, 1970), 582–85

Anno Mardis 50,000,000, o.s. I, Bardianna, of the island of Vamba, and village of the same name, having just risen from my yams, in high health, high spirits, and sound mind, do hereby cheerfully make and ordain this my last will and testament.

" 'Imprimis:

" 'All my kith and kin being well to do in Mardi, I wholly leave them out of this my will.

" 'Item. Since, in divers ways, verbally and otherwise, my good friend Pondo has evinced a strong love for me, Bardianna, as the owner and proprietor of all that capital messuage with the appurtenances, in Vamba aforesaid, called 'The Lair,' wherein. I now dwell; also for all my Breadfruit orchards, Palm-groves, Banana-plantations, Taro-patches, gardens, lawns, lanes, and hereditaments whatsoever, adjoining the aforesaid messuage;—I do hereby give and bequeath the same to Bomblum of the island of Adda; the aforesaid Bomblum having never expressed any regard for me, as a holder of real estate.

" 'Item. My esteemed neighbor Lakreemo having since the last lunar eclipse called daily to inquire after the state of my health: and having nightly made tearful inquiries of my herb-doctor, concerning the state of my viscera;—I do hereby give and bequeath to the aforesaid Lakreemo all and sundry those vegetable pills, potions, powders, aperients, purgatives, expellatives, evacuatives, tonics, emetics, cathartics, clysters, injections, scarifiers, cataplasms, lenitives, lotions, decoctions, washes, gargles, and phlegmagogues; together with all the jars, calabashes, gourds, and galipots, thereunto pertaining; situate, lying, and being, in the west-by-north corner of my east-southeast crypt, in my aforesaid tenement known as 'The Lair.'

" 'Item. The woman Pesti; a native of Vamba, having oftentimes hinted that I, Bardianna, sorely needed a spouse, and having also intimated that she bore me a conjugal affection; I do hereby give and bequeath to the aforesaid Pesti:—my blessing; forasmuch, as by the time of the opening of this my last will and testament, I shall have been forever delivered from the aforesaid Pesti's persecutions.

. . .

" 'Item. Knowing my devoted scribe Marko to be very sensitive touching the receipt of a favor; I willingly spare him that pain; and hereby bequeath unto the aforesaid scribe, three milk-teeth, not as a pecuniary legacy, but as a very slight token of my profound regard.

" 'Item. I give to the poor of Vamba the total contents of my red-labeled bags of bicuspids and canines (which I account three-fourths of my whole estate); to my body servant Fidi, my staff, all my robes and togas, and three hundred molars in cash; to that discerning and sagacious philosopher my disciple Krako, one complete set of denticles, to buy him a vertebral bone ring; and to that pious and promising youth Vangi, two fathoms of my best kaiar rope, with the privilege of any bough in my groves.

" 'All the rest of my goods. chattels and household stuff whatsoever; and all my loose denticles, remaining after my debts and legacies are paid, and my body is out of sight, I hereby direct to be distributed among the poor of Vamba.

" 'I have no previous wills to revoke; and publish this to be my first and last.

" 'In witness whereof, I have hereunto set my right hand; and hereunto have caused a true copy of the tattooing on my right temple to be affixed, during the year first above written.

" 'By me, BARDIANNA.' "

"Babbalanja, that's an extraordinary document," said Media.

"Bardianna was an extraordinary man, my lord."

"Were there no codicils?"

"The will is all codicils; all after-thoughts; Ten thoughts for one act, was Bardianna's motto."

"Left he nothing whatever to his kindred?"

"Not a stump."

EDITOR JAMES GORDON BENNETT'S CRITICISM OF
ASTOR ON THE BASIS OF HIS LAST WILL AND TESTIMONY

James Gordon Bennett, editor of the *New York Herald,* had never been an admirer of John Jacob Astor. Even in 1845, his newspaper had pointed to a study that had given Astor's wealth as $25 million at a time when one-fifth of the population of New York City (some 80,000 people) were so poor as to need public assistance. So Bennett had long been known for his excoriation of big business and management, which the narrator of "Bartleby" is so happy to be a part of, proudly dropping the name of John Jacob Astor as a man with whom he has done business and who knows well the narrator's good qualities. When John Jacob Astor's will was finally made public in April 1849, almost a year after his death, it was Bennett's paper that secured the big story by reprinting the will on its front page. Bennett, who had not joined other mainstream journalists after Astor's death in praising his enterprise in creating a fortune from humble beginnings, now unleashed his wrath on the man whom he viewed as having cheated the people of New York City. Instead of returning a significant amount of his vast fortune to humanity, he had taken extra precautions to insure that almost all of it would go to his heirs. He had designated less than five percent for charity or public causes, the largest being $400,000 to the Astor Library.

FROM JAMES GORDON BENNETT, "ASTOR'S WILL," *NEW YORK HERALD*, 5 APRIL 1849, QUOTED IN SIGMUND DIAMOND, *THE REPUTATION OF AMERICAN BUSINESSMEN* (GLOUCESTER, MASS.: PETER SMITH, 1970), 32–33

The will of John Jacob Astor is a curious document, both in its language, composition and grammar, as well as in its bequests. During the greater portion of the last years of his life, he was the associate and Maecenas of Washington Irving, Mr. Cogswell, Mr. Halleck, and several other literary, philosophical and poetical gentlemen connected with the literary latitude and longitude of New York. The results of their doctrines, their views, their ideas, their talk, appear in the will; and judging from that document, we must say that we don't think too much of their teachings. If we had been an associate of John Jacob Astor...we should have given him some instructions in political economy, at least of a very different character from what it appears he has imbibed from those whom he lived among. The first idea we should have put into his head, would have been that *one-half of his immense property—ten millions, at least—belonged to the people of the city of New York.* During the last fifty years of the life of John Jacob Astor, his property has been augmented and increased in value by the aggregate intelligence, industry, enterprise and commerce of New York, fully to the amount of one-half of its value...Having established this principle, we would have counselled John Jacob Astor to leave at least the half of his property for the benefit of the city of New York...leaving ten millions to be given to his relatives—a sum quite enough for any reasonable persons, of any rank of life in this country. But instead of this, he has only left less than one-half a million for a public library. What a poor, mean and beggarly result from associating with such literary men, philosophers and poets!

We cannot, therefore, pronounce the highest species of eulogy upon the character of the late John Jacob Astor. He has exhibited, at best, but the ingenious powers of a self-invented money-making machine; and the associates, advisers, and counsellors of his later years, seem to have looked no further than to the different pins, cranks and buttons of this machine, without turning it to any permanent benefit to that community from whose industry he obtained one-half the amount of his fortune, in the indirect values added to his estates in the course of years.

HORACE MANN ON RICH MEN, MEANINGFUL SACRIFICE, AND JOHN JACOB ASTOR

The matter of a rich man's charity comes up in "Bartleby" when the narrator sees himself as the charitable benefactor of his employee Bartleby, whom he allows to remain in his Wall Street law chambers even though Bartleby prefers not to work. The narrator regards charity not primarily as a way to alleviate Bartleby's suffering, but as a way to buy himself a good conscience. Charity, he emphasizes, is useful to the one being charitable. In 1849, shortly before Mann made his speech to the Boston Mercantile Library Association, the subject of a rich man's charity was very much in the news with the publication of Astor's will. Mann holds up Astor as the worst kind of rich man, lacking any true sense of philanthropy, in sharp contrast to an earlier businessman named Stephen Girard, a true philanthropist who gave away his wealth to the public instead of, like Astor, hoarding it for his children alone.

Following the publication of Mann's speech, Astor's grandson published a lengthy rebuttal, designed to counteract any damage that Mann had delivered to Whig candidates up for election.

FROM HORACE MANN, *A FEW THOUGHTS FOR A YOUNG MAN* (BOSTON: LEE AND SHEPARD, 1887), 52–60

Now I wage no war against wealth. I taint it with no vilifying breath. Wealth, so far as it consists in comfortable shelter and food and raiment for *all* mankind; in competence for every bodily want, and in abundance for every mental and spiritual need, is so valuable, so precious, that if any *earthly* object could be worthy of idolatry, this might best be the idol. Wealth, as the means of refinement and embellishment; of education and culture, not only universal in its comprehension, but elevated in its character; wealth, as the means of perfecting the arts and advancing the sciences, of discovering and diffusing truth, is a blessing we cannot adequately appreciate; and God seems to have pronounced it to be so, when He made the earth and all the fulness thereof,—the elements, the land and sea, and all that in them is,—so easily convertible into it. But wealth, as the means of an idle or a voluptuous life; wealth, as the fosterer of pride and the petrifier of the human heart; wealth, as the iron rod with which to beat the poor into submission to its will,—is all the curses of Pandora concentrated into one. It is not more true, that money represents all values, than that it represents all vices.

Great wealth is a misfortune, because it makes generosity impossible. There can be no generosity where there is no sacrifice; and a man who is worth a million of dollars, though he gives half of it away, no more makes a sacrifice, than (if I may make such a supposition) a dropsical man, whose skin holds a hogshead of water, makes a sacrifice when he is tapped for a barrel.

. . .

But in speaking of the criminality of hoarding vast wealth, whether to gratify acquisitiveness or to maintain family pride, regardless of the suffering it might relieve, the vice it might reclaim, the ignorance it might instruct, or the positive happiness which, in a thousand ways, it might create, one grand exception should be made. Perhaps you have demanded that this exception should be intimated, at an earlier point; but I have reserved it to the present time, in order to give it a distinct enunciation, and to do it ample justice. Like every other act, the right or wrong of amassing property depends upon the motive that prompts it. If a man labors for accumulation all his life-long, neglecting the common objects of charity, and repulsing the daily appeals to his benevolence, but with the settled, determinate purpose of so multiplying his resources that, at death, he can provide for some magnificent scheme of philanthropy, for which smaller sums or daily contributions would be insufficient, and then he becomes a self-constituted servant and almoner of the Lord, putting his master's talent out at usury, but rendering back both talent and usury, on the day of account; and who shall say that such a man is not a just and faithful steward, and worthy of his reward? But the day is sure to come which will test the spirit that has governed the life. On that day, it will be revealed, whether the man of vast wealth, like Stephen Girard, has welcomed toil, endured privation, borne contumely, while in his secret heart he was nursing the mighty purpose of opening a fountain of blessedness so copious and exhaustless, that is would flow on undiminished to the end of time; or whether, like John Jacob Astor, he was hoarding wealth for the base love of wealth, hugging to his breast, in his dying hour, the memory of his gold and not of his Redeemer; griping his riches till the scythe of death cut off his hands, and he was changed, in the twinkling of an eye, from being one of the richest men that ever lived in this world, to being one of the poorest souls that ever went out of it.*

*I make this reference to Mr. Astor from no personal motive whatever. So far as my own feelings are concerned, it gives me pain to mention his name. I select him "to point a moral" only, because I suppose him to have been the most notorious, the most wealthy, and, considering his vast means, the most miserly, of his class, in this country. Nothing but absolute insanity can he pleaded in palliation of the conduct of a man who was worth nearly or quite twenty millions of dollars, but gave only some half million, or less than a half million, of it for any public object. If men of such vast means will not benefit the world by their *example* while they live, we have a right to make reprisals for their neglect, by using them as a warning after they are dead. In the midst of so much poverty and suffering as the world experiences, it has become a high, moral, and religious duty to create an overwhelming public opinion against both the parsimonies and the squanderings of wealth.

WALL STREET AND WEALTH IN THE TWENTY-FIRST CENTURY

The unbridled and voracious procuring of wealth in the manner of John Jacob Astor, whose presence hangs over Melville's "Story of Wall Street," was not just an 1850s issue. In 2002 and 2003, the inordinate salaries, stock options, and general perks garnered by the nation's chief executive officers heading the wealthiest corporations were the stuff of headlines. The U.S. economy boomed in the 1990s. Many ordinary workers in America invested in stocks to pay for their children's educations and their retirements. And many pension funds were heavily invested in the bullish stock market. As long as the economy was thriving, seemingly to everyone's advantage, heads of companies enjoyed free rein in their pursuit of the almighty dollar, and there was little scrutiny of their compensation from stockholders or the government. But the stock market suddenly began to slide in 2001. And the terrorists' attacks on September 11, 2001, sent the stock market downward. Further disastrous news came to a head in November 2001 when Enron, one of the nation's largest corporations, had its credit rating sunk to high-risk junk-bond levels, came to be investigated by the Securities and Exchange Commission, and, on December 2, 2001, filed for bankruptcy. On December 3, Enron laid off 4,000 employees, many of whose pensions had been heavily invested in Enron shares and were now worthless. Investigations revealed that Enron stock has been criminally inflated and that executives, while urging their employees to invest in Enron stock, had quietly been unloading their own shares before the bubble burst. Following the collapse of Enron came the collapse of other large companies like WorldCom, and the jobs and savings of thousands of Americans who worked for them came down with them. Moreover, the savings of millions more whose pension funds had been heavily invested in these companies also suffered. Simultaneously, the once thriving high-tech industry, which had produced so many millionaires, now came tumbling down, costing thousands of jobs. Airlines, teetering on the brink of bankruptcy, began laying off thousands of employees. On a single day, American Airlines laid off 5,000 flight attendants. In the summer of 2002, the stock market plunged to one of the lowest levels in decades. By the summer of 2003, unemployment in the United States had risen to the highest level since the 1930s.

Against this economic disaster made worse by corporate malfeasance, the salaries, pensions, stock options, and general behavior of company executives began increasingly to come under scrutiny. Not only did CEOs like Kenneth Lay of Enron and Bernie Ebbers of WorldCom escape prison terms despite their companies' criminal activity, they were able to retain millions of dollars worth of property while their employees were thrown on the street without income or pensions. As a consequence, the public became interested in knowing the income of the nation's CEOs. It was revealed that in the year 2000, the average worker got an annual raise of 3 percent, while the average CEO got a raise of 22 percent. In addition to salaries, CEOs made an average of $14.9 million in stock options in 2000. Below are some of the salaries in 2000 of CEOs of large corporations:

Michael Dell of Dell Computer	$235 million
Sanford Weill of Citigroup	$216 million
Gerald Levin of Time Warner	$164 million
John T. Chambers of Cisco	$157 million

The average compensation package for CEOs in 2002 was $10.83 million. Drug companies in 2002 paid their CEOs up to $74 million a year.

The point has been made that in the 1980s, CEOs made about 40 times the salary of the average worker. By 2002, CEOs made 400 times the salary of the average worker.

Some people in the financial community argue that CEOs deserve large salaries because they make huge profits for the company and create jobs. But the figures argue otherwise. In 2002, Levi Company paid their CEO, Phil Marineau, $25.1 million, slightly more than the total profit for the year. Companies where many CEOs have high salaries have not realized profits. Just a few examples: In 2000, William Esrey, CEO of Sprint, a long-distance company, was paid $53 million in cash and stock, while his company's stock fell by 70 percent. Michael Eisner, CEO of Walt Disney, received a $5 million *bonus* in 2002, even though Disney stock fell by 34 percent. David D'Alessandro of John Hancock Financial Service engineered himself an $8.2 million pay raise with company profits falling off 32 percent. Jeff Barbakow, whose Tenet HealthCare is under federal investigation and whose profits have been falling, made $189 million in 2002. He was forced out of his position in summer of 2003.

In 2003, profits fell precipitously, and corporations continued to cut jobs and salaries of workers. But in some of these cases, the total compensation of CEOs remained astronomically high. Don Carty, CEO of American Airlines, cut $1.8 billion in jobs and salaries of workers in April 2003. The very next day, he arranged a new lucrative deal for himself and other executives. But in this case, the outrage was so thunderous that Carty was forced to resign.

Despite plummeting profits and the country's record-breaking unemployment (by the summer of 2003 it was worse than at any time since the Great Depression) the average CEO received a 14 percent raise in 2002. The average salary for a CEO in 2002 was $13 million. In the top echelon, the average was $33.4 million. This was in addition to their stock options—stock they could buy at low cost and sell at a profit. In 2003, for example, the CEO of Juniper Networks, in addition to his enormous salary, cashed in his stocks for a profit of $7.5 million.

The following headlines and excerpts from the *New York Times* in the spring and summer of 2003 illustrate the backlash against the excessive wealth of CEOs in the face of unemployment, bankrupt pension funds, and falling profits: one article from April 4 on Richard M. Scrushy of HealthSouth, and one from September 18 on Richard A. Grasso, chief executive of the New York Stock Exchange. A final excerpt from the *New Yorker* magazine indicates the continued pursuit of excessive wealth even in times of the nation's economic hardship.

RICHARD M. SCRUSHY, CEO OF HEALTHSOUTH

In 2001, Richard M. Scrushy, chairman and CEO of HealthSouth, received a salary of $3,961,169, a bonus of $6,500,000, and $58,322 in other compensation, for a total yearly take from HealthSouth alone of $129,199,197. Part of his contract included a supplemental pension benefit, a founder retirement benefit that he would receive even if he were fired for cause, which would guarantee him $2,376,701 a year. The company, which paid him over $129 million a year, contributed only $120 per employee to the employees' saving plan. Thus, the CEO's salary and bonus alone were more than twice the total amount it paid for all its employees' pensions.

In 2003, Richard Scrushy was fired for accounting fraud but does not yet face criminal charges. The following excerpt from a *New York Times* article states that further investigations have revealed that Scrushy augmented his income from HealthSouth with a separate corporation specializing in real estate.

FROM GRETCHEN MORGENSON WITH MILT FREUDENHEIM, "SCRUSHY RAN HEALTHSOUTH REAL ESTATE ON THE SIDE," *NEW YORK TIMES*, 4 APRIL 2003

Richard M. Scrushy derived great wealth and considerable power from his position as the founder and chief executive of the HealthSouth Corporation, the nation's largest rehabilitation hospital company. But HealthSouth was not the only public company Mr. Scrushy founded that generated wealth for him and a handful of his trusted colleagues.

In 1994, Mr. Scrushy and two partners created Capstone Capital Corporation, a publicly traded real estate investment trust that invested in hospitals, outpatient centers and other health care properties, most of which had been owned by HealthSouth and other companies associated with, Mr. Scrushy. By purchasing cheap stock before the initial offering and selling properties to the REIT, Mr. Scrushy and his partners profited handsomely in deals that are likely to attract more scrutiny from investigators now that Mr. Scrushy has been accused by securities regulators of fraudulently inflating earnings at HealthSouth. He has not been criminally charged.

RICHARD A. GRASSO, CHAIRMAN OF THE NEW YORK STOCK EXCHANGE

In the last week of August of 2003, the public learned that the man in charge of regulating the nation's financial community was receiving $140 million in deferred pay and retirement benefits—an inordinately high salary that had been determined by a board that included people Grasso was responsible for regulating. In the course of the investigation that ensued, it was found that five years earlier, Grasso had sat on the board of a company, Computer Associates International, that he was technically overseeing as head of the New York Stock Exchange. At that time, Computer Associates International proposed paying its senior executives more than $1 *billion* in stock, this just before the company's stocks fell and its chief executive, Charles B. Wang, was forced to resign after being accused of improper accounting.

The following excerpt, on the front page of the *New York Times,* announces Grasso's resignation.

FROM GRETCHEN MORGENSON AND LANDON THOMAS JR., "CHAIRMAN QUITS STOCK EXCHANGE IN FUROR OVER PAY," *NEW YORK TIMES,* 18 SEPTEMBER 2003

Richard A. Grasso resigned yesterday as chairman and chief executive of the New York Stock Exchange after three weeks of blistering criticism of his pay package.

Mr. Grasso had a remarkable rise at the exchange, from a clerk earning $82.50 a week in 1968 to its top executive in 1995. When it was announced last month that he was taking out $140 million in deferred pay and retirement benefits, a furor erupted as critics noted that he was not just a market leader but a regulator whose pay was set by some of the people he oversaw. The outrage over his pay threatened to engulf the exchange itself.

THE POWER AND WEALTH OF THE CEO IN AUGUST 2003

The *New Yorker* column in the "Talk of the Town" section from which the following excerpt is taken points out that the multibillion-dollar scandals of the twenty-first century have forced a government, inclined to favor big business, to become tougher on chief executives who criminally inflate the stock of their companies and maneuver astronomical salaries and stock options while profits are falling and employees are being fired. Nevertheless, the writer notes that some CEOs whose greed and irresponsibility have damaged the lives of employees and the nation's economy continue to go unpunished. William Donaldson, mentioned in the first paragraph, is the chairman of the Securities and Exchange Commission.

FROM JOHN CASSIDY, "BUSINESS AS USUAL," *NEW YORKER*, 4 AUGUST 2003

In Washington last week, William Donaldson suggested that the worst corporate scandals are behind us. That may be, but elsewhere in the capital it has emerged that Freddie Mac, the federally sponsored company that was set up to enable moderate-income Americans to buy their own homes, has been massaging its earnings and paying its former chief executive, Leland Brendsel, five million dollars a year. In California, Tenet Healthcare, the nation's second-biggest hospital chain, has been accused of defrauding Medicare of hundreds of millions of dollars. Tenet's former chairman, Jeffrey Barbakow, cashed in stock options worth a hundred and eleven million dollars in 2002, which made him the highest-paid executive in the country. Since the news broke of a federal investigation into Tenet's finances, stockholders have seen the value of their investments fall by seventy-five per cent. In hailing the progress of the Corporate Fraud Task Force, the White House claimed last week that "C.E.O.s and other executives who fudged the numbers and deceived investors are being held accountable." But, so far, neither Brendsel nor Barbakow has been charged with any wrongdoing.

QUESTIONS AND PROJECTS

1. Write an essay on the possibility that the sphere of home exerts a positive influence on the individual.

2. Contrast the domestic sphere with the workplace.

3. Consider the impact of wealth on an individual, drawing from your knowledge or experience. Is wealth more likely to bring heartache or happiness to those who possess it? Have a class debate on the issue.

4. Who suffers, if anyone, in the life of a person single-mindedly pursuing wealth? Family? Associates? Employees? Write a drama illustrating your point.

5. After doing research, write a definition of capitalism. Have a class debate on whether capitalism should have free reign in a society or whether it should be limited.

6. Define the word *sinecure*. Are there positions in society today, somewhat like the nineteenth-century Master in Chancery, for which handsome salaries are paid but little actual work is required, just to hold a title?

7. Conduct some research on the economic philosophies of the Whigs and the Democrats in the mid-nineteenth century. Using what you find, stage a political debate, in period dress, between a Whig and a Democrat running for office. Afterward, members of the audience should decide who won, stating their reasons.

8. Andrew Carnegie, another wealthy baron like John Jacob Astor, expressed his idea about the wealthy individual's obligation to society in an essay titled "The Gospel of Wealth." Read Carnegie's essay and contrast his philosophy with the actions of Astor.

9. Examine the legalese of Astor's will. Try to translate it into English. Why do you suppose the will (other legal documents) are not written in plain English in the first place? Does this will, the kind of work Bartleby and his associates would have copies, have a bearing on the story?

10. Follow carefully the financial pages of a city newspaper for a week. Make a report on items relevant to executive pay.

FURTHER READING

Adams, Donald R., Jr. *Finance and Enterprise in Early America*. Philadelphia: University of Pennsylvania Press, 1978.

Atkins, Nelson. *Fitz-Greene Halleck*. New Haven, Conn.: Yale University Press, 1930.

Blackmar, Elizabeth. *Manhattan for Rent, 1785–1850*. Ithaca, N.Y.: Cornell University Press, 1989.

Bryce, Robert, and Molly Ivins. *Pipe Dreams: Greed, Ego, and the Death of Enron*. New York: Public Affairs, 2002.

Cochran, Thomas C., and William Miller. *The Age of Enterprise: A Social History of Industrial America*. New York: Macmillan, 1942.

Colton, Calvin. "Labor and Capital," *The Junius Tracts*, no. VII, 1844, quoted in *Ideology and Power in the Age of Jackson*, edited by Edwin C. Rozwenc, 357. New York: Anchor Books, 1964.

Diamond, Sigmund. *The Reputation of American Businessmen*. Cambridge, Mass.: Harvard University Press, 1955.

Haeger, John Denis. *John Jacob Astor: Business and Finance in the Early Republic*. Detroit: Wayne State University Press, 1991.

Hightower, Jim. *Thieves in High Places*. New York: Viking, 2003.

Huffington, Arianna. *Pigs at the Trough*. New York: Crown Publishers, 2003.

Jeter, Lynne W. *Disconnected: Deceit and Betrayal at WorldCom*. Hoboken, N.J.: Wiley, 2003.

Meyer, Marvin. *The Jacksonian Persuasion*. New York: Vintage, 1960.

Miller, Douglas T. *The Birth of Modern America*. New York: Bobbs-Merrill, 1970.

Myers, Gustavus. *History of the Great American Fortunes*. New York: Modern Library, 1936.

Palast, Greg. *The Best Democracy Money Can Buy*. Sterling, Va.: Pluto Press, 2002.

Pessen, Edward. *Jacksonian America*. Homewood, Ill.: Dorsey, 1969.

———. *Most Uncommon Jacksonians*. Albany: State University of New York Press, 1967.

———. *Riches, Class, and Power before the Civil War*. Lexington, Mass.: D. C. Heath, 1973.

Porter, Kenneth Wiggins. *John Jacob Astor: Businessman*. Cambridge, Mass.: Harvard University Press, 1931.

Remini, Robert V. *The Age of Jackson*. New York: Harper and Row, 1972.

Ronda, James. *Astoria and Empire*. Lincoln: University of Nebraska Press, 1990.

Rozwenc, Edwin, ed. *Ideology and Power in the Age of Jackson*. New York: Anchor Books, 1964.

Smith, Matthew Hale. *Sunshine and Shadow*. Hartford, Conn.: J. B. Burr, 1869.

Spann, Edward K. *The New Metropolis: New York City, 1840–1857*. New York: Columbia University Press, 1981.

Strong, George Templeton. *The Diary of George Templeton Strong*. 2 vols. Ed. Allan Nevins and Milton Halsey Thomas. New York: Macmillan, 1952.

Swartz, Mimi, and Sherron Watkins. *Power Failure: The Inside Story of the Collapse of Enron*. New York: Doubleday, 2003.

Zinn, Howard. *The People's History of the United States*. New York: HarperPerennial, 1980.

3 _____

Work without Hope: The Office Worker

[H]e copied for me at the usual rate of four cents a folio (one hundred words). (19)

Or, if he wanted anything, it was to be rid of a scrivener's table altogether. (8)

His poverty is great; but his solitude, how horrible! (22)

"Bartleby" is a tale told by a Wall Street businessman about the employees who work in his office. In the course of his story, the narrator provides details about their working environment and working conditions—the jobs they are responsible for and how they perform them, the hours they work, and the pay they receive. He reveals the typical attitude of a boss toward "his" employees and their relationship to him. He reveals what he does not fully understand, that the three scriveners have been irreparably damaged by the spiritually cold world where the almighty dollar comes before the human needs of its operatives. "Bartleby" is one of our few portraits of office workers in the nineteenth-century United States.

Typical workers in the eighteenth century had been self-employed artisans and cottage workers—blacksmiths, silversmiths, weavers, tailors—who produced merchandise on a small scale. But the profile of the worker began to change in the nineteenth century. The factory system in the United States dates from about 1790 but did not impact the work force significantly until the 1820s, well after the building of the first textile mill at Waltham, Massachusetts, in 1813. The cottage industries where cloth was produced by hand on looms gave way to a new technology that had produced factories where workers became extensions of the machines they operated. The phenomenal business growth in the first 50 years of the nineteenth century, which made millionaires like John Jacob Astor, had necessitated workers on a large scale to work in the burgeoning textile, iron and steel, and other industries and on the railroads traversing the continent. Suddenly tens of thousands were needed to

Two Wall Street clerks in the nineteenth century, seemingly correcting copy. Fifth Avenue Theatre Business Office, 1899. Museum of the City of New York, The Byron Collection 93.1.1.15535.

be operatives in the cotton and woolen mills in New England, the iron and steel mills of Pennsylvania, and the railroads and canals throughout the country. In New York City, new growing wealth and population gave rise to retail merchants and salespersons, housekeepers and stewards, nurses and midwives, laundresses, hairdressers and barbers, seamstresses, and textile workers.

The demand for workers in the cities was met by the rural population in the United States and immigrants from Europe. Young women from rural areas poured into textile-mill towns like Lowell and Lawrence, Massachusetts, and into cities like New York to work as domestics. Young men left farms that could not sustain large families and sought work in the cities so desperately in need of laborers. A flood of immigrants into the United States began to lower the high demand for some wage earners in the 1840s. At the same time, this influx lowered wages, enabling unscrupulous employers to run their businesses to reap maximum profit for themselves with little or no regard for their workers and to replace activists with cheaper and more pliant immigrant labor.

The plight of most factory workers during the nineteenth century was notorious. There were, in effect, no laws and regulations protecting this sudden influx into the market from exploitation by their employers, who believed it was their God-given right to make as much money as possible. To maximize profits for factory owners and corporations, workers were paid extremely low wages, required to work long hours, and subjected to chemicals and machinery that endangered them. The earsplitting banging of the shuttles in a room of 40 or more looms destroyed the hearing of those who worked there day after day. Phosphorous ate away the lower jaws of the young girls who worked in match factories. Men fell into vats of molten metal, and men, women, and children were maimed when their hair or limbs were caught in a factory's machinery. For all these reasons, the nineteenth-century laborer was not expected to live into middle age. In the middle of the struggle for abolition of Southern slavery, wage earners in the North were called factory slaves. The first major push for legislation on behalf of the worker was for a 10-hour day.

A nineteenth-century office on Canal Street. Nicaragua Canal commission office, 1895. Museum of the City of New York, The Byron Collection 93.1.1.7385

The introduction of many machines in factories turned the men and women who operated them into machines themselves. In "Bartleby," Melville sees this transformation into machines in the lives of office workers as well—human beings who have been turned into caricatures by their employers—human beings who find it necessary to rebel against their dehumanization in small and large ways.

In the bustling New York City of the 1840s, energized by the building of the Erie Canal, the growth of financial institutions to supply capital to industry resulted in the immense growth of a category of white-collar wage earners that existed for the first time in significant numbers. To accommodate the vast financial complex that had arisen to put investment capital to use, an army of office workers, including copyists, clerks, office boys, bookkeepers, accountants, and real estate and insurance agents were required in the many insurance, stocks and bonds brokers', real estate, and lawyers' offices on Wall Street and in what were called *counting houses* in England. Ironically, Matthew Smith's 1869 description of the office of William B. Astor, John Jacob's son, sounds very like the environment in which Bartleby and other clerks in the financial district worked:

On Prince Street, just out of Broadway, is a plain one-story building, looking not unlike a country bank. The windows are guarded by heavy iron bars. Here Mr. Astor controls his immense estate. In 1846, Mr. Astor was reputed to be worth five millions. His uncle Henry, a celebrated butcher in the Bowery, left him his accumulated wealth, reaching half a million. By fortunate investments, and donations from his father, he is supposed to be worth forty millions. His property is mostly in real estate, and in valuable leases of property belonging to Trinity Church. At ten o'clock every morning Mr. Astor enters his office. It consists of two rooms. The first is occupied by his clerks. His sons have a desk on either side of the room. In the rear room, separated from the front by folding doors, is Mr. Astor's office. (*Sunshine and Shadow,* 187)

There were two classes of office workers in both England and the United States in the nineteenth century. One class came from the ranks of privilege. These were young men whose wealthy fathers placed them in offices to perform as clerks, at the same time becoming educated in the law or high finance. When historians speak of the opportunity of clerks to rise in the world, this is the class of which they speak. Such young men lived in comfortable surroundings in their parents' homes and had the money and leisure to spend on urban entertainments, education, and literary pursuits. George Templeton Strong, whose diary of his years on Wall Street provides an invaluable picture of the times, was such a clerk, first working in his father's law firm. This class of clerks moved up to better, professional positions in their 20s. Thus, those in their ranks were always young. A second class of clerks, while expected to be educated in language and arithmetic and write in a clear, readable hand, came from the lower classes and were often the sons of artisans, who saw office work as an advancement over hard labor with one's hands. B. G. Orchard, in his 1871 survey *The Clerks of Liverpool,* describes what seems to have been universally expected of clerks and scriveners for lawyers:

> The Law, though in popular estimation respectable and mysteriously dreadful, is about the poorest grazing ground a clerk can feed on. Lawyers and law stationers do not need men of talent, nor do such to them; for the work not done by the principals or the managing clerk is of the dreariest routine character, and the incomes earned by the legal gentlemen being, on the average, smaller than those that reward the enterprising exertions of employers in other businesses, it is only natural for them to save all they can in office expenses. (35)

For most of these men, there was little or no advancement. Like Turkey, they grew old in these office jobs. Their wages were slightly better than those of factory workers, but not high enough to lift them out of poverty. Melville, as an inspector in the New York Custom House, a position much superior to a lawyer's scrivener, carried home the princely sum of four dollars a week in 1867. The possibility of an employer's being able to attract numerous men of privilege to his office to learn the trade, often without having to pay them anything, kept the salaries of the lower-class clerks low and the jobs few and unstable.

The lower-class clerks, like those portrayed in "Bartleby," unlike their upper-class counterparts, often lived all their lives in straitened circumstances. If they married, their wives had to work (usually at home), and they could never afford the luxuries of attending the city's theatrical and musical productions.

Melville was undoubtedly inspired to write "Bartleby" by a sketch titled "The Lawyer's Story," which appeared in February 1853 in both the *New York Times* and the *New York Tribune.* A story of a young law clerk and his sister, the narrative attests to the danger and poverty experienced by many members of this class of workers. The clerk and his sister exist marginally, taking temporary jobs for as long as employers have need of them and then finding themselves out of work, struggling to keep themselves alive. In their case, starvation is not the only danger, for she is kidnapped by the madam in a house of prostitution and he is cheated and imprisoned by a criminal. Neither of these dangers to those young and poor were unknown in nineteenth-century New York City.

The work environments of these clerks and copyists did not put them in danger of losing life or limb as they might in a factory, but they experienced their own kind of psychological despair, leading to widely recognized work-related physical ailments, as can be seen in Turkey's alcoholism and Nippers's stomach ulcers. Some of this can be explained by the false promise that these jobs held out for young men of rising in the world to more lucrative, respectable positions in the financial sector. After all, John Jacob Astor, the myth went, had come from humble beginnings to become the richest man in America. The reality, however, was that it was the rare clerk in this class who ever rose above their demeaning positions.

The myth, long held in America, was that the Jacksonian years constituted the era of the common man, that anyone, especially a white-collar worker who served as a clerk, accountant, or copyist, who was determined and worked hard, could rise in the world, that most of America's rich men had once been poor themselves. This seems to have been true of some men in the eighteenth and early nineteenth centuries. Benjamin Franklin's father seems to have been a candle maker of modest means, and John Jacob Astor's father was supposedly a struggling merchant. But during the so-called democratic age of the common man in the nineteenth century, in 1845, evidence shows that only two of New York City's 100 wealthiest men (worth $250,000 or more) came from poor backgrounds. By examining over 1,000 case histories of well-to-do citizens, historian Edward Pessen concluded the following: "Vastly rich or fairly rich, celebrated or obscure, it mattered not: the upper 1 per cent of wealth-holders of the great cities—the rich of their time—almost universally were born to families of substance and standing" (*Riches, Class, and Power before the Civil War,* 86). Another myth was the myth of equality of opportunity. Most of the successful businessmen and professionals of the day had much greater opportunities in terms of family wealth, social standing, useful family connections, and educations as young men than did those of humble beginnings.

Those in the narrator's employ demonstrate the dead-end jobs of the clerical force. Turkey illustrates the English immigrant in the workforce, trapped until old age in a poverty-level dead-end position. Hear the speech he delivers to the narrator, who has just tried to deprive him of a half-day's work:

> "True; but, with submission, sir, behold these hairs! I am getting old. Surely, sir, a blot or two of a warm afternoon is not to be severely urged against gray hairs. Old age—even if it blot the page—is honorable. With submission, sir, we *both* are getting old." (7)

Nippers and Ginger Nut are typical of the young men whom capitalists of the time insisted could rise to desirable Wall Street positions from humble clerkships. Despite the discouraging example of Turkey, Nippers struggles to better himself by scaring up what we would now call paralegal jobs at the justices' courts and the Tombs. For his heroic efforts, the narrator describes him as having "diseased ambition" (9). Ginger Nut, a 12-year-old office boy, has been placed in the narrator's office to study law. George Templeton Strong, working in his wealthy father's law office, on October 9, 1838, describes one of the law clerks in his father's employ as "a very well-regulated piece of copying machinery" (*The Diary of George Templeton Strong,* vol. 2, 92). He describes himself in the office as "a kind of professional steam engine" (vol. 2, 171).

While the pay of the white-collar worker was assumed to be better than that of the factory worker, neither was paid sufficiently well to escape living in tenements. These were of two types. One type of tenement was made from what was once a large one-family residence that had been subdivided multiple times to house as many as a dozen families. A New York State Assembly report on tenement houses found a particularly filthy tenement just behind Trinity Church on Wall Street. This building, with no plaster on the walls, rotten stairways, and a leaking roof, housed 70 people.

Most of what we assume about the life of copyists and clerks in nineteenth-century America actually comes from portraits of the English work scene, notably those of Charles Dickens. In "A Christmas Carol," published in 1843, we see a glimpse of the working conditions and the home life of Bob Cratchit, a rich man's clerk. And in *Bleak House* (1852–53), Dickens paints the picture of the squalor in which a law copyist has lived and died. One of the few hints we have of clerks in the United States comes from an 1857 collection of essays under the title *The Man of Business, Considered in His Various Relations,* written by Protestant ministers. Another account, provided by a former clerk, about her work some 30 years after Bartleby's time, still provides a picture of working conditions and an environment that seems consistent with that described by Melville.

The section on the nineteenth-century white-collar wage earner ends with the case of Fitz-Greene Halleck, John Jacob Astor's business manager, an artist whose creativity seemed dormant as long as he worked in a Wall Street office.

A CLERK'S LIFE IN LONDON

Charles Dickens had himself worked as a clerk in a law office and as a short-hand reporter for a newspaper. In 1843, in "A Christmas Carol," his story of the redemption of a miser named Scrooge, he characterized the life of a lower-class clerk: his depressing work environment, his terror at losing his job, and his low wages that are not enough to support his family and provide his sick son with the proper medical care. Cratchit makes "fifteen Bob a week," on which he supports five children in a four-room house.

The first excerpt from "A Christmas Carol" is a description of Bob Cratchit's workplace. The second is an exchange between the clerk and his employer, who begrudges him his one Christmas holiday.

There are parallels between "Bartleby" and Charles Dickens's *Bleak House,* with its subject of a seemingly unending legal case and its portraits of lawyers and workers in their offices. David Jaffe, in *"Bartleby the Scrivener" and "Bleak House"* (10), points out that the various clerks mentioned in *Bleak House*— Mr. Boythorn, Guppy, and Smallweed—resemble Turkey, Nippers, and Ginger Nut. But Dickens's *Bleak House* chapter "The Law-Writer" is a particularly grim look at the life and death of Nemo, one of Bartleby's professional contemporaries in London. The chief characters in this excerpt are a lawyer named Tulkinghorn, who is attempting to find a "law-writer" who has copied some documents for him; Snagsby, who runs a legal-stationery shop and arranges for the copying of documents; and Krook, keeper of the Rag and Bottle shop, where the law copyist Nemo rents a room.

FROM CHARLES DICKENS, "A CHRISTMAS CAROL," IN *CHRISTMAS BOOKS BY CHARLES DICKENS* (NEW YORK: JOHN W. LOVELL, 1880)

The door of Scrooge's counting-house was open that he might keep his eye upon his clerk, who in a dismal little cell beyond, a sort of tank, was copying letters. Scrooge had a very small fire, but the clerk's fire was so very much smaller that it looked like one coal. But he couldn't replenish it, for Scrooge kept the coal-box in his own room; and so surely as the clerk came in with the shovel, the master predicted that it would be necessary for them to part. Wherefore the clerk put on his white comforter, and tried to warm himself at the candle; in which effort, not being a man of a strong imagination, he failed. (9)

...

At length the hour of shutting up the counting-house arrived. With an ill-will Scrooge dismounted from his stool, and tacitly admitted the fact to the expectant clerk in the Tank, who instantly snuffed his candle out, and put on his hat.

"You'll want all day to-morrow, I suppose?" said Scrooge.

"If quite convenient, sir."

"It's not convenient," said Scrooge, "and it's not fair. If I was to stop half-a-crown for it, you'd think yourself ill-used, I'll be bound?"

The clerk smiled faintly.

"And yet," said Scrooge, "you don't think *me* ill-used, when I pay a day's wages for no work."

The clerk observed that it was only once a year.

"A poor excuse for picking a man's pocket every twenty-fifth of December!" said Scrooge, buttoning his great-coat to the chin. "But I suppose you must have the whole day. Be here all the earlier next morning."

The clerk promised that he would. (14)

FROM CHARLES DICKENS, *BLEAK HOUSE* (LONDON: MACDONALD, 1855)

"You copied some affidavits in the cause for me lately."

"Yes, sir, we did."

"There was one of them," says Mr. Tulkinghorn, . . . the handwriting of which is peculiar, and I rather like. . . . I looked in to ask you who copied this?"

"Who copied this, sir?" says Mr. Snagsby. . . . "We gave this out, sir. We were giving out rather a large quantity of work just at that time. . . . To be sure! I might have remembered it. This was given out, sir, to a Writer who lodges just over on the opposite side of the lane."

. . . "*What* do you call him? Nemo?" says Mr. Tulkinghorn.

"Nemo, sir. Here it is. Forty-two folio. Given out on the Wednesday night, at eight o'clock; brought in on the Thursday morning, at half after nine."

"Nemo!" repeats Mr. Tulkinghorn. "Nemo is Latin for no one." (131, 132)

. . .

[Tulkinghorn and Snagsby go in search of Nemo and are directed to a room upstairs in the Rag and Bottle shop.]

It is a small room, nearly black with soot, and grease, and dirt. In the rusty skeleton of a grate, pinched at the middle as if Poverty had gripped it, a red coke fire burns low. In the corner by the chimney, stand a deal table and a broken desk; a wilderness marked with a rain of ink. In another corner, a ragged old portmanteau on one of the two chairs, serves for cabinet or wardrobe; no large one is needed, for it collapses like the cheeks of a starved man. The floor is bare; except that one old mat, trodden to shreds of rope-yarn, likes perishing upon the hearth. No curtain veils the darkness of the night, but the discolored shutters are drawn together; and through the two gaunt holes pierced in them, famine might be staring in—. . . (134, 135)

[Nemo, they discover, is dead of an opium overdose.]

THE OFFICE IN NINETEENTH-CENTURY AMERICA

In his book *White Collar: The American Middle Classes,* C. Wright Mills refers to oral accounts of the office situation in the nineteenth century after the Civil War. At this time, women had become clerical workers in a field that they would soon come to dominate. Although the account is of an office in the 1880s, some 30 years after "Bartleby," it gives the reader one of the few impressions of the office in the nineteenth century, seemingly dark, drafty, and deadening.

FROM C. WRIGHT MILLS, "THE OLD OFFICE," IN *WHITE COLLAR: THE AMERICAN MIDDLE CLASSES* (NEW YORK: OXFORD UNIVERSITY PRESS, 1951)

Just the other day the first typist in the city of Philadelphia, who had served one firm 60 years, died at the age of 80. During her last days she recalled how it was in the earlier days. She had come into the office from her employer's Sunday school class in 1882. She remembered when the office was one rather dark room, the windows always streaked with dust from the outside, and often fogged with smoke from the potbellied stove in the middle of the room. She remembered the green eyeshade and the cash book, the leather-bound ledger and the iron spike on the desk top, the day book and the quill pen, the letter press and the box file.

At first there were only three in the office: At the high roll-top desk, dominating the room, sat the owner; on a stool before a high desk with a slanted top and thin legs hunched the bookkeeper; and near the door, before a table that held the new machine, sat the white-collar girl.

The bookkeeper, A. B. Nordin, Jr. recently told the National Association of Office Managers, was an "old-young man, slightly stoop-shouldered, with a sallow complexion, usually dyspeptic-looking, with black sleeves and a green eye shade...Regardless of the kind of business, regardless of their ages, they all looked alike..." He seemed tired, and "he was never quite happy, because...his face betrayed the strain of working toward that climax of his month's labors. He was usually a neat penman, but his real pride was in his ability to add a column of figures rapidly and accurately. In spite of this accomplishment, however, he seldom, if ever, left his ledger for a more promising position. His mind was atrophied by that destroying, hopeless influence of drudgery and routine work. He was little more than a figuring machine with an endless number of figure combinations learned by heart. His feat was a feat of memory." (190, 191)

THE YOUNG CLERK: 1857

In a collection of essays by clerical writers titled *The Man of Business, Considered in His Various Relations,* one, "The Merchant's Clerk Cheered and Counseled" by James W. Alexander, is directed to the youthful employees in the financial community. Alexander acknowledges that there are two classes of clerks and that upper-class young men are in the distinct minority. So his remarks are primarily meant for the rural or small-town boy who leaves his family behind to find work in New York City. Alexander's primary concern is to warn naive young men against the vice of the city that can tempt them in their loneliness and destroy their careers.

While Alexander stresses the evils of alcohol, prostitution, and bad companions, he seems to turn a blind eye to the evils of the system, encouraging the young clerks to avoid complaining, work hard, and be cheerful and hopeful, that by so doing they will rise to better positions in the business world.

FROM JAMES W. ALEXANDER, "THE MERCHANT'S CLERK CHEERED AND COUNSELED," IN *THE MAN OF BUSINESS, CONSIDERED IN HIS VARIOUS RELATIONS* (NEW YORK: ANSON D. F. RANDOLPH, 1857)

The young men engaged in the commercial houses of this metropolis are innumerable; the numbers rise by tens of thousands. Hence we are justified in giving a character somewhat local to these remarks, believing that the youth of other cities are not so diverse in nature or situation as that they may not derive benefit from advices calculated for the meridian of New-York. Within limits so narrow, much can not be said; but all that is offered proceeds from true sympathy and earnest good will.

Of the countless throng of city clerks, some are living under the parental roof, but the great majority have come from the country. An increasing centripetal force bears the youth of rural districts towards the great emporium. While this infusion of fresh blood into the old veins is useful in many ways to the receiving party, it involves losses and exposures on the part of those who come. Each of them has left a beloved circle, which, alas! he has not yet learned to prize, and has entered into a comparatively homeless state.

* * *

This coast is strewed with blackened hulks and gaping timbers, which went out of port all flaunting with pennons. The newly-arrived boy or young man plunges into trouble and danger the hour he sets foot in the city. All is strange and much is saddening; but he must choke down unmanly griefs, and he knows little of his worst enemies. The single circumstance that parental care is henceforth removed, or made slight by distance, leaves him stripped of armor in a battle-field.

Whatever comes of it, put your shoulder to the wheel for a few months; by that time some of the rough places will have become plain. Wear the yoke gracefully. Every moment of this weariness and trouble will turn out to your lasting profit, especially in regard to character. There are certain things which you will be ashamed to class among hardships. Such are early rising, which you should practise for pleasure and longevity, as well as religion; exercise in the open air, or on your feet; hard work, tending towards knowledge of business; punctuality, without which you can never attain wealth or honor; and tedious employment in affairs which secure you confidential regard. In all these temptations to discontent, let me venture an observation on life, which I confess it cost me many years to comprehend. Uneasiness in the youthful mind arises from a fallacy that we may express thus: "Work now, but rest and pleasure hereafter." Not merely the clerk, but the millionaire, thus deludes himself: "I will bear these annoyances in view of the refreshing and luxurious respite of my hereafter." In opposition to all this, let me declare to you, that these hours, or days, or years of repose, when the mighty oppressive hand of the giant Business is let up, will be none the less sweet, for your having taken a genuine satisfaction in your work as you went along. You will not make the journey better, if, like famous pilgrims to Loretto, you put peas in your shoes. FORM THE HABIT OF SEEKING PLEASURE IN WORK, HAPPINESS IN THE DUTY OF THE HOUR.

The period when the young man is about coming of age is very important. Now it is, if ever, that he is most tempted to slip his neck out of the yoke, and most harassed with wishes prompted by false independence. No man can calculate the mercantile disasters arising from the preposterous wishes of young men, without experience, ability, connections or capital, to rush into business for themselves. Wise delay in such cases is promotive of success. The number of principals is far too great in proportion. It is not every man who is formed to be a leader, and some are clearly pointed out for subordinate posts as long as they live. But as these are often the very persons who will be slowest to take the hint, let it be the maxim of all to adventure no sudden changes; to wait for undeniable indications of duty and discretion; to attempt nothing of the sort without the full approval of older heads; and, above all, to play the man in regard to the unavoidable annoyances of a subaltern place.

. . .

It is the more necessary for the young in a strange city to be resolute and decided in this matter, because he has to make head against a strong torrent of circumstances. Those who have mastered this tide, and reached success, are too often indifferent about the poor fellows who are still struggling. Again I must say, with much earnestness, the state of society in our cities, is not favorable to the improvement of clerks. In a great number of instances, they may be said to be homeless. Their solitary chambers afford no invitations, except to sleep. There is often no cheerful apartment where they can feel themselves to be welcome. The mansions of their employers are, of course, out of the question.

POETIC RENDERINGS OF THE SILENCING OF THE ARTIST
BY WALL STREET

Bartleby has often been interpreted as a figure of Melville himself, who had been silenced by Wall Street values when he had not been able to make a living writing and when he could not satisfy the mass audience of readers eager for popular fiction. Melville had had youthful experiences in working in clerical positions, once briefly in his brother's law office and once for a merchant in Hawaii. Later he had turned to the writing of fiction and poetry. But his great novel, *Moby Dick,* now considered an American masterpiece, was then found puzzling, and his novel *Pierre* infuriating. In *Pierre* he had started out trying to cater to the public taste and, in spite of himself, had parodied the kind of romance the public craved. Even his closest friends and family were flabbergasted and annoyed by *Pierre.* They considered him to be mentally unstable, like Bartleby, and tried their best to get him out of the isolation he had gone into at Arrowhead in Massachusetts. Ironically, some 13 years after Melville published "Bartleby," he also ended up, like Bartleby, working in an office in New York's financial district, in the Custom-House, within three blocks of Wall Street.

An argument could also be made that Bartleby, as representative of the silenced artist, is John Jacob Astor's business executive, Fitz-Greene Halleck, who was widely known as a poet. In his need to make a living, Halleck had come to New York and eventually found his position with Astor, for whom he worked for 16 years. As long as he was required to serve the business interests of Astor, he did not publish poetry, and many of his admirers saw his creativity and talent as having been sacrificed to the god of Wall Street. Halleck had been very much in the news in 1849 and 1850 when it became known that Astor had left him only $200 a year, an undeserved slap in the face. There were a few theories about why Astor treated Halleck so miserably in his will. One reason may have been that in 1836, in his widely read pamphlet *Fanny,* Halleck had made fun of Astor's son-in-law, the Reverend John Bristed, the father of Astor's favorite grandchild, to whom he left a large legacy.

James Grant Wilson, Halleck's biographer, discovered two poems, written in the 1840s, deploring Halleck's "dead letters."

A poem by Anne Lynch, dated 1847, speaks of the high purpose of the poet who can "lift our spirits from the dust." But "the one among the throng" she speaks of is Fitz-Greene Halleck, who has dropped his lyre and sings no more. The world's citizens, presumably, have lost his ability to uplift them. She ends the poem with a plea that he sing again. A second undated, anonymous poem speaks more directly to the poet's sacrifice of his talent to Wall Street and John Jacob Astor.

FROM ANNE LYNCH, "ON HALLECK," QUOTED IN JAMES
GRANT WILSON, *THE LIFE AND LETTERS OF FITZ-GREENE
HALLECK* (NEW YORK: D. APPLETON, 1869), 471–72

I see the sons of Genius rise,

The nobles of our land,

And foremost in the gathering ranks

I see the poet-band.

That priesthood of the Beautiful,

To whom alone 'tis given

To lift our spirits from the dust,

Back to their native heaven.

But there is one amid the throng

Not passed his manhood's prime,

The laurel-wreath upon his brow,

Has greener grown with time.

And in his eye yet glows the light

Of the celestial fire,

But cast beside him on the earth

Is his neglected lyre.

The lyre whose high heroic notes

A thousand hearts have stirred

Lies mute—the skilful hand no more

Awakes one slumbering chord.

O poet, rouse thee from thy dreams!

Wake from thy voiceless slumbers,

And once again give to the breeze

The music of thy numbers.

Sing! for our country claims her bards,

She listens for *thy* strains;

Sing! for upon our jarring earth

Too much of discord reigns.

FROM "DESCRIPTION OF THE POET HALLECK," QUOTED
IN JAMES GRANT WILSON, *THE LIFE AND LETTERS
OF FITZ-GREENE HALLECK* (NEW YORK: D. APPLETON,
1869), 393

Methought that brow, so full and fair,

Was formed the poet's wreath to wear;

And as those eyes of azure hue,

One moment lifted, met my view,

Gay worlds of starry thoughts appeared

In their blue depths serenely sphered.

Still to his task the bard applied,

Unrecked, unheeded all beside;

And as he closed the solemn sheet,

I heard his murmuring lips repeat—

Total a semi-million clear

Income received for one short year;

Aladdin's wealth scarce mounted faster

At its spring-tide than thine, Herr Astor.

CONTEMPORARY BARTLEBYS

Major changes have occurred in the field of clerical work since Bartleby's day. Clerical workers, especially in financial and insurance institutions, have increased substantially. In the mid-nineteenth century, clerical workers constituted less than one percent of all wage earners. By the end of the twentieth century, one-tenth of all workers were in clerical positions. And from the first of the twentieth century to the last, almost all clerical workers were female instead of male. The introduction of the typewriter altered the main work of the office in the early part of the century. But the office worker was now under provisions of what the blue-collar labor force called the *speed-up,* being under tremendous pressure to perform at greater and greater speed. Typists were hired only if they could reach speeds of a certain number of words a minute. The individualism of the handwritten document was no more. Now a machine stood between the task to be done and the finished product. Moreover, the deadening conditions affecting the typist were the same as those that plagued Turkey and Bartleby: a single error on a page—the omission of a line, say—might require the retyping of the entire document. With the introduction of the word processor, the deadly necessity of retyping entire documents came to an end. But the machine domination of the office has become even more intense. The breakdown of the machine paralyzed work, for instance.

Divisions of labor into typists or word processors, bookkeepers, receptionists, underwriters, bank tellers, programmers, and so on heighten the perfunctory, disjointed nature of white-collar work so that the worker rarely sees his or her place as an intelligence in the finished task.

Another discouragement in the twenty-first-century office is the often subtle but firm control that management has over clerical work. This is most clearly demonstrated in the arrangement of the enormous offices that have superseded the small ones of the nineteenth century. In the typical work situation, there are rows and rows of desks for clerical staff in the middle of an immense room. Around the edges of the room, facing the clerical staff, are the desks of division managers, monitoring their work.

The development of office cubicles, first apparent in the computer industry, has become another means of control and intensifies the mechanical nature of work, for it stifles human social connections and communication. In this arrangement, workers are isolated from each other and from the outside world. Bartleby looked out on a blackened wall. The cubicle worker is boxed into a small space by walls.

One of the greatest discouragements, experienced especially by Nippers in "Bartleby," is the inability to rise to a better position from office worker. A few twentieth- and twenty-first-century clerks are promoted to higher managerial positions, but most of these are males, and many, as in the nineteenth century, are children of owners who have been charged with learning the business from the bottom up. For the great majority, changes, when they occur, are lateral.

The connection between the operation of office machines and the killing off of aspiration is made by David Lockwood in *The Blackcoated Worker*, a study of the British office worker:

> But in selecting staff by modern methods for well-defined mechanical duties, the employer runs the risk of eliminating those who have not the physical qual-ifications for the use of certain machines, but have on the other hand the gifts of intelligence and character which would permit them to reach the higher rungs of the ladder. The inverse is equally true: owing to such methods, the employee employed as a machine operator receives a strong impression that he is meant exclusively for this unimportant function and must remain his whole life in an inferior post. (91)

The following excerpts from an essay by Maarten de Kadt, once a white-collar worker in an insurance office, illustrate the controls exercised over the Bartlebys of the contemporary world.

CONTROL AND SURVEILLANCE

Maarten de Kadt provides a detailed analysis of the work situation in one of the nation's largest employers of white-collar workers—the insurance industry. Despite the image of white-collar workers as upwardly mobile, educated members of the middle class, de Kadt, a former underwriter, sees the office as "a clerical work factory." As in "Bartleby," constant surveillance, division of labor, and mechanization of tasks negate the intelligence, creativity, freedom, and responsibility of the worker.

FROM MAARTEN DE KADT, "INSURANCE: A CLERICAL WORK FACTORY," IN *CASE STUDIES ON THE LABOR PROCESS*, ED. ANDREW ZIMBALIST (NEW YORK: MONTHLY REVIEW PRESS, 1979)

An underwriter used to be responsible for the main decision-making function in the insurance business. I remember being told countless times that we as underwriters were the heart of the insurance operation. In recent years much of underwriting has become a clerical operation. While many of the work procedures which were common more than two decades ago are still in use, a large part of the work has become standardized and can in many cases be done simply by referring to various tables and charts; much has been computerized. (242)

The Newark office in which I worked was a typical medium-sized insurance company office. My desk was in the middle of a large open floor of an office building. By 9:05 a.m. the steady click, click of many typewriters could be heard. The telephones had started to ring. Most of the windows to the outside world were in the offices of the managers. Those offices were arranged around the outside of the floor. Not only could these managers look outward, but they could look inward as well: each of these offices had windows overlooking the open floor. The desks on the open floor were arranged in columns and rows. On one side of my desk there were five more desks, on the other there were four. Behind me there were three rows of desks and in front there were eleven more. This part of the office was laid out in a matrix of about ten by fifteen desks. Here 150 employees did their daily work. (244)

. . .

Management surveillance, while the most effective form of control, was not the only one. . . . Management also used the division of labor to control the work. The office contained two kinds of division of labor. Each section had its own hierarchy of supervision and surveillance . . . (245)

. . .

The control over the clerical labor process and over clerical workers in the insurance factory . . . remains one of control by humans over other humans. . . . The clerical work factory has been designed to keep down the cost of record keeping while maintaining control over the workers who keep records. (256)

QUESTIONS AND PROJECTS

1. Write a detailed job description for the narrator to use in filling a position in his office.

2. In an essay, explore the similarities between Bartleby's position and that unfolded in current documents on the white-collar worker.

3. Keeping in mind issues discussed in this chapter regarding work, construct a volume of interviews with working people for which each student contributes his or her own interview.

4. Have a class project of writing a history of working people in a local industry.

FURTHER READING

Anderson, G. *Victorian Clerks.* Manchester, England: Manchester University Press, 1976.

Fried, Albert, ed. *Except to Walk Free.* Garden City, N.Y.: Anchor Books, 1974.

Jaffe, David. *"Bartleby the Scrivener" and "Bleak House."* Hamden Court, Va.: Archon, 1979.

Kocka, J. *White Collar Workers in America, 1890–1940.* London: Sage Publications, 1980.

Lockwood, David. *The Blackcoated Worker: A Study in Class Consciousness.* Oxford: Clarendon Press, 1989.

Mills, C. Wright. *White Collar: The American Middle Classes.* New York: Oxford University Press, 1951.

Orchard, B. G. *The Clerks of Liverpool.* Liverpool: J. Collinsoa, 1871.

Pessen, Edward. *Riches, Class, and Power before the Civil War.* Lexington, Mass.: D. C. Heath, 1973.

Rozwenc, Edwin C., ed. *Ideology and Power in the Age of Jackson.* Garden City, N.Y.: Anchor Books, 1964.

Smith, Matthew Hale. *Sunshine and Shadow.* Hartford, Conn.: J. B. Burr, 1869.

Strong, George Templeton. *The Diary of George Templeton Strong.* 2 vols. Ed. Allan Nevins and Milton Halsey Thomas. New York: Macmillan, 1952.

Zimbalist, Andrew, ed. *Case Studies on the Labor Process.* New York: Monthly Review Press, 1979.

Zinn, Howard. *A People's History of the United States.* New York: HarperPerennial, 1980.

4

Worker Resistance

Nothing so aggravates an earnest person as a passive resistance. (72)

"Bartleby" is essentially the story of how the narrator/employer reacts to his workers' resistance to their "dull, wearisome, and lethargic" jobs. There is Turkey's alcoholism, blots, and refusal to give up his half day's work. There is Nippers's moonlighting and symbolic adjustments and readjustments of his desk. And, especially, there is Bartleby in his firm refusal to correct, copy, do the simplest errand, or leave the office—all expressed in the radical phrase "I prefer not to."

Bartleby's "passive resistance," which so exasperates his employer, is an echo of one of Melville's contemporaries, Henry David Thoreau, who promulgated a concept of resistance to governmental authority through nonparticipation. In his essay, Thoreau wrote of passive resistance. Melville almost certainly knew who Thoreau was, and, while Bartleby may not be equivalent to Thoreau, he most certainly partakes of the nonviolent resistance inspired by Thoreau's civil disobedience. Thoreau titled his essay "Resistance to Civil Government," a title that was changed by others to the one it is now known by: "Civil Disobedience." Thoreau's idea took shape in the summer of 1846, shortly after the Mexican War began, when, after years of refusing to pay his state poll tax to a government that supported Southern slavery and then the war, he was jailed. In 1848, he gave a lecture that had primarily to do with resistance to government. And in the next year, it was published by Elizabeth Peabody, the sister-in-law of Nathaniel Hawthorne, once Melville's closest friend. Rather than adopting the violent methods of John Brown to resist slavery (although Thoreau greatly admired John Brown), he initially took the road of peaceful, nonviolent civil disobedience by merely refusing to pay his taxes. Civil disobedience came to mean the strategy of refusing to obey an unjust law in order to bring attention to it and repeal it. The strategy also included peaceful acquiescence to whatever penalty, like imprisonment, one's law-breaking incurred.

In addition to his rebellious preferences, Bartleby has further identification with Thoreau in that Thoreau's entire life was lived in passive resistance to a national society based on materialism and business. Although he was Harvard-educated and the son of a merchant, Thoreau preferred not to live his life as a professional or a businessman. He preferred not to own property or accumulate capital or to be a part of what the Reverend John Todd called a *society of interdependence.* He spent his days doing independent surveying for the county, often without being asked or paid, and taking children on nature outings. His whole experiment in independence at Walden Pond was a philosophical renunciation of the larger society of capitalistic getting and spending.

Thoreau's strategy of civil disobedience was widely used in the nineteenth century by many others fighting for social change, particularly women's suffrage and temperance. The peaceful demonstrators were in sharp contrast to the violent ones like Carry Nation, who took an ax to the bars.

Two prominent struggles against governments in the twentieth century are notable for having given credit to Thoreau in their own staunch adoption of civil disobedience or nonviolent resistance in objecting to government policies. The first was India's Mohandas Gandhi, who drew from Thoreau's thought, among others, in his struggle for basic human rights and independence from Britain for the Indian people, something not achieved until 1947. Gandhi's struggle began in the late nineteenth century and continued for over 50 years. He used two guiding principles, which, translated into English, mean "truth and firmness" and "noninjury." His nonviolent strategies included large demonstrations, boycotts of British goods, refusals to pay tax on British goods, massive sit-ins in the streets, and noncooperation with the colonial government, which led to resignations of Indians in public offices and the boycotting of government agencies and courts.

Another struggle made use of Thoreau's ideas of nonviolence as they were refined by Gandhi. This was the civil rights movement, which fought for basic rights, including suffrage, justice, and integration for African Americans. Its most prominent leader was Martin Luther King Jr. Instead of armed raids, bombings, destruction of property, and assassinations, King's methods of resistance were nonviolent sit-ins, boycotts, legal suits, and marches, beginning with the bus boycott in Montgomery, Alabama, which first drew King into the movement. Dr. King's activities also included a march of 200,000 on Washington, D.C., in 1963 and a 1965 march from Montgomery to Selma, Alabama.

Gandhi's and King's nonviolent resistance infuriated and provoked violent reactions from their adversaries, but inspired sympathy on the part of many citizens and resulted in positive change.

Nonviolent civil disobedience was also successfully used by the overwhelming majority of peace activists against the Vietnam War in the 1960s. Often invoking Thoreau, who had opposed the Mexican War, these resisters, from the ranks of young and old, borrowed tactics from the civil rights movement, staging sit-ins in public buildings and massive marches, including the largest in U.S. history—a march on Washington, D.C., on November 15, 1969, that involved 250,000 people.

LABOR RESISTANCE

Bartleby is a passive resister who refuses to (prefers not to) perform his job or leave his place of employment, prefiguring the protesting worker in the twentieth century. To the Bartleby-like sit-downs and strikes, labor added the picket line. While many strikes and labor demonstrations did turn violent, most were peaceable, the violence generally being generated as a response on the part of owners and managers.

Striking workers usually walk off the job, leaving the factory or field, but in a sit-down strike, used widely in the 1930s, workers remain in the workplace until their demands are met. The effect is to bring factory operations to a halt and keep the owners from bringing in scabs to do the work. In the 1930s, sit-downs were effectively used by workers in a number of industries, including rubber, steel, automobile, and textile factories. The first of the sit-down strikes of the 1930s was in the Firestone rubber plant in Akron, Ohio, in late January 1936, chiefly over the dismissal of one of the workers, a man named Dicks. The men went into work at the conveyor belts, and then at a prearranged time, one of the men gave a signal and they stepped back from their work, their noisy world now motionless and silent. As foremen raced to inform management, the men made a pact to police the factory, making sure that everything in the factory would be left clean and in good working order, and that there would be no drinking or rowdy behavior. As news of the sit-down circulated and other rubber plants threatened to join them, management agreed to their demands to reinstate Dicks with back pay and to open salary negotiations.

One of the most famous sit-down strikes was in 1936 and 1937, undertaken by automobile workers in the General Motors plants in Flint, Michigan. The sit-downs began when management refused to discuss the workers' grievances. Workers took over a Fisher Body plant in Cleveland, Ohio. Two days later, workers began sit-in strikes in two Fisher Body plants in Flint, eventually involving 136,000 automobile workers in nationwide strikes. A month later, with the sit-in still not resolved, workers occupied another crucial General Motors plant. Workers were scrupulous in protecting the property they had occupied. Their families and supporters on the outside provided them with food. Finally, on February 11, 1937, a settlement was reached between the workers and General Motors.

Workers who occupied plants in sit-downs were, however, charged with trespassing on the owners' property. And in 1939, sit-down strikes were declared illegal, so workers turned from the sit-down strike to the slow-down: they came to work, but slowed down operations to lower the factory's total production.

SABOTAGE

Assembly-line work, like that used in many factories, inspired a type of worker resistance known as *sabotage*. Nothing so completely accomplished the dehumanization and depersonalization of a worker, the beginnings of which we find in "Bartleby," as the assembly line. It divided labor into discrete, mindless motions so that, for example, a worker might be charged with doing nothing all day but the turning of one-sized screws into the same small parts of an automobile—over and over and over again. In chopping up work into minuscule, repetitive functions, the worker became a mindless machine with no connection to or pride in a final product. The assembly line allowed the owner total control over the worker, especially because management could set the pace of the operation, speeding up the conveyor belts and pace of assembly to tremendous speeds in order to produce more products in less time, a situation parodied by Charlie Chaplin in the film *Modern Times*. One of the songs sung by workers asked Mr. Foreman to please slow down the assembly line.

The connection with Bartleby echoes in David Gartman's lines from "Origins of the Assembly Line and Capitalist Control of Work at Ford":

> Since its origin, the assembly line has been killing auto workers in a number of ways. Death might come in the literal form of an industrial accident on the relentless, driving line, as it did recently at a GM assembly plant in California. Or it might be the "spiritual" death brought on by a lifetime of boring, monotonous, and meaningless work. The assembly line has also meant the death of an important aspect of working-class power, for it has been a crucial factor in the demise of a tradition of skilled, intelligent labor. (193)

Resistance to the assembly line took the forms of the old sit-downs and slow-downs, but also, interestingly, what were called *skippies*. During a skippy, workers would decide to "skip," or leave out crucial screws at particular points in the manufacturing process, resulting in numerous seriously flawed products.

INDEPENDENT RESISTANCE

A skippy was only one rebellious action in a larger category of resistance called sabotage, which is rarely used by organized labor but often used by single individuals. In the workforce, the term usually means some action on the part of a worker that ends up screwing up the quantity, quality, or service that the industry or business exists to produce. For example, the failure to place a screw in a vital place on an automobile weakened it. The "accidental" dropping of a crate of fragile merchandise at the dock shattered the contents. An act of sabotage may be putting something into the machinery that will break it down, perhaps for just long enough to give the workers a rest. It may be no more than putting vinegar into a loom for weaving silk. Sabotage as a practice on the part of workers has probably existed since the dawn of the workforce, but the term originates from the French word for wooden shoes, *sabots,* which disgruntled European workers once threw into the machinery to damage it.

Sometimes individual workers seem scarcely aware of their own sabotage in a system of work whose humiliations they might feel but have not intellectualized. Others plan a single act of sabotage in retribution for a particular grievance, or they plan more than one action in retribution for a pattern of grievances: being passed over for a raise, being chewed out in front of coworkers, being burdened with additional projects, being forced to do demeaning tasks.

OFFICE SABOTAGE

The factory is not the only place where sabotage in the workplace occurs. There is ample reason and opportunity for sabotage among white-collar workers in the office. From the book *Sabotage in the American Workplace,* edited by Martin Sprouse, come personal histories of sabotage on the part of many different kinds of workers, including those who are the modern-day equivalents of Bartleby, working in insurance offices, law offices, banks, and stock brokerage houses. A programmer for a bank hacks into the payroll, causing it to disappear and infect the bank's whole computer system. A technical writer creates a novel on company time. Paralegals, handling clients, collect money to pay the clients' doctors but pocket most of the rest of the money that would end up with the law firm they work for. An insurance file clerk lets the paperwork for an individual's policy go through even though the client has not kept up the premiums. A secretary for a cosmetics company leaves the office early but records a full day's work. A file clerk destroys notices of court appearances.

A WHITE-COLLAR PERSPECTIVE

The following interview with Chris Carlsson is a look into the resistance underground in the white-collar world. Carlsson is now an independent writer, editor, and producer of graphic and multimedia design. From 1981 to 1994, he was a prime mover in establishing, producing, and editing *Processed World*, a freestyled, radical magazine of satire, art, fiction, and reportage on white-collar issues, directed chiefly, though not exclusively, to the disaffected office worker. The interview with Carlsson is a description of the conditions that provoke sabotage, the resister's attitude toward the office and office work, and the means of undermining the system.

FROM CHRIS CARLSSON, INTERVIEW WITH AUTHOR, SAN FRANCISCO, CALIF., 13 OCTOBER 2003

CJ: Tell me something of your history as a white-collar worker.

Carlsson: Well, I didn't graduate from college. I dropped out of college in 1979. And at that point, I already had experience working at information desks. But my first real experience as a white collar worker was as a sales clerk at Waldenbooks in Springfield, Pennsylvania in 1974. In college I worked at the Information Desk at SF State University. One of the first jobs I had after I dropped out of college was working at the Downtown Community College Center at 4th and Mission in San Francisco. And its purpose was to train the white-collar worker.

CJ: What used to be called a business college.

Carlsson: Yes, essentially it was a city business college, part of a community college. And I was already involved in various radical political groups and involved with street theater, so that combination with my situation led me to a job paying six or seven dollars an hour. While there I did take a class in IBM mag card—it was the precursor of screen display word processing, looked kind of like an IBM Selectric. It had a machine next to it that read cards, like sizable punch cards. There you had to memorize where you were on the page. So if you made a typo, you had to line advance, line advance, line advance, word advance, word advance, word advance, until you got to the right place to make the corrections and then print. I was already a pretty good typist because I had learned typing when I was in the ninth grade. Used to make a living for a long time actually—I was a typist. I kind of had a personal commitment to not selling my brain. I was willing to sell my body but not my brain. So I wouldn't consider—wouldn't look for jobs that required me to be engaged creatively. I was in such an oppositional stance to the world that I was in. I thought, what can I do minimally, so that essentially, I would be formally, though not totally dominated by capital.

CJ: I understand that you are an advocate for the white-collar worker.

Carlsson: Actually, its not part of my job—its part of my avocation. My main bread and butter these days is the ILWU newspaper.

CJ: Tell me about Processed World.

Carlsson: In 80 and 81—some other white-collar workers and I first started *Processed World* magazine. It was originally set up to be a channel, a forum for horizontal communications amongst people in the office world because we recognized that A) we had this typical work force of lifer types who had been there for a while and didn't have much aspirations to do anything else with their lives. And then there was a tremendous body of workers like us who—discontented liberal arts graduates or drop outs who had learned one thing in college which was how to fill out forms. So whether they were philosophers, or dancers, or historians, or all the different possible categories we could possibly be in was who they really were and found themselves day in and day out having to do something else to pay their bills. And we were in that same category, so we said, "Let's create a magazine to begin to talk about the political implications of that." And the possibility of providing strong leverage in some kind of working class revolt, which was more or less a fantasy for us that we'd be part of that. Not to mention the fact that what set us apart from normal workers is that we were also very oriented toward pleasure and this notion of sacrifice and working for the class and dedicating your own life for other people was not our point of view at all. Our point if view was *our* lives. *Our* lives sucked. And it could be a lot better. And one of the reasons it sucked was because we were doing completely stupid things—that not only did we not want to do these things, but *nobody* should do these things. There were these huge industries that should be abolished tomorrow: banking, insurance, real estate, advertising, shoddy production in every part of the economy. So we had this deep critique of the economy that very few people ever articulated or shared—to this day. And, the magazine, therefore, didn't just provide a place for political discussion of issues, though that was part of its function, it was a forum where people could sort of vent about these things on the job, but it was also a place where people could express themselves creatively—when you didn't have any future to being able to express yourself creatively. If nothing else, it allowed *us* to do that. But other people too. And we tapped a nerve and got a tremendous response.

And there was quite a vibrant underground culture around it. Gatherings at bars during the week for several years. We would gather in the streets on Friday. We'd dress in strange costumes and dance around the streets with signs like "IBM: Intensely Boring Machines" and "Data Slaves." And we sort of short circuited the normal problems of underground media which is finding your audience and being able to communicate with it. So we were actually out on the streets—every Friday anonymously distributing the magazine and soliciting participation from writers and editors to get involved. It was an open forum in which everyone could participate. So over the course of thirteen years we probably had four hundred people that were part of the collective. Those people in the collective were actually working as tech writers or secretaries or word processors or whatever. All of us were smart people with backgrounds and skills and doing various things to figure out how to make a living in a really very unfriendly world and not give away our whole brain and all of our creative possibilities and still maintain some sense of our humanity and create a life worth living right now.

CJ: What happened to the magazine?

Carlsson: It succeeded to some extent and our part of it was that during the time we published it, from 81 to 94, the rest of the left disintegrated and vanished. We ended up being one of the last ones standing. And the culture sustaining it pretty much shriveled up and died. By the nineties, the level of engagement and response to the magazine dropped off really noticeably. We were getting far fewer letters to the editor. We were once flooded with mail and suddenly we weren't being flooded with mail. It just wasn't happening. I don't know if that's because the culture shifted to the right. I voted to stop the magazine but I was out voted by the rest of the then-collective. However, they weren't able to keep publishing, so issue 32 in 1994 was the last until we did a special twentieth anniversary issue in 2001.

During the time when we started, I wrote an article on workplace transience called the rise of "The Rise of the Six Month Worker" a look at the dialectical relationship between people like me who wanted to work less and liked to come in and be casual—and the needs of capital which was also needing to casualize the work force. And it was pretty clear that to us that that was true, but at that point in the eighties we were seeing a process beginning to radically Taylorize office work, which depended on temporary workers to cushion that process of workplace restructuring.

CJ: I came across an article that described office work in an insurance company as a white collar factory. Is that an overstatement?

Carlsson: Not at all. I think that was the model for office work. The first ideas about how to organize office work were based on the factory model.

CJ: How so?

Carlsson: I think originally they put people in giant rooms. People were sitting in rows of desks, sitting at computers or typewriters. When I came into the office world, we were already in cubicles.

CJ: What effect did this have? Did it contribute to a certain amount of isolation?

Carlsson: Well communication continued to be established through the internet, and earlier, by using the Xerox machine to circulate information. Xeroxes were floating around every office. And there is communication between office workers through email.

CJ: Now there's surveillance of employee's email, is there not?

Carlsson: There is surveillance, but there are many ways around it with software. Its not that hard to disguise time theft and personal communication. Those people had a lot of autonomy, but they were controlled in other ways. And in fact it was actually parallel to what we found out in *Processed World* (that referred to itself as the magazine with the bad attitude). Anyone could do the work. It wasn't a matter of skills or anything else. It came down to attitude. If they have a bad attitude, they're fired. There is this compulsion to produce—over produce—better than anybody else.

The concept of working as a team was introduced ostensibly to democratize work and take advantage of incentive, but, in fact, became just as controlling as division of labor. So this team mentality is way more insidious than waiting for the boss to catch you. It's not only that you are under optimum pressure by your co-workers all the time but that you crack the whip on yourself, knowing that they will be put out if you don't do your part.

CJ: So, given the character of white-collar work, that you've just described, you decided to undermine it.

Carlsson: Well yes, for example, I was working as a temporary with Arthur Anderson and quite a few other jobs and did that for the better part of a year and a half. And we had a little slogan: "a ream [of paper] a day keeps the paper bills away." The office world back then was tremendously wasteful. And I think it still is. But I haven't been in it in a long time and I understand the success we had exploiting the excess fat of the land is not so available to the people after us.

Another example: at the Downtown Community College, I mentioned, I worked as an information clerk. It was mindless. I wasn't allowed to read, even when there was nothing to do. So I was sitting there at the information desk and came up with a little satire that later appeared in *Processed World,* called "The Heel Business School: The Training Institute for the Clerical Working Class," and it went on and on with that kind of rhetoric and there was a message from the director for me to come to her office. There was a scandal. The director called me in and fired me—I was quitting anyway. So, that was my early experience.

CJ: About this time you and your friends decided to form a resistance movement.

Carlsson: Yes, it all started with a little brochure I wrote shortly after I left my job. It was called "The Inner Voice"—a joke done in the style of an invoice about the prices to pay for being an office worker in downtown San Francisco. My girl friend and I put this out, and we handed it out in the Financial District in 1980. We imagined we might be part of a white-collar working class organizational revolt with our rather delusional left-wing mentality. We were communists with a small "c."

And resistance was the point of *Processed World.* When we launched the magazine in 1981, we were part of the whole zine revolution and that culture of the late eighties and nineties was based on a kind of resource theft. Part of how the office worker survived was by taking your personal phone calls, playing on the internet, using your email, and, you know, writing letters and writing novels, doing whatever you want to do with all those resources and I think that remains true to this day although the success with which people do that, subject to much greater surveillance, and the ability to loot the supply closet is limited in most companies because it has been so thoroughly looted for so long.

CJ: So, what you are telling me is that sabotage occurs even given the mentality of a white collar work force, poorly paid perhaps, fairly compliant, typically obeisant to management.

Carlsson: Oh yes.

CJ: What kind?

Carlsson: Well, there're two main ways people resist in an office. Time theft is the most obvious and widespread. In most offices, most people look busy. They seem to be working but actually aren't. Writing articles or writing their own novels or writing to their mothers or whatever it is. People find ways to create space, use mutual solidarity to protect each other, come in late, leave early, take long breaks and lunches, make time to do their own research (perhaps for a new job, for their kids' school, what have you). The other kind of sabotage is the kind where you break your machine. For a lot of office workers it's hard to really break their machine because they depend on it. But it's always easy to just pull back and announce, "My machine is fouling up," when it isn't really. There are lots of ways to physically damage a computer: The keyboard is vulnerable to spilled drinks, disk drives don't like magnets, paper clips can scratch magnetic media. But usually people don't do that themselves because it just makes more work for them. A very easy act of sabotage that I saw many times was the simple placement of an "out of order" sign on a floor's copying machine. There's nothing wrong with it at all, but suddenly business has to stop on that floor for the rest of that day and maybe the next day and the day after that while they wait for a technician to say its all right. But it has an effect. So there's that kind of sabotage.

There's a lot of stuff at the level of misinformation. Say you're doing data entry on the job or perhaps you're working on a mass mailing. It's incredibly easy to enter the wrong information, transpose numbers in an address or phone number. Anytime you type someone's name in, you do it slightly differently. Disinformation is probably vastly more deliberate and widespread than anyone can see or measure.

As companies try to save money with temporary workers, they invite a breakdown in control because the temporary worker has zero loyalty to the firm. Are you going to be gone in a few weeks? If you are, why would you care about the integrity of the data or the long term consequences of bad information?

The damage done is immeasurable and difficult to discover. I think many workers are not fully aware of their own resistance. I was different. It was my mission. I deliberately did stuff like that. Some people who do these things don't think in these terms, but a lot of people do. That's the nature of this whole question of attitude. It turns on keeping the job or getting ahead or not getting a raise or not getting the raise you think you deserved. Essentially there are a lot of ways to get even that are hard to catch.

CJ: Maybe we should end with words from Martin Sprouse's introduction to his book, Sabotage in the American Workplace: *"As long as people feel cheated, bored, harassed, endangered, or betrayed at work, sabotage will be used as a direct method of achieving job satisfaction—the kind that never has to get the bosses' approval."*

QUESTIONS AND PROJECTS

1. Conduct your own interview with a white-collar worker, addressing specifically the subject of worker dissatisfaction and resistance.

2. Write an essay titled "Worker Resistance in 'Bartleby the Scrivener.'"

3. Conduct research on the sit-down strike in American history and write a term paper from the information you uncover.

4. Interview a local union leader about his/her organization's opinion of the refusal to work as a labor strategy.

5. Throughout history, the government has on occasions outlawed strikes. Have a debate on whether strikes are in the best interests of the country's citizens.

6. Conduct research on the philosophy of resistance used by Martin Luther King Jr. and write a research paper from your findings. Contrast King's view with that of others in the struggle for racial justice who did use violence.

7. Debate the question of whether violence is ever justified in resistance.

FURTHER READING

Barnett, Louise K. "Bartleby as Alienated Worker." *Studies in Short Fiction* 2 (fall 1974): 379–95.

Busch, Frederick. "Thoreau and Melville as Cellmates." *Modern Fiction Studies* 23 (summer 1977): 239–42.

Conkling, Chris. "Misery of Christian Joy: Conscience and Freedom in 'Bartleby, the Scrivener.'" *Literature and Belief* (1981) I: 79–89.

Flynn, Elizabeth Gurley. "The Conscious Withdrawal of the Workers' Industrial Efficiency." IWW Publishing Bureau, October 1916. http://sniggle.net/Manifesti/sabotage.php.

Gartman, David. "Origins of the Assembly Line and Capitalist Control of Work at Ford." In *Case Studies on the Labor Process,* ed. Andrew Zimbalist. New York: Monthly Review Press, 1979.

Martin, Brian. *Nonviolence versus Capitalism.* London: War Resisters' International, 2001.

McKenney, Ruth. *Industrial Valley.* New York: Harcourt, Brace, Jovanovich, 1939.

Oliver, Egbert S. "A Second Look at Bartleby." *College English* 6 (May 1945): 431–39.

Rogin, Michael. *Subversive Genealogy: The Politics and Art of Herman Melville.* Berkeley: University of California Press, 1985.

Short, Raymond W., and Richard B. Sewall. *A Manual of Suggestions for Teachers Using Short Stories for Study.* New York: Henry Holt, 1956.

Sprouse, Martin, ed. *Sabotage in the American Workplace.* San Francisco: Drop Press, 1992.

Zelnick, Stephen. "Melville's 'Bartleby': History, Ideology, and Literature." *Marxist Perspectives* 2 (winter 1979–80): 74–92.

5

Religious Justification of Wall Street Practices

Gradually I slid into the persuasion that these troubles of mine, touching the scrivener, had been all predestinated from eternity. (35)

In "Bartleby," Melville makes specific references to New York City entities—one to John Jacob Astor and one to Trinity Church. As readers, we are obliged to ask why, in a piece of short fiction, the author made those choices. This chapter explores a context for those references as a means of better understanding Melville's intent.

In "Bartleby," religion encroaches on the financial world repeatedly, a situation that reflects a reality of nineteenth-century society in the United States. The successful businessman was usually an ardent churchgoer who believed it to be his God-given duty to make money. Similarly, the typical minister cultivated contacts with the wealthy, at the same time vigorously reinforcing a widely held conviction that the rich man's success was a consequence of his being especially loved by God.

The significant, overt allusions in the story to religion and the church establish the alliance so descriptive of Melville's milieu. However, these allusions would have been more readily apparent to the New Yorker of Melville's day than to a reader 150 years later. One of these references is to the sermons of the Reverend Joseph Priestley, a highly respected scientist who discovered oxygen, and the Reverend Jonathan Edwards, the most readily recognizable figure of the religious "Great Awakening" in the United States. The narrator finds justification for his inaction in sermons by these widely read ministers, who preached that all things were predetermined by God. The narrator also makes specific reference to Trinity Church, an Episcopalian church situated at the end of Wall Street, a short walk from the stock exchange. The narrator is on

A nineteenth-century photograph of Wall Street with Trinity
Church looming at the end of it. Collection of the New York
Historical Society.

his way to Sunday services there to hear a notable minister when, on a detour
to his nearby office, he finds Bartleby living there. His encounter with Bartleby,
living alone in the office, he says, "disqualified [him] for the time from church-
going" (25). The businessman of Melville's day would also have seen the earlier mention of John Jacob Astor as a glance at the connection between business
and the church since Astor, while not a member of Trinity Church, had well-
known, lucrative business connections with Trinity Church, which will be discussed below.

    "Bartleby" is also rich in explicit and implicit references to religious scrip-
ture. The narrator is reminded of John 13:34, a verse from the New Testament: "A new commandment I give unto you, that ye love one another" (King
James Version, all subsequent quotations are also from this version). Another

biblical quotation, of Job 3:14, appears when, at the time of Bartleby's death, the narrator says Bartleby is sleeping "[w]ith kings and counsellors" (45). And there are also *implicit* references to scripture, including Matthew 25, which ends, "Inasmuch as ye do it unto the least of these, my brethren, ye do it unto me," and 2 Corinthians 3:6, which teaches that the *letter* of the law kills, but the *spirit* of the law gives life. There is also an oblique reference to Peter's denial of his friendship with the imprisoned Jesus in the narrator's denial that he knows Bartleby.

BUSINESS AS GODLY

The Protestant Church in the nineteenth century, according to Henry F. May, believed in "the sanctity of private property, the virtue of competitive enterprise, and the legitimacy of gain" (*Protestant Churches and Industrial America,* 6). The businessman in the 1850s was able to lust and scramble for riches with few impediments, little censure from an overwhelmingly religious public, and a relatively free conscience. This was made possible by the natural evolution of what came to be identified as the *Protestant Ethic.* One of the tenets of Protestantism, on which New England was founded, was that every person was enjoined by God to work hard in a calling. From the religious point of view, it followed that success was not just the result of hard work, talent, and luck, but a sign of righteousness and God's special regard for the successful merchant. It also followed that poverty was a sign of shiftlessness, error, and God's displeasure with the poor. As the Protestant Ethic evolved further, many in the religious community came to regard wealth as the surest proof of success in the calling and the most comforting evidence of God's love. Those whom God loved, it was argued, he rewarded. The doctrine reached an absurd extreme in the last decades of the nineteenth century, when it was argued that the greatest glory to God was not a saint, not a martyr, not a sister of mercy, but a multimillionaire.

This doctrine joined business and church, entrepreneur and clergyman, in a zealous, mutually advantageous alliance. As Henry F. May writes, "the most articulate and influential sections of American religion were intimately associated with the mercantile wealth and financial conservation of the eastern seaboard" (6). From the nation's ministers, the businessman received high praise and ardent justification for his avarice. Reformers who fought against social inequities and workers obviously unhappy with their poverty in the employ of industry were vilified as enemies of God's divine plan, wherein some were intended to make the money that kept society in order and in motion and some were meant to do the hard labor and stay in their places. What was good for the financial world was good for everybody. The more money that could be generated the better, and those who complained were ill informed and ill intentioned.

A typical sermon, whose title is self explanatory, was published in New York City in 1836: *The Book of Wealth in Which It Is Proved from the Bible That It Is the Duty of Every Man to Become Rich,* by Thomas P. Hunt.

TRINITY CHURCH AND JOHN JACOB ASTOR

The specific mention of Trinity Church in "Bartleby" raises the relationship of business and religion in nineteenth-century New York City, an issue that may frequently have been lost on readers in another time and place. Trinity, one of the early Church of England (or Anglican or Episcopalian) congregations in the Northeast, stands prominently at the end of the short thoroughfare known as Wall Street.

Oddly enough, the businessman-church connection is secured by the intimate association between Trinity Church and John Jacob Astor. Astor Sr. was not an Episcopalian and was not connected to Trinity Church as a member of the congregation, but his immediate family and heirs were active members of Trinity. John Jacob Astor Jr. was a vestryman at Trinity from 1865 to 1884 and a warden from 1884 to 1886. William Astor was a vestryman from 1887 to 1897. But the elder's connections with Trinity were largely (and important) matters of business.

Trinity was from its inception a wealthy church, having been provided with an enormous patent from Queen Anne in 1705, for 32 acres in lower Manhattan. To this 32 acres it soon, by purchase and through gifts, acquired a total of 100 acres. By the end of the eighteenth century, Trinity Church was the owner of at least 1,000 lots. Its holdings covered more than 31 streets from the Battery to 14th Street. So vast were its holdings that it was a corporation as well as a church and is frequently referred to as Trinity Corporation.

Like other Episcopalian churches in the eighteenth and nineteenth centuries, it had a distinct character. In the eighteenth century, its congregation was composed of members of the British ruling class sent to administer the colonies and American Tories who sympathized with the British. Together these were among the wealthiest residents in the city. Trinity continued to attract wealthy parishioners in the nineteenth century. If the finery and elegance and the coolness of the wealthy congregation were not enough to discourage a working-class or low-middle-class person from attendance, Trinity's expensive pew fees, required of all attendees, certainly were. The impediment of high pew fees was a concern of John McVickar, a member of Trinity Church and a Columbia

College professor, who established small mission churches in Manhattan for less elegant believers. Trinity, the church of the wealthy, was willing to contribute money to sustain places of worship elsewhere in Manhattan for the poor, but not, evidently, to lower barriers to the poor to come inside its own sanctuary. In 1847 it ceased its contributions to the City Missionary Society, despite the appeals of John McVickar.

While Trinity kept the poor at arm's length, however, it formed alliances with the city's wealthy that worked to their great benefit. The church had a practice of selling to individuals the right to lease (or rent) multiple lots to which it continued to hold title. One of the church's business partners in this respect was Aaron Burr, vice president of the United States from 1801 to 1805, who killed Alexander Hamilton in a duel and was charged with (and acquitted of) treason because of his questionable financial schemes. But in 1804, Burr fell on hard economic times, forcing him to sell his rights to lease Trinity Church's land to none other than John Jacob Astor. Astor eventually negotiated his right to lease vast amounts of Trinity's land until 1866. He, of course, subleased the property to others at much higher rates to make a handsome profit. To illustrate, he and his heirs paid only $269 a year for 350 lots. He neither improved the property nor paid taxes on it, encouraging or requiring the tenants who rented from him to construct new buildings on the property. If they fell behind in their payments or came to the end of their leases, they lost their buildings. Astor was able to raise the rent for the next lessee, and Trinity became the owner of the new constructions. By the end of the nineteenth century, when improvements were made on land that Trinity leased directly to occupants, it reimbursed the renter for improvements when the lease came to an end. But not so with Astor in the 1840s and his heirs in the 1850s. With the money he made from Trinity's land, he bought land in north Manhattan that he rightly judged would eventually be more valuable. In this way, Astor created his real estate fortune.

By 1840, Trinity Church was the chief owner not only of some of the most elegant real estate but of many tenements in New York City. At the turn of the twentieth century, it leased residential rooms and apartments in 334 tenements. There were, in addition, hundreds of tenement houses on land owned by Trinity, but for which it had sold the rights to lease to individuals like John Jacob Astor's heirs. Matthew Smith described its holdings as including "wharves, ferries, dock privileges, and depots; immense blocks on Broadway, of marble, granite, iron, and brown-stone; splendid stores, hotels, theatres, churches, and private mansions" (*Sunshine and Shadow*, 278). Its real estate in 1855 was estimated at 15 million dollars, based on figures it provided to the legislature, but many in New York believed this to be a deliberate understatement. Its entire worth, according to Smith, was believed to be "from forty to a hundred millions."

Throughout the 1840s and 1850s, in the years surrounding Melville's writing of "Bartleby," Trinity was a constant subject of fierce argument in the New York press that took the church to task for its blatant help in making the rich, especially Astor, richer. One critic, Mike Walsh, in his radical newspaper the *Subterranean,* declared that Trinity should be made to give some of its vast properties to the city's poor. In 1845, he attacked both Trinity and Astor for hoarding enough wealth to support in comfort every person in the United States.

Criticism from many quarters intensified in 1846, when Trinity ceased most of its support of charities and missions to use its vast resources to build what would be called a massive cathedral on a magnificent scale. The church's scorning of the poor and favoritism of the rich at that time is described by Morgan Dix, a former rector of the church, in *A History of the Parish of Trinity Church in the City of New York*:

> And the property which they hold in trust has increased so prodigiously in value that the facility to turn its management to individual profit or sectarian ends, and the impunity from all investigation or punishment, tend to present temptations which may not always be successfully resisted.
>
> The floating rumors, in some cases too well substantiated, of large sums paid to relieve favorites of their debts or of succor extended to long-established and comparatively wealthy parishes whose delegates in Convention had voted with Trinity, while the merest pittance was refused to a poor free church.... the giving of money as a reward and the withholding it as a punishment,—these things were, it was claimed, entirely foreign to the intentions and expectations of its royal founders. (vol. 4, 266)

In the same year, 1846, a group of Episcopalians under the leadership of Robert B. Minturn and Luther Bradish made headlines by taking Trinity Church to court, claiming that its title to so much land in Manhattan was illegal: the resources given it by the crown of England in colonial times was intended to support all the Episcopalian churches in New York, not just one congregation. In the course of the trial, the group dragged Trinity Church publicly through the mud, demonstrating that in its exploitation of the poor and favoring of the rich, it was neither Christian nor democratic. Edward K. Spann, in *The New Metropolis: New York City, 1840–1857*, writes this about the trial:

> Their challenge brought more than a decade of controversy in which Trinity's title to its land was challenged in the courts, investigated in the legislature, and debated in the press. Again and again, the title was upheld, although less out of

sympathy for Trinity than out of a desire to defend existing property rights. The great wealth held by such religious corporations as Trinity was undemocratic and unchristian, said one judge.... The rights of property were saved, but not before the public was treated to the spectacle of a high-toned brawl over the use and abuse of wealth. (230)

But Trinity's courtroom success in holding on to its vast resources did not end the controversy. In 1848, Clinton Roosevelt unsuccessfully urged the state of New York to lay claim to the church's land to pay off the city's debts and to reduce taxation on its citizens.

The exorbitant pew fees at Trinity also continued to be discussed publicly. Matthew Smith wrote, "Pew rents are very high, and a man on a small salary, with a small income, might as well attempt to live on Fifth Avenue as to attend a fashionable place of worship" (491). It was not until 1854, the year after the publication of "Bartleby," that one of the church's leaders proposed doing away with the pew fees at Trinity.

In the middle of this ongoing public controversy, in 1853, Melville wrote and published a short piece of fiction subtitled "A Story of Wall Street," choosing for his narrator to plan to attend Sunday services at Trinity Church. This detail underscores the fiction's criticism of the pervasive glorification of great wealth, justified and encouraged by religion and the church. In a society manipulated by the rich and the church, Bartleby, Melville, and their kind have no place. Finally, Bartleby prefers not to participate in such a world.

The following excerpts document the alliance of wealth and religion reflected in "Bartleby." The first is an editorial from the *American,* a pro-labor newspaper, berating wealthy churches for helping businessmen justify exploitation. The next two are sermons by the Reverend Horace Bushnell and the Reverend John Todd, both praising the pursuit of wealth. The last is a church-generated report on Trinity's tenements.

"MAMMON IN THE PULPIT, CHRISTIANITY OUTCAST"

On September 25, 1897, an editorial in the liberal newspaper called the *American* took wealthy churches to task for courting the rich and ignoring the poor. In the writer's sentiment that Christianity was being twisted to bring comfort to those who exploited the masses, one is reminded of the narrator's misuse of biblical injunctions to love one's neighbor. The lawyer follows the letter of the law of charity without its spirit. And the sermon he would have heard at Trinity Church on Sunday, had he actually gotten there, would probably, as this writer suggests, laud the wealthy parishioners who paid the minister's handsome salary.

FROM WHARTON BARKER, "MAMMON IN THE PULPIT, CHRISTIANITY OUTCAST," IN *THE GREAT ISSUES: REPRINTS OF SOME EDITORIALS FROM THE* AMERICAN, *1897–1900* (PHILADELPHIA: WHARTON BARKER, 1902)

But how many are there who are willing to purchase riches by preaching what the rich are pleased to hear, by condoning the sins of the rich against mankind, by teaching that to live by preying upon the fruits of others' toil is no crime under the laws of Christianity, by calling upon the poor to submit contentedly as they may, but, above all, peacefully, to such despoilment!

How many, we ask, are the men who have purchased places in our churches, purchased salaries and the bodily comforts that riches bring, by teaching the lessons and precepts of Christ, not as he taught them, but as the rich, who disobey those precepts, would have them taught, who have purchased their places not only by foregoing to scourge from the pulpit those who gather riches by preying upon others, but by aiding the rich in this despoilment, this aggrandizing of their riches, by teaching the downtrodden that they have no cause for complaint, even though they be ground down to poverty, that there is nothing un-Christian in this building of the riches of the few upon the poverty of the many? (153)

. . .

The rich hear what they want to hear, hear that they have lived up to the precepts of Christianity though they have transgressed the great precept of Christianity by enslaving men they are told to regard as their brothers,... They hear falsehood not the truth. (157)

. . .

So are the churches made repugnant to the poor and the oppressed. Fashionable society, fond of the display of wealth, scorns to worship with the poor, repulses them from the church door by the cold sneer of assumed superiority.... [S]o are the poor repulsed within the churches where they are made to feel that money rules, where they are made to feel that they are in the presence of Mammon. (160, 161)

THE VIRTUE OF THE RICH, THE VICE OF THE POOR

The narrator of "Bartleby" can easily justify his behavior as an employer and his place in New York's financial community by appealing to religion. One might well wonder if the noted preacher he plans to hear in Trinity Church would be someone like the Reverend Horace Bushnell. In 1847, Reverend Bushnell preached a sermon in Hartford, Connecticut, urging the city to prosper. It is one of the clearest religious statements of the justification of the pursuit of wealth and the alliance of the businessman and the clergyman. In the course of the sermon, Bushnell gives a green light to the greedy and a slap on the wrist to the poor.

FROM HORACE BUSHNELL, *PROSPERITY OUR DUTY: A
DISCOURSE DELIVERED AT THE NORTH CHURCH,
HARTFORD, SABBATH EVENING, JANUARY 31, 1847*
(HARTFORD, CONN.: CASE, TIFFANY AND BURHAM, 1847)

For it is the duty of every man to be a prosperous man, if by any reasonable effort he may. God calls us to industry, and tempts us to it by all manner of promises. He lays it upon us as a duty to be diligent in business, to seek out ways of productive exertion, to make our five talents ten, and our ten talents twenty. He is pleased with thrift and makes it the sister of virtue. Every shiftless character, therefore, is a character so far lost to virtue. Give me then, as a minister of God's truth, a worldly, money-loving, prosperous, but strenuous and diligent hearer . . . (6)

. . .

Thus it is in every poor community that has run itself down, by a lack of character and enterprise. Reduced to poverty by a want of industry and virtue, their poverty becomes, in its turn a temptation, exasperates their depravity and makes them scoffers, at last, even against the principles of virtue. The want of character first makes them poor, and then the destruction of the poor is their poverty. . . . Having too little virtue to thrive, they must yet live; and therefore they descend to the basest employments and trades, that they may gain their bread. The loss of hope is followed by shame. Having no industry to earn a living and no character to lose, they are ready, of course, to steal. (9)

. . .

Prosperity and virtue are interwoven, by God, in the scale of being itself. Virtue is the appointed spring of prosperity,—prosperity the badge and flower of virtue. (12)

THE CHURCH'S PRAISE OF WEALTH

From reading the Bible, one might expect a Christian minister's sympathies to lie with the meek, "who will inherit the earth," or with "the least of these," with whom Jesus identified. But the following selection by the Reverend John Todd, a doctor of divinity, suggests that his sympathies lie with the successful—that is to say, the wealthy American businessman. Though Todd acknowledges that businessmen have obligations to society, his position is that God intended society to be constructed in a hierarchy and intended specific talents for specific people. Some were meant by God to lead and some to serve. Thus, some were meant to enjoy the fruits of wealth and some were not. His attitude worked well with the narrator's simplistic reading of Jonathan Edwards, who so comforted him: if the poor suffer and the rich flourish, we can do little about the situation, because everything is already determined by God from the beginning of time.

FROM JOHN TODD, "MEN OF BUSINESS: THEIR POSITION, INFLUENCE, AND DUTIES, TO THEMSELVES, TO SOCIETY, AND ESPECIALLY TO THEIR EMPLOYEES," IN *THE MAN OF BUSINESS, CONSIDERED IN HIS VARIOUS RELATIONS* (NEW YORK: ANSON D. F. RANDOLPH, 1857)

Let it be once settled in the mind that Infinite Wisdom has seen fit to have mutual dependence among his creatures, and then we can see why under his government there should be diversities of gifts—why there should be different stations and positions in life; some high and some low; some honored and some unknown; some rich and some poor; some to plan and some to execute. (2, 3)

. . .

Instead of doing away with these diversities of gifts, and breaking up the arrangements of Divine Providence, the Gospel comes in to regulate and guide them, and make them all work in beautiful harmony.... Some are fitted by the providence of God, by natural talents, by capital, one or both, to be employers, and some are fitted to be employed. (4)

. . .

In a land where the Gospel has roused up the human mind, educated it universally, and created great industry, there will be great wealth... All this goes to create and call out men possessing a peculiar kind of talent, a peculiar natural endowment; and these constitute a distinct and a very important class. I mean what is commonly called the BUSINESS MEN of the age. It embraces a great variety of occupations and employments. I include in it all who give their time and thoughts to a particular branch of business, such as bankers, insurance companies, merchants of all descriptions, capitalists, manufacturers, railroad and canal contractors, master mechanics, ship-masters, and all who employ others to manage movable property. (5)

. . .

The money power of the world is committed to one class of men. I have sometimes heard it asserted that it is mere accident and chance that one man makes money while his neighbor can not. But I know better. It is a talent. The Bible calls it a "power." "Thou shalt remember the Lord thy God; for it is He that giveth thee *power* to wealth." A peculiar talent is necessary, just as a peculiar talent is necessary for a profession. (25, 26) . . . Now is it clear that God, in his great wisdom, has raised up a class of men, scattered all over the earth, to attend to its financial concerns, and to transact the business to be done? (26)

TRINITY CHURCH'S TENEMENTS

At the time of the appearance of "Bartleby," Trinity Church, to which the narrator is heading on a Sunday morning, was one of the largest owners of tenements in New York City. These were buildings housing multiple families. Throughout New York City in the nineteenth century, the very word *tenement* was synonymous with squalor and filth. A report in 1887 describes the rooms of New York tenements as without sun or light, "swarming with vermin," its rooms blackened with filth, rooms with collapsing walls and ceilings, "crowded with sick and dirty children" (*The Tenement House of New York City*, 7–8).

In 1909, Reverend Manning of Trinity Church insisted that Trinity's tenements be inspected and improved, suggesting that its property, especially that leased to John Jacob Astor and his family, was in "unsanitary and questionable condition" (Ogden, *Trinity's Tenements*, 16). The following is an excerpt from the committee charged with investigating Trinity's tenements. Obviously, the church had not in the past maintained its properties admirably. Its vast real estate was maintained for business and profit.

FROM DAVID B. OGDEN, *TRINITY'S TENEMENTS* (NEW YORK: TRINITY CHURCH, 1909)

Summary and Conclusions.

In the report it has been sought to show clearly the existing condition of the Trinity properties, including their defects and their good qualities. According to the conditions disclosed in the investigation, the houses may be grouped into three classes.

The first includes buildings in good condition throughout or with only minor defects, such as small leaks in the roof, barely enough to stain the ceiling, defects in outside rain pipes, one or two rooms the walls of which need repapering or repainting. Most of the houses—that is 208 buildings, being 62% of the whole number examined—belong to this class.

The second class includes buildings with some or many defects, ranging from houses almost in the first class to houses almost in the third class. In this class there are 112 houses or 34% of the whole.

The third class includes houses in bad condition. This class includes 14 houses, being 4% of the whole.

. . .

There are defects in about one-third of the houses, which need improvement and cause criticism to be made of the owner; but on the other hand they are on the average in the class with buildings of the vicinity and frequently are much better. If they were torn down the probable result would be that the tenants would move into other houses in the same neighborhood, to which they are closely bound by business, political, church and other affiliations, and in these they would be more over-crowded, and would pay higher rents for accommodations probably not so good.

In the twelve houses now reported in bad condition the defects are largely defects of maintenance. Walls and ceilings are dirty, plaster is broken, plumbing fixtures are foul and in poor repair. There are some unlighted interior rooms also, but the greater number of defects are not inherent structural defects and the responsibility for them cannot always be definitely fixed.

. . .

In general, it may be said that sensationally bad conditions were not found in the tenements and smaller dwelling houses owned and controlled by Trinity Church. A very considerable majority are in good condition; a minority have defects, and a very few are in bad condition. It seems probable, however, that the residence houses on leased Trinity ground—numbering between two and three hundred—over which Trinity has no control, are, like many other tenements throughout the city, often in very bad condition. This is especially probable in the case of the houses on land held under leases which will soon end, where the owners do not wish to make repairs and improvements in buildings which will soon pass out of their hands. Until all the houses on Trinity's land are kept in good condition, they will always be made a ground of reproach to the church.

QUESTIONS AND PROJECTS

1.   Read an excerpt from Jonathan Edwards's "Freedom of the Will" (which you can usually find in anthologies of American literature). Clarify his thesis with your class. Then have a debate on his thesis.

2.   Write an essay answering why this sermon comforted the narrator.

3.   Consider the difference between "the letter of the law" and "the spirit of the law." Make a list (from your own experience or hypothetical), of specific examples of this concept.

4.   Write an essay on the concept of the spirit of the law in "Bartleby" with specific reference to 1 Corinthians 13.

5.   Have a class debate on the validity of Horace Bushnell's title. Is it the will of God or is it moral that "prosperity" is our duty?

6.   Conduct a class discussion on the various reasons why people contribute to charity. Bring up specific examples.

FURTHER READING

Bates, Ernest Sutherland. *American Faith.* New York: W. W. Norton, 1929.

Blackmar, Elizabeth. *Manhattan for Rent, 1785–1850.* Ithaca, N.Y.: Cornell University Press, 1989.

Dix, Morgan. *A History of the Parish of Trinity Church in the City of New York.* vol. 4. New York: G. P. Putnam's Sons, 1906.

Everett, John Rutherford. *Religion in Economics.* New York: King's Crown Press, 1946.

May, Henry F. *Protestant Churches and Industrial America.* New York: Harper and Brothers, 1949.

Rosenberg, Carol Smith. *Religion and the Rise of the American City.* Ithaca, N.Y.: Cornell University Press, 1971.

Smith, Matthew Hale. *Sunshine and Shadow.* Hartford, Conn.: J. B. Burr, 1869.

Spann, Edward K. *The New Metropolis: New York City, 1840–1957.* New York: Columbia University Press, 1981.

Sweet, W. W. *The Story of Religion in America.* New York: Harper, 1930.

The Tenement House of New York City. New York: Albert B. King, 1891.

Weber, Max. *The Protestant Ethic and the Spirit of Capitalism.* Trans. Stephen Kalberg. Los Angeles: Roxbury Publishing, 2002.

6

Homeless

> Yes, thought I, it is evident enough that Bartleby has been making his home here, keeping bachelor's hall all by himself. (22)

Bartleby is one of our most graphic portraits of a homeless man in the mid-nineteenth century. Instead of sleeping in the doorway of a building or beneath an underpass or on the steps of a church, Bartleby sleeps in the office where he is employed. His employer first notices that Bartleby is "*always there*...first in the morning, continually through the day, and the last at night" (20). But the narrator's revelation that Bartleby is a homeless, 24-hour occupant of the office does not come until he stops by his office one Sunday morning on the way to church. A disheveled Bartleby comes to the door, blocks his lawyer employer's admittance, and asks him to come back later. Upon returning, the narrator finds that Bartleby has temporarily disappeared, leaving evidence that he has been living in the office: "Bartleby must have ate, dressed, and slept in my office" (22). An impression in the cushion of an old sofa suggests that Bartleby has slept there. He also finds hidden away a blanket; supplies for polishing his shoes; a basin, soap, and towel; and some ginger cookies and cheese. "Yes, thought I, it is evident enough that Bartleby has been making his home here, keeping bachelor's hall all by himself" (22). After weeks have gone by without the narrator's having been able to dislodge Bartleby, the bizarre idea crosses his mind that Bartleby will live in the office for years and "in the end perhaps outlive me, and claim possession of my office by right of his perpetual occupancy" (36). In his ruminations, the narrator makes a distinction between different kinds of homeless people when he contemplates having Bartleby arrested as a "vagrant," and then, realizing that vagrant means a homeless person who goes from place to place like a hobo, sees that Bartleby is really the opposite of a vagrant:

—a vagrant is he? What! he a vagrant, a wanderer, who refuses to budge? It
is because he will *not* be a vagrant, then, that you seek to count him *as* a vagrant. (37)

The narrator experiences the frustrations that many who work with the
homeless undergo, when he finds Bartleby continuing to "haunt" the building where the office was once located and asks him, "[W]ill you go home with
me now—not to my office, but my dwelling—and remain there till we can
conclude upon some convenient arrangement for you at our leisure?" (41).
Bartleby, of course, refuses. The irony is that homelessness becomes a metaphor
for the threat of dehumanization in the tale. And all the characters, except perhaps Ginger Nut, give the impression of being homeless in some essential,
metaphoric way.

A HISTORICAL LOOK AT HOMELESSNESS

The early religious settlers in America had little patience with the poor,
whom they classified as idle or lazy, whether they were wanderers or stationary, and homelessness was not easily tolerated within the confines of colonial
communities. But homelessness, like poverty itself, did not disappear. Citizens acting from both charity and pragmatism began to realize this, and the
homeless began to be consigned to workhouses and almshouses in the eighteenth century. Throughout the nineteenth century, a large portion of the
homeless—children, the insane, criminals, and the poor—were lodged in these
institutions. The narrator, at one point, considers that Bartleby should go to
an almshouse. Sailors constituted one of the most significant parts of the homeless population, and it is not surprising that the first homeless shelters in New
York City, the Sailors Snug Harbor, was established in 1814 for seamen. Others were placed as workers on farms. With each economic depression, like the
ones in 1819, 1837, and 1857, the homeless population grew. The problem
worsened significantly after the Civil War with displaced veterans and poverty-
stricken immigrants. Many were simply kept in jails. For instance, one report
indicated that 435,000 homeless people were housed in New York police stations in 1874–75.

After the Civil War and the economic depression of 1873, homeless men in
particular became vagrants, wandering from place to place. Others began to
gravitate to certain areas within every city called *skid rows*. Here men could
find low-cost houses, soup kitchens, employment agencies, and the company
of others like themselves. Charitable organizations like the Salvation Army
supported the homeless, built hotels for them, and helped them get jobs from
their bases in skid row. With each economic resurgence, the homeless problem diminished. With every economic setback, homelessness returned.

Homelessness soared to dramatic levels—between 2 and 5 million—with the Great Depression of the late 1920s and 1930s. At this time, the fathers and sons of many families hit the road, becoming homeless, to find work wherever they could or to escape the heavy responsibilities of supporting wives and children. The economic recovery in the late 1930s and the world war that followed it caused a sharp decline in homelessness and vagrancy. Franklin Roosevelt's New Deal was the beginning of welfare programs that decreased the inevitability of the poor from sliding into homelessness and assisted those who were already homeless to get back on their feet. Among these programs were Social Security, Unemployment Compensation, the G.I. Bill of Rights, and the Veterans' Administration.

HOMELESSNESS IN 2003

Since the late 1970s, homelessness has become one of the most acute urban problems in the United States. In 1983, the number of homeless people in New York City alone was estimated at over 100,000. As in the Great Depression of the 1930s, economic adversity is one of the chief reasons. In times when unemployment soars—in 2003 it was the highest since the Great Depression—so does homelessness. When a single individual or a family is thrown out of their quarters because the bank forecloses on a mortgage or they cannot pay rent to their landlord, they, then, face the problem of seeking shelter in a housing market where rentals, even of shacks, have soared to astronomical proportions. Moreover, gentrification, in cities where affordable housing has been torn down in urban renewal, has caused a shortage of affordable housing.

Another major reason why we find the homeless living on the streets of cities is the policy, begun in the 1960s, of discharging patients from (and refusing to admit new patients to) long-term care in mental institutions, as care has been transferred to local agencies. Large numbers of these mentally ill people ended up homeless on the streets. Deinstitutionalization has also occurred in prisons and jails, which have discharged prisoners who also end up living on the streets. The homeless population continues to swell with Vietnam veterans suffering from post-traumatic stress disorder following combat, as will be apparent in the interview that follows. So the homeless people who live in the streets and temporary shelters of the country's urban areas come from the ranks of the unemployed and underemployed, the mentally ill, the substance abusers, petty criminals, and those whose families have been disrupted.

The following interview with Johnny Baskerville zeroes in on problems of the homeless man in the twenty-first century, in this case the Vietnam veteran, and the problems of the people who are charged with helping them.

ANALYZING HOMELESSNESS, GUIDING THE HOMELESS

For nine years, Johnny Baskerville has been a counselor and provider for veterans, who constitute one-third of the homeless in the twenty-first century. Working in the middle of downtown San Francisco in an agency called Swords-to-Plowshares, Baskerville sees clientele—primarily men—who live in shelters, on the street, and in run-down hotels in the city. What he has to say enlarges our view of the current problem of homelessness. And often, "Bartleby" lurks in the background. The combat veterans that see Baskerville have usually had a past trauma that has rendered them mentally incapable of coping with the world. The same can be said for Bartleby, who has been deeply, psychologically traumatized by his job in the Dead Letter Office. Like the men Baskerville counsels, Bartleby obviously has no family. When the narrator asks him if he will tell him something about his birth, his past, Bartleby says, "I would prefer not to." Many of the people Baskerville sees are not making enough money to afford housing. Doubtless, Bartleby could scarcely afford to rent a room on his pay of four cents for 100 words. Certainly he couldn't afford to rent a room when he decides to stop copying altogether. Like the current homeless person on the street, Bartleby has finally located, in his employer's office, a place of safety to set up camp. His manner of gathering together essentials—soap, shoe polish, blanket—is the pattern of today's homeless man who sets up a safe camp beneath an overpass and pushes the sum total of his belongings in a grocery cart. Like the man who prefers to live "under the stars," Bartleby prefers to be alone, instead of in the crowded tenements that would likely be his only option.

FROM JOHNNY BASKERVILLE, INTERVIEW WITH AUTHOR, SAN FRANCISCO, CALIF., 22 OCTOBER 2003

CJ: Could you first tell me about your present position?

Baskerville: Currently I am lead case manager for a veteran specific organization. We're called Swords-to-Plowshares. The organization itself provides a myriad of services, what could be considered a continuum in our own right. We provide social services within this component. A large part of our veteran constituency is homeless, and unemployed. We provide social services, and we also provide employment services. We have a substance abuse treatment facility located on Treasure Island. We have a permanent housing facility with one hundred units at The Presidio. We also provide legal services, but the legal services are limited to discharge upgrades and service related disabilities. We don't provide assistance in civil or criminal cases.

CJ: Could you just give me a general idea of your experiences with homeless people before we move to particulars?

Baskerville: Well, the whole homeless issue is a very complicated issue. I'm not a homeless advocate. I don't consider myself an activist or a homeless apologist. I'm a service provider who sees many different clients—veterans, many of whom are homeless. I think the big issue that comes up is, "What is the nexus for homelessness?" I think people look for one easy reason for homelessness. And, honestly, there are a lot of reasons. One of the reasons is, obviously, lack of available housing. One of the reasons is that people are unemployed or underemployed. Another reason is that people have psychosocial problems, including mental health and substance abuse. Big problems with substance abuse within the community that I serve. Whether or not that has anything to do with their military service—I'm not sure. I can tell you that the amount of homeless veterans in San Francisco mirrors the national average: thirty-three percent or almost one-third of the homeless population are veterans. One-third of the population with mental health problems are veterans. Mental health problems are big contributors to the homeless problem, a big issue in San Francisco.

CJ: You've been working in this capacity for how long?

Baskerville: I've been working at Swords-to-Plowshares for nine years. Nine years working with this population.

CJ: Obviously, not all homeless men fall into the same category. Could you identify some of these categories?

Baskerville: There's a whole segment of the homeless population who I probably don't see. Most of my constituency does, in fact, have some type of mental problem that's contributing to their situation. A lot of my folks have burned some of their bridges with their family members. A lot of relationship damage has been done. Another category is a man who is the victim of down-sizing; he is one or two pay checks away from being in serious financial trouble. But in that category, you might find a man who has a good support network—family and friends. If *they* fall on hard times, and they become homeless, well, they don't immediately fall into the social services network. They have friends, they have family, they have other options they can follow, so there's that whole invisible part of the homeless population we don't even see. And a lot of people don't know about, that's not even counted. The people that I see, for the most part,—there are some other things going on. There's unemployment, but there is something else that's happening where they really can't connect with family. They can't get that temporary bridge housing until they can get back on their feet.

CJ: In your experience, is there a particular kind of emotional or social problem that manifests itself?

Baskerville: Yeah, when you talk about—within the veteran's community—there's a large percentage of our veteran's are Vietnam era veterans. A lot of those veterans are combat veterans with diagnosed or undiagnosed PTSD—which is Post Traumatic Stress Disorder. A veteran with that particular disorder has experienced combat. A lot of these veterans came home and just did not want anything to do with the military, including the VA hospital. Many of them have been able to acclimate to society for many years. Then years after their military service, they've spun out of control. Found themselves losing everything.

CJ: They operate "normally" for years?

Baskerville: Sure. Only to the outside world. But to their family members, their wives, who obviously suffer along with their spouses with this disorder—they know. The wives, the spouses, the children, the family members knew that their men—and its mostly men—are having this problem. So that's a diagnosis that we see that contributes to homelessness.

CJ: How does it manifest itself?

Baskerville: Well, PTSD will manifest itself with flashbacks. Also broken sleep. Surprisingly enough—we have this very popular event here in San Francisco called "Fleet Week." Fleet Week is when the fleet comes to town and the Blue Angels fly over. If you check with emergency services, you'll find there's an increase in admission of combat veterans during Fleet Week. There's a decrease in the number of veterans we see here for normal social services, because during Fleet Week, a lot of veterans leave town. Of course, a lot of them can't get out of town and can't get away from it. A lot of them end up in the facilities because those sounds of jets flying overhead spark some of those memories of jets flying overhead when they were in combat. Its very frightening for some of the men who served and have this disorder. They may or may not know that something is going on with them. Maybe it was diagnosed at one time. But because of their lack of ability to seek treatment—weren't able to get treatment—. We just know that Fleet Week has certain ramifications to the men that we serve. And, of course, we obviously are not going to discontinue Fleet Week, but I just don't think people realize how stressful it is for so many combat veterans to hear those planes flying overhead. I've had men tell me about it, you know.

CJ: Could you talk a little about the homeless person's relationship to their shelter? Have you ever come across a homeless person that has a phobia about leaving their shelter?

Baskerville: Well, you're not really talking in this case about city or county sponsored shelters. What you're describing is the homeless person has set up a camp site and that's where they live. I wouldn't describe it as a phobia. But the dynamics of that are: if you're homeless and if you're living in the street, you have to find a safe place to stay. Some places are safer than others. And it has to do with the time of year. So safe places like a doorway in an abandoned building that has a nice big overhang and it's a deep doorway and it's a well-lighted street is a safe place to live. And you don't—everybody wants that. And it's just like in the real world. It's location, location, location. And that's what it's about. So if you're a homeless guy and you get all your stuff and you put it in this safe place—well-lighted and a deep alcove, where there aren't citizens that are going in or out and making you move, then you want to keep that space. And you will probably not leave that space.

And there's an example of that not fifty feet up the street here. There's a homeless gentleman who sleeps right on Market Street, and the building that he sleeps in front of is one of those closed electronic places with the metal grate in front of it. He lives there and he never ever leaves there. He never moves. He's there all the time. I come to work in the morning and he's there, and I leave at night, and he's still there. Now, I imagine nature must call at some time, and he's got to move, but you know, he protects his space. And I think what happens, this dynamic of what happens in the community, is that if you stay in one place long enough, your contemporaries who are homeless come to recognize that it's your space, and they give you respect for that space, and nobody'll take your space. His space isn't really a prime space, because it doesn't offer a lot of privacy so there wouldn't be a lot of people vying for it.

Or you'll find people who'll fine a real isolated space in the weeds, so to speak, in a forested type of area where they set up their hooch, they set up their campsite. People become very possessive of their sites.

CJ: Is there an emotional attachment to those sites?

Baskerville: Yes, I think there is. I think there is. I think you *live* there. That's where you *live*. And people will go through some rather elaborate routines. You pitch a tent, you set up clotheslines. I know from walking around the city a lot—just to exercise. I don't know whether—call it stupid or foolish or having the heart of a gunslinger—I choose to walk off the beaten path. I walk through some uncongested areas, by overpasses, and where they're doing construction. And you'll see campsites where people have actually set up clotheslines. They might even have generators. They'll have cook stoves. Like they're going camping. So they've made the best of the situation that they've found themselves in. A lot of them feel—wouldn't it be safer, wouldn't it be better to be in a shelter? The most common response to that is that, number one, they don't feel safe in the shelters. And, number two, they lose their freedom of movement by being in the shelters.

CJ: They lose control over their lives?

Baskerville: Right, which, you know, if you really think about it, you're not subject to that control when you go home and close the doors where *you* live.

So it's—I think the person says, "I'll endure this discomfort of living in the elements, but I'm free to do as I please." And there's a part of me that can understand that platform—that a lot of the homeless advocates launch from. The freedom to choose. I, myself, am a lot more pragmatic, because I'm a provider. I see things.

CJ: Obviously, there are men who aren't interested in breaking out of this cycle?

Baskerville: Jeez, I don't know. I think the number is probably pretty small. People, given their choices of living in their own place where they have their own key and can lock their own door and shut out the world, as most of us are able to do,—I think most people, if given the opportunity, would choose that. I think most people would. There are folks who obviously do not choose to do that. As a provider, my thinking is, five years ago, is that everybody would want to do that. But I instigated housing for people who had lived in the streets for many years, and got people into places. But some of them ultimately left and went back to living outside under the stars. I just think they could have possibly been uncomfortable in that environment. You know, most of the housing options I came up with were SROs, as exotic as a one-room flat.

CJ: What is an SRO?

Baskerville: I'm sorry. That's a "single room occupancy" hotel. So if you really think about it. If you're really living in a communal type with a lot of people—I think the reason why some go back to living under stars is their desire not to be around a lot of people. Maybe they're uncomfortable around people, and they find their comfort in this solitude, being by themselves. They can come in and interact with people when they want to, but they like to be by themselves.

CJ: As a provider, can you think of instances when you've gotten very frustrated with an individual?

Baskerville: Oh yes. Oh yes. I mean, for me, it doesn't happen that often. I think—well, actually, I was frustrated this morning. Well, there you go! But I have a gentleman that I work with and in one of the models that's accepted within the community is the model of harm reduction. And the idea of harm reduction is to meet the person where they are right now and try to provide services for them where they are right now. If you can bring them forward from where they are, that's fine, but you try to protect their health and their safety and look out for their welfare where they are. So, I have a guy who I've been working with for years. And he was in the streets, homeless, and receiving social security. Every month his check went to smoking crack cocaine. What would happen was during the month the dealers would give him credit, so when he got his check, they would immediately come and say you owe us four hundred dollars, you owe us three hundred and fifty dollars—whatever number they made up. So in a of period time, he would smoke it all up and live in the street, and yadda, yadda, yadda. So what I did: he was declared incompetent to handle his funds, so he was mandated to have a payee. When that happened, it gave me a little bit of control over his funds. Then what I did was, I put him in a hotel. And he has been living in that hotel for the last six years—until today—when he got evicted. That's another story. But what we would do: he is also a schizophrenic and it happens that when he used drugs, he wouldn't take his meds. We entered into a contract—he and I—whereby he comes in every day and he picks up and takes his meds. And in turn he picks up ten dollars, fifteen dollars, twenty dollars which we keep in a safe for him. It allows him to stretch his money out over the month. He no longer is threatened by any dealers, because it didn't take them very long to realize that he wasn't good for it because his money resources were cut off so his money lasts a whole month. Now I know he's going to use that ten or fifteen dollars to buy crack, but that's a lot better than him smoking up three or four hundred dollars in one day. I recognize that he's going to buy ten or fifteen dollars worth of crack per day. But he's also taking his meds every day. Prior to that, he had had multiple hospitalizations in the psych ward. He hasn't had a hospitalization in the psych ward for six years. He's been treated in out-patient clinics with a lower level of care. My job—I'm mandated by the Department of Public Health—to try to keep people from having to go on to a higher level of care. My job is to meet people in this out-patient setting, and to the best of my ability, to try to keep them from being hospitalized in San Francisco General Hospital. That costs between 12 and 17 hundred dollars a day. So I figure that, you know, that we've done our job with this particular client. He hasn't been hospitalized for six years. Prior to that, he was hospitalized—oh my God—dozens of times, because what would happen is that if he would become psychotic and have to be brought to the hospital, he would be there anywhere from forty-eight hours to seven days.

CJ: So what happened today?

Baskerville: Well, what happened was: the hotel he's living in was a dump. Now, granted, he doesn't help very much, because in spite of the good things I've done with him, I've never been able to get a handle on his hygiene and grooming. Just never was able to. But the hotel is a dump anyway. So I think about three years ago, I went by there and I said this place is a dump. We're not going to pay four hundred dollars. We're only going to pay three hundred dollars. And that went on great for a few years. And then all of a sudden they came to us and said he should be paying five. So we got into this big legal battle with them. This huge legal battle. And what ultimately happened was we couldn't come to terms with the money that was owed to them in back money. So he was actually evicted. He voluntarily left. I can find funds for rental assistance. But I just could not see giving these blood suckers who run these dumps—these dumps that most farmers would not put their cattle into—most horsemen would not want to put their horses in, even like a work horse. So I moved him to another hotel. Actually I've got an interview with him on the 29th for supportive services where he can receive support services on site. The only problem is that I see him in the morning to do what I do with him but I have always felt that he would thrive a lot better if he was in a hotel that had some kind of support services on site. Now my veteran X is always going to be him. He's a sweet guy and I've known him for seven years. And he's like my friend now. We're not necessarily going to hang together or anything like that but he relies on me. He relies on me and I like him a lot and I don't want to see him die. So that's what I do. I just try to keep him from dying because, you know, he's a combat veteran and he's a man of honor though he's in a very bad place right now. At one time, he was a strapping, nineteen-year-old with a marine uniform on, going off to fight a war. He's just pretty fucked up but he's got friends here at Swords.

CJ: Do you have any knowledge of white-collar workers who secretly live in their workplaces?

Baskerville: I don't have any first hand knowledge of it, but I have a sense that it probably happens. If you're a white collar worker and you find yourself homeless, and you have no support network, you would likely live in a combination of your workplace and your car. How you would probably survive is, you would probably sleep in your car and you would get to work early and you would clean up at work. You wouldn't necessarily live at work. People would probably figure that out. But we have a tremendous number of people who live in their vehicles. And they use the facilities in the community to wash up and clean. And places to eat. And they live in their cars. And I will reveal, just personally, that I was homeless for awhile myself. And thank God I had a car. And the seats went all the way down. The thing I really, really wanted was something like those old bench seats that went all the way across. But I had bucket seats. If I had had bench seats, I would have been in hog heaven. But, yeah, a lot of people live in their cars. There are parts of this city where you can go to where you can find a community of people living in their cars.

Another point about homeless in San Francisco—when I first came to San Francisco, I was meeting people who were on general assistance, who were in housing. They had places to live. And most people lived in what I called SROs, single-room occupancy hotels. General Assistance was $340 a month and they paid these hotels $300 a month for rent and they got $40 to live on. And they had food stamps. And they lived in these places for years—for years. But what happened is that when the market started exploding, even before the dot com era, the rents started going up. And what happened was that when the working poor could no longer afford the market rates of a one-bedroom apartment, they started matriculating down to the hotels. And what happened was, when you started having people that could pay more than General Assistance, the rates started going up. And now there's not a person whose on General Assistance unless he's living in some kind of subsidized housing. But they can no longer live in these hotels. So these SRO hotels, which used to be the primary source of housing for people on General Assistance, underemployed, VA pension, SSI, very low income—those units that used to go for $300 a month five and a half or six years ago, now they're costing $600 a month. And believe me they haven't taken the time to do any up-grades. There's maybe been a slap of paint here or there, but for the most part, they are the same dumps now that they were then, but getting $600 a month. And, to me, although some people would say that shelter is not housing, the reality is that people actually live in the shelters. It has to be clean, safe as it can be. If you're on general assistance, and you don't live in a shelter, then you live in the street or live some place.

CJ: Is there one particular individual that you've worked with that sticks in your mind and heart more than anybody else?

Baskerville: Well, yeah. The ones that stick in my mind are the ones that died. I had a veteran by the name of Jesse and Jesse was a mess. He was HIV. He had hepatitis C. He didn't have any teeth, but he had this smile. Jesse had served two tours in Vietnam. When he was eighteen years old. But what was unique about Jesse is that he had huge support from his family. His sister loved him to death. As I said, he was HIV and I think the HIV had gone to his brain. Part of the reason I liked Jesse so much was because I liked his sister. Here was a guy who—whenever anybody would see him, would walk around him but his family still loved him. His sister said, "My brother Jesse wasn't like this before he went to Vietnam." I think that's why I'm an anti-war person, to this day because I know what war does. Jesse would walk around with a blanket around him and he was a mess. And he would come in and he had this real passive/aggressive way of trying to get things from you. We do money management here. For a while I tried to be Jesse's money manager but it was impossible, just impossible. If someone doesn't buy into it, it doesn't work. Anyway, Jesse—his memory started going, and he left a note that he was going to Baltimore to see his cousin. His sister called me and I told her. And she said, "Well, he hasn't seen those people in years." Well, he did manage to negotiate and get on a bus and get to Kansas City. She lives down South, North Carolina or someplace like that, and she got on a plane and went looking for him and stayed there for seven days. Well, what ended up happening is that Jesse died, in a field. And the rats ate him. And I just think about that. Here's a guy who in the prime of his life, gave two years of his life for the protection of his country. And it's not necessarily anybody's fault that he ended up like he did, other than the fact—I truly believe—that if he had not heeded the call to go to a questionable war, he wouldn't have ended up in a field in Kansas City. And I've always felt that Jesse's name should be on the Wall—the Vietnam Wall in Washington, D.C. It just took him twenty years to succumb to his wounds. But he is as surely a victim of Vietnam as the guy that came home in a box. So Jesse was just an incredibly talented guy. He could paint. He could sing. But he had a Post Traumatic Stress Disorder, probably a little bit of schizophrenic, probably from the substance abuse. He did everything. He drank. He did it all. But I think it was just to push down the pain. Just to push it down as far as he could.

CJ: Have you had any suicides among the homeless you have seen?

Baskerville: Oh yeah. Yeah, I had a veteran who came in here, and God, I knew it. I was just so busy, so busy with so many. And I had a bad feeling about him. A bad feeling. He'd come in and he'd talk and went to an out-patient mental health clinic. And his pathology was more what you call access to characterlogical stuff. Well, its more a personality disorder—depression or schizophrenia. I hesitated to open him up into the mental help system which probably wouldn't have done him a lot of good. But he never said to me that he was suicidal. He never said to me, "I have a plan." He never shared that he was thinking about taking his life. And I had him in a hotel down in the financial district. And he had a lot, a lot of problems—girlfriend problems, employment problems. No family. And he ended up going to San Francisco General Hospital. And I really truly believe they bum-rushed him out of there. Veterans, lots of time when they go into community based facilities, especially when the community is strapped, they figure, "He's a veteran—let's send him to the VA." I think that's bullshit. I think if a man has done his time in the military, if anyone is entitled to double-dip, it's a veteran. If a veteran walks into a community facility, they shouldn't be questioned, you know? This particular veteran could not receive VA benefits for whatever reason—didn't have a good discharge or whatever. But he was released from the hospital and went to the Golden Gate Bridge and jumped. Actually I've had two jumpers from the Golden Gate Bridge. And I think of this guy, Darryl, after it happened, I said to myself, I should have seen that, but I think if I confuse my sorrow that he's dead and have it roll over into some kind of guilt, then I might as well turn in my keys and go home. Because this is going to happen. This is going to happen. These are the people that I see.

CJ: Do you have to struggle with that? With the proximity of guilt?

Baskerville: Yes, even though I said what I did, I feel guilty about that. I really should have seen it. And I'm not a clinician. And I talked to somebody about it. And I described to her what happened and she said, "I probably couldn't have seen it, Johnny. Nobody could have seen it." But I do believe that somebody at San Francisco General Hospital should have seen it. They are just so much at capacity there and the system is just so overworked, over loaded, I think they just missed it. I think they may have mistaken him for a malingerer. Sometime the homeless realize the criteria for being hospitalized and they get themselves hospitalized to take a seven-day break. This is like the bane of the existence of the staff up there. They are there to serve people with genuine problems and they get malingers and it pisses them off. But I think they missed this guy. To the best of my knowledge he didn't have any problems with drugs or anything either. He was just lost. He looked lost. He just always looked lost. So, yeah, I still feel guilty about it, though people have told me I shouldn't. But shit, you know, the guy died. Not necessarily on my watch, but he didn't *have* to die. Well, maybe he did have to die. Maybe it was just preordained that that was going to happen.

But looking over our shoulders, I and the other people who work here made a huge difference in people's lives—huge. But for every case like these two stories I told you, there are hundreds more that did well. You know, from guys bringing me pictures—I knew a guy who was sleeping in the streets, sleeping in his own vomit and piss. And he'll come back years later with his newborn son and his wife and tell me he just bought a house. Hey, you know. That's what makes it worthwhile—when I lose the Jesses and the Dennises—if all I did was have people die, I couldn't do this, but I believe I have saved lives. I truly do. I truly, truly save lives, and that's the difference.

QUESTIONS AND PROJECTS

1. In an essay, explore the idea suggested in the essay above that homelessness is used as metaphor in "Bartleby."

2. Make a report of homelessness in your own town or city as a major class project.

     A. Create a demographic of areas where homeless people live.

     B. Explore the major causes of homelessness in your area.

     C. Make a list of agencies that deal with homelessness and their methods for confronting the problem.

     D. Arrange for someone who works with the homeless to speak to your class. Prepare questions for him or her to incorporate into your report.

3. Identify controversies involved in dealing with the problem of the homeless. Look into conflicting philosophies about assisting the homeless, conflicts over laws affecting the homeless, and conflicts between merchants and tourism on the one hand and homeless advocates on the other.

FURTHER READING

Caton, Carol L. M. *Homeless in America.* New York: Oxford University Press, 1990.

Dunham, H. W. *Homeless Men and Their Habitats.* Detroit, Mich.: Wayne State University Press, 1953.

Glasser, Irene. *Homelessness in Global Perspective.* New York: G. K. Hall and Co., 1994.

Momeni, Jamshid A. *Homelessness in the United States.* Westport, Conn.: Greenwood Press, 1989.

Ringenbach, P. T. *Tramps and Reformers, 1873–1916: The Discovery of Unemployment in New York.* Westport, Conn.: Greenwood Press, 1973.

Robertson, Marjorie J., and Milton Greenblatt, eds. *Homelessness: A National Perspective.* New York: Plenum Press, 1992.

7

Agoraphobia

What I saw that morning persuaded me that the scrivener was the victim of innate and incurable disorder. (25)

It becomes apparent to the narrator that his employee, Bartleby, suffers from a mental disorder of some kind. On the Sunday morning when he finds Bartleby is sleeping in the office, he concludes, "What I saw that morning persuaded me that the scrivener was the victim of innate and incurable disorder" (25). Several days later, he thinks of him as "a demented man" (27). He describes Bartleby to a police officer as "unaccountably eccentric" (42), and to the grub man in the Tombs as "deranged" (44). Over and above Bartleby's refusal to correct copy or help with errands around the office, and later to do any work at all, are other strange behaviors: he never speaks unless to answer, he never reads, and he spends considerable time staring at a blank wall. His most pronounced symptom, however, is his refusal ever to leave the office. Even after the lawyer, in exasperation, moves his belongings out and relocates his office, Bartleby remains behind, refusing to leave even as another tenant attempts to set up business there—"haunting the building generally, sitting upon the banisters of the stairs by day, and sleeping in the entry by night" (39).

When the narrator tries to talk Bartleby into securing another position, and Bartleby protests that there is too much confinement in the jobs the narrator suggests, there is an instant reaction: " 'Too much confinement,' I cried, 'why you keep yourself confined all the time!' " (40). To other suggestions, Bartleby replies, "I like to be stationary," and "No: at present I would prefer not to make any change at all" (41).

At Arrowhead, in western Massachusetts, Melville's behavior was often something like Bartleby's. While writing *Pierre* in 1852, he confined himself to his room alone and had little to do with extended family or friends, who rarely entered his inner sanctum. He seldom came out even to join his family for meals. Instead, his meals were placed outside his room door, from where he retrieved them later. His withdrawal in 1852 and in 1853 while he worked on another project continued to alarm his family, who feared he was emotionally unstable. His mother, wife, brothers, uncle, father-in-law, and close friends were in frequent, urgent consultation about what should be done about him and what could be done to alleviate his urgent financial situation. His mother described his condition to his uncle, who was desperately trying, with Melville's brother, to find a consulship for him: "The constant in-door confinement with little intermission to which Herman's occupation as author compels him, does not agree with him" (quoted in Howard, *Herman Melville*, 204).

Although Melville never reached the level of isolation and confinement of Bartleby, there is little question that Bartleby's mental disorder, known as agoraphobia, was utmost in Melville's mind at the time he composed the story: his friend, George J. Adler, a German philosopher whom he had met on a sea voyage in 1849 and had become immensely fond of, had developed agoraphobia and had to be admitted to Bloomingdale Asylum a few months before the publication of "Bartleby" (see Howard, 208).

A phobia is fear of a particular situation or object that a person realizes is not dangerous or hurtful, but still summons up terror when he or she encounters it. Agoraphobia literally means a terror of the marketplace, essentially fear of a bustling, busy area. It has, typically, come to mean an unnatural fear of anything beyond the protective walls of home—the open street, a crowded store, a noisy social gathering, a bus or subway, and so on. People with other phobias, like fear of birds or flying or spiders or heights, can usually avoid them and function fairly normally. But agoraphobics usually cannot function in the world by just avoiding a specific object. A relatively normal life is beyond their reach because they are compelled to be housebound. The prospect of leaving the protection of the house induces intense feelings of apprehension, anxiety, dizziness, or intense discomfort. If they are forced to leave the house, they will become more apprehensive the farther away they go. For this reason, agoraphobia is considered the most severe and debilitating of phobias, and the hardest to treat. Boundaries of some kind—like a wall or a line of trees—seem to alleviate the fears of many agoraphobics. They seem to fear that they will become panic-stricken if they encounter a strange situation outside their four walls, and that if panic overtakes them, they will lose control. One characteristic of agoraphobics is an overwhelming fear of making a mistake and being humiliated. To keep from making mistakes, they avoid commitments and change. By refusing to take positive action, they feel that they are better in control of their lives. To resist making commitments, they emotionally isolate themselves.

Agoraphobia tends to develop in one's early 30s. It affected more men than women before the twentieth century; afterward, it began to be found more frequently in women. Whether it strikes man or woman, it is a crippling disorder that interferes with normal function. Typically, the agoraphobic person cannot go outside the house to work, cannot go out to shop or do errands, cannot attend social functions outside the house, cannot drive children to schools or doctors. It is estimated that from 50 to 80 percent of people suffering from phobias are agoraphobic.

Clinicians also report that most of the agoraphobics they have dealt with exhibit bizarre personality traits. Symptoms of agoraphobia often include what clinicians term *depersonalization* and *derealization,* the first having to do with the inner world of agoraphobics and the second having to do with the outer world. When agoraphobics experience these states, which can last for a few seconds to a few months, they feel unreal, strange, and disconnected from their surroundings.

Occasionally, agoraphobia is brought on by an identifiable childhood trauma, as described in one of the first case studies of agoraphobia, in 1919. A man named Vincent related that his fears began in childhood when a boy in his village was murdered. Vincent's symptoms appeared shortly thereafter and continued throughout his life.

Those who suffer from the disorder have symptoms of clinical depression as well as anxiety. They complain of feeling hopeless, irritable, and having difficulty sleeping. The incidence of suicide among agoraphobics is high, reaching some 20 percent. Deaths by accidents and other unnatural causes are also quite high.

In this selective description of agoraphobia, we find many of the symptoms of Bartleby's disorder: he refuses to issue out of the office even for food (his food being brought to him apparently by Ginger Nut); he "prefers" not to subject himself to any change; he avoids commitment, refusing social contact by never speaking unless spoken to; he gives evidence, the narrator believes, of having experienced trauma during his experience in the Dead Letter Office; he is eccentric; he chooses to isolate himself emotionally; at one time the narrator believes that Bartleby has lost his sight, likely a result of derealization, meaning a separation from reality; and he seems to suffer from depression and chooses to end his own life.

The following excerpts are accounts of the disorder related by agoraphobics. The first reveals agoraphobia's root in panic and anxiety that drives a young wife into seclusion. The second enlarges on depersonalization and derealization.

JANE'S PANIC AND AGORAPHOBIA

Robyn Vines begins a book titled *Agoraphobia: The Fear of Panic* with testimony from Jane, an Englishwoman who first sought help for her disorder when she was 41 years old. Jane was a wife and mother of four children and was described by Vines as once an active and social member of her community.

Like many agoraphobics, Jane's condition begins with panic attacks, which lead to misdiagnosis and overmedication. She finally, like Bartleby, isolates herself.

FROM ROBYN VINES, "JANE," IN *AGORAPHOBIA: THE FEAR OF PANIC* (LONDON: FONTANA/COLLINS, 1987)

I had my first panic attack eighteen months ago when I was thirty-nine years old. It was like a giddy turn, but much worse. My heart was pounding, I couldn't get my breath and my legs were shaking so much that I felt I was going to fall down. I was working at the time and the only thing I could do was to go and lie on the floor in the ladies' toilet until it had passed. I went to the doctor and he put me on drugs: melleril, diazepam and iron tablets. They didn't help and the situation got worse. I had to stop work and found that I was beginning to avoid things and staying home more than I should. Then, six months ago, I awoke in the middle of the night and found that I couldn't breathe. My husband called an ambulance and they took me to hospital where I stayed a week. There was no need for it. They said it was anxiety and I now know that it was. After that, I found I couldn't go to church any more, or to the supermarket, shops, pictures, or really out anywhere. It was terrible and I felt really awful all the time. (15)

RUTH'S EXPERIENCE WITH DEPERSONALIZATION

When Ruth Hurst Vose, also an Englishwoman, wrote her book *Agoraphobia,* she had a perspective that many of those who wrote on the subject lacked: she herself suffered from the disorder. So when she describes one of the defense mechanism that the body and mind of the agoraphobic experiences, she can speak from her own experience. Although she found it to be an unpleasant experience that horrified her family, she realizes that depersonalization was a saving "cut-off mechanism." Without it, she believes she would have suffered a total breakdown.

It is not a stretch of the imagination to realize that Bartleby experiences this distance between himself and reality and feels a curtain drop between his inner and his outer self. He becomes a machine, not only because that is what this culture requires of him—to be a writing machine—but because becoming a machine blunts the pain a human being is doomed to experience.

FROM RUTH HURST VOSE, "DEPERSONALIZATION," IN *AGORAPHOBIA* (LONDON: FABER AND FABER, 1986)

When things really did go over the top and I could take no more agoraphobic punishment, nature provided me with a most necessary haven. I would quite simply and unconsciously cut off from my feelings, a process described by psychiatrists as "depersonalisation."…[I]t is important to stress that if this cut-off mechanism did not exist, the mind would really suffer a severe breakdown. One has only to imagine what would happen to a pressure cooker if the safety valve got blocked.

Depersonalisation is not a pleasant experience in anyone's book.

. . .

The loneliness of depersonalisation is intense—after all, you have given up on everyone including yourself—and the pain and hurt are indescribable. Physically, I could not move, my blood flowed so slowly that my limbs were icy cold and my face quite white, and I could only see about a square inch in the centre of my normal range of vision. Everything around me became totally unreal, and I neither knew nor cared who or what anything was. (60–61)

QUESTIONS AND PROJECTS

1.   Conduct thorough research and write a paper on the subject of agoraphobia, using some case studies that seem appropriate to "Bartleby."

2.   As a team, imagine and write a report of a psychiatrist who has examined Bartleby.

3.   Imagine what may have gone through Bartleby's head as he departed the Dead Letter Office. Write an account of this.

4.   Imagine and write an account of a diary that Bartleby kept during his stay in the narrator's office.

FURTHER READING

Chambless, Dianne L., and Alan J. Goldstein, eds. *Agoraphobia: Multiple Perspectives on Theory and Treatment.* New York: John Wiley and Sons, 1982.

Copps, Lisa, and Elinor Ochs. *Constructing Panic: The Discourse of Agoraphobia.* Cambridge, Mass.: Harvard University Press, 1995.

Hecker, Jeffrey E. *Agoraphobia and Panic.* Boston: Allyn and Bacon, 1992.

Howard, Leon. *Herman Melville.* Berkeley: University of California Press, 1951.

Thorpe, Geoffrey L., and Laurence E. Burns. *The Agoraphobic Syndrome: Behavioural Approaches to Evaluation and Treatment.* New York: John Wiley and Sons, 1983.

8

"Billy Budd": Acceptance or Resistance?

STRATEGY FOR AN INITIAL DISCUSSION OF "BILLY BUDD"

ASSIGNMENT:

Complete the reading of "Billy Budd"

Be prepared to argue one side of the following issue:

> Captain Vere does or does not take the right course of action in the case of Billy Budd.

Be prepared to support your position with specific references to the text.

Remember that every student in the class will be expected to contribute to the discussion.

SUGGESTIONS FOR THE INSTRUCTOR ON THE DAY OF THE DISCUSSION:

Direct seating to be arranged in a *tight* circle.

Take your own seat outside the circle.

Remind the students that they will be marked on the frequency of their participation, rather than the quality or erudition of their remarks, so they need not remain silent for fear of saying "the wrong thing."

To open the discussion, have students who believe that Vere did what he should or had to do raise their hands. Likewise for those who disagree with this position. If one side consists of only two or three students, ask for a few volunteers to make the sides a bit more equitable.

Assign one student to be alert to students who are having difficulty breaking into the discussion and interrupt the discussion to give those a chance to speak their minds.

After the discussion starts, be as inconspicuous as possible. Do not break into the discussion yourself, even if there are silences. Keep your eyes downcast as much as possible, glancing up only to identify speakers in order to mark your records.

RULES FOR STUDENTS:

It is up to you to initiate the discussion and to make yourself heard. Do not raise your hand or look to your instructor for permission to speak. Feel free to break in at any time in order to be heard. Feel free to challenge ill-informed or misguided statements.

"BILLY BUDD": ACCEPTANCE OR RESISTANCE?

The first section of "Billy Budd" that Melville composed, ironically, became the last part of the novella—the ballad called "Billy in the Darbies." He began working on the prose narrative of Billy around 1888, probably inspired by a number of things. One was the publication in June 1888 of an article by Lieutenant H. D. Smith on the *Somers* mutiny, a case that bears resemblance to Melville's tale and one in which his cousin Guert Gansevoort had been involved. Another was the recent publication of the autobiography of Thurlow Weed, which revealed Weed's talks with Gansevoort about the controversial executions of supposed mutineers aboard the *Somers*. Furthermore, in 1889, while he was working on the story of Billy Budd, an article appeared in *Cosmopolitan* titled "The Murder of Philip Spencer," one of the men executed for mutiny on the *Somers*. Melville continued revising the story until he died in 1891, leaving "Billy Budd" unfinished. The first version, edited from the manuscript, was not published until 1924. Many versions followed as well as many interpretations. The version most faithful to Melville's manuscript, showing his notes in detail, has been edited and annotated by Harrison Hayford and Merton M. Sealts, Jr.

The Structure of "Billy Budd"

The first one-fourth of "Billy Budd" is devoted primarily to an analysis of the three main characters—foretopman Billy Budd, Captain Edward Fairfax Vere, and Master-of-Arms John Claggart—as well as a presentation of the historical context of the story that takes place in 1797. The narrative begins in this first section with the impressment of Billy from the merchant ship the *Rights-of-Man* onto the *Bellipotent,* an English warship engaged against the French.

The second section, parts 9 through 17, develops the story of Billy's nagging troubles aboard the *Bellipotent,* including warnings from the old sailor, Dansker, which Billy can't understand; further development of Claggart's character and motives that might explain why he plots against Billy; Billy's spilling of his soup; the midnight approach by a sailor acting on Claggart's orders; and the response of some of the sailors friendly to Claggart.

The third section encompasses Claggart's charge against Billy, Billy's blow to Claggart's head, the preparation for a drumhead court, and Billy's trial and sentencing.

The final section includes the visits to Billy from Captain Vere and the chaplain, his execution, the phenomena surrounding his death, and three sequels. The sequels develop the circumstances of Vere's death from wounds delivered by the French warship called the *Atheist,* the official report of Billy's case in a naval chronicle, and the ballad of "Billy in the Darbies" (*darbies* meaning "chains").

The Setting

The French Revolution, which replaced an age-old absolute monarchy with a republic based on equality, fraternity, and liberty, is prominent in the background of "Billy Budd." The *Bellipotent* in 1797 is fighting for the English against France as part of the War of the First Coalition, a group of European countries fearful that the democratic ideals promulgated in the French Revolution would spread to other parts of the world. The wars between revolutionary France and monarchical England, called the Napoleonic Wars, continued until 1815, with the defeat of Napoleon by Lord Wellington at the Battle of Waterloo. A pivotal figure in understanding "Billy Budd" is Admiral Horatio Nelson, who defeated the French at the Battle of the Nile just one year after Billy's execution aboard the *Bellipotent.* Nelson died a hero's death in 1805 at the Battle of Trafalgar. The ruling class's revulsion and fear of revolutionary ideas in France is alluded to repeatedly in the story of Billy Budd.

Two other crucial events that bear on the story of Billy Budd are the English sailors' uprising at the English anchorage called the Spithead and their mutiny at the Nore, situated near the mouth of the Thames, which occurred shortly before Billy's impressment. Both events, which terrified the naval leadership and the British crown and aristocracy, were seen as the result of infection from the French Revolution. In fact, these were uprisings coming more from practical than philosophical concerns: impressment, rotten food, insufficient food, shoddy clothing, and brutal punishments.

Point of View

The subtitle, "An Inside Narrative," is the reader's first clue that Billy Budd's story is being told by a naval insider. Subsequent clues bear this out. That the narrator is or has been a naval officer is borne out by his command of nautical language and the workings aboard ship as well as by his knowledge of the gossip of boardrooms, which only a man of rank would be privy to. He knows the opinion captains on other ships have of Captain Vere and his handling of the case of Billy Budd. That he is formally educated suggests that he is not a common seaman. He has a grasp of history and mythology and a nodding acquaintance with philosophy.

His detailed knowledge of what led up to Billy's trial and the particulars of what occurred in the secret inner sanctum of the drumhead court gives the impression that an investigation was conducted into the affair, an investigation of which he may have been a part. Just before Melville began writing "Billy Budd," authorities and the public had reopened the investigation into suspected mutiny aboard the *Somers,* with which his cousin had been involved.

The narrator's attitude is difficult to fathom. Obviously he has been steeped in the traditions and values of the English ruling class. The French Revolution and the spread of its sentiments throughout Europe he regards as an unfortunate threat to the status quo. He claims the mutinies in England in the wake of the French Revolution were "more menacing to England" than the French Revolutionary government (Melville, 303). Indeed, he writes that when the mutineers raised the British flag with the cross and union crossed out, they were "transmuting the flag of founded law and freedom defined, into the enemy's red meteor of unbridled and unbounded revolt" (303). In connection with his regard for established tradition and law, he sometimes seems to portray Captain Vere as a brave, intelligent, and benevolent leader. The narrator even gives the benefit of a doubt to the naval chronicle that horribly maligned Billy as fomenting rebellion and then stabbing Claggart with a knife. The narrator, inexcusably, writes coyly of this outrage: "doubtless for the most part it was written in good faith" (382).

What confounds the reader, however, is the narrator's sometimes veiled, sometimes overt and unmistakable language, scattered throughout his story, that there was justifiable motivation for the mutinies. He labels the mutineers' actions as arising from "[r]easonable discontent growing out of practical grievances" (303). To put down the uprising at the Spithead, the government conceded that there were "glaring abuses" to be redressed (304). He goes on to detail the grievances, insinuating his sympathy for the mutineers: "Yes, the outbreak at the Nore was put down. But not every grievance was redressed. If the contractors, for example, were no longer permitted to ply some practices peculiar to their tribe everywhere, such as providing shoddy cloth, rations not sound, or false in the measure; not the less impressment, for one thing, went on" (308). He frankly acknowledges the evils of impressment and the forcing and welcoming of criminals aboard British warships. Moreover, in comparing the philosophers behind the French Revolution with the politically conservative Captain Vere, he writes that their "minds [were] by nature not inferior to his own" (312).

And, equally puzzling, at the same time that he praises Captain Vere, he obliquely but surely damns him for committing a gross injustice in the case of Billy Budd. In his concluding sequels, he declares that the *Atheist* is "the aptest name...ever given to a warship" (381), implying the godlessness of the whole system that thrives on war.

Fundamentally, the narrator comes across as a kindly fellow with much more compassion for the common sailor than others of his class demonstrate. His weakness is his timidity and his reluctance to be openly critical of a fellow officer, the king, or the traditional class system that has fostered him.

The narrator's character might well have been suggested by Melville's own cousin, Guert Gansevoort, who was involved in a similar and notorious court-martial that resurfaced in the news at about the same time that Melville began writing "Billy Budd." Like the narrator, Gansevoort seemed to be a compassionate, insightful person who was still too limited by his own allegiances in a hierarchical military system to denounce unequivocally the injustices in it.

Characterization

The subtitle, "An Inside Story," signals the reader that this is a psychological study of the characters. Melville spends over one-fourth of his narrative in establishing character. Characterization is essential in setting up the tale's conflict and creates a symbolic system of competing forces. Billy was Melville's central interest as he first began writing his story, and he starts the story with the idea of Billy as he makes reference to a legendary "Handsome Sailor" who emerges on many a ship. Such a sailor is usually strong, attractive, a natural man; outstanding in his performance of his duties; jovial; and, above all, a magnet to whom his shipmates are drawn. Billy is such a character aboard the *Rights-of-Man*. More than that, he is cherished not only by his shipmates, but by Captain Graveling himself, because he is a "Peace-Maker" (296). Upon coming aboard the merchant ship, he uses his fists to put a troublemaker in his place, so making peace aboard the ship and earning the allegiance of Red Whiskers, the old troublemaker himself.

Billy is, above all else, innocent, being frequently compared to Adam before the Fall. For instance, he is completely trusting. Even though Dansker warns him of Claggart, Billy is never the least suspicious of him, right up to the moment when Claggart begins to accuse him of fomenting mutiny. His innocence is shown in his happy-go-lucky, good-natured total lack of cynicism. There is also a suspicion that Billy is "innocent" in the sense that he is intellectually a child. The narrator reports that Billy is described as having a "lingering adolescent expression" (299), is called "Baby Budd," (293) and that some men aboard the *Bellipotent* make fun of him behind his back. The narrator suspects that he has "not yet . . . been proffered the questionable apple of knowledge" (301). Billy is repeatedly compared to animals. The narrator says he has about as much self-consciousness as a Saint Bernard. The comment comes up repeatedly at trial that Billy is mentally incapable of fomenting mutiny, as Claggart charges he has done. Although Billy may have had a highborn mother, he is a foundling, has no education, and appears to be illiterate, as were most common sailors of his day. Billy, the typical Handsome Sailor, is a thoroughgoing seaman with little or no knowledge of things that occur on land. On shore, one would immediately know that he was a sailor.

While Billy is compared to Jesus, he is, obviously not Jesus, because he has two interconnected flaws. He has a pronounced speech impediment, a stutter, and a hair-trigger temper. Confronted with injustice, he will react quickly and violently. The pounding he gives Red Whiskers foreshadows his reaction to Claggart's false accusation.

Again, as in "Bartleby," Melville seems to identify Billy with Christ to invoke the Christian humanism in the words of Jesus: "Inasmuch as ye do it unto the least of these, my brethren, ye do it unto me."

Claggart

While Billy figuratively and literally dwells high up, in the foretop, Claggart dwells below deck. In every particular he is the opposite of Billy Budd. Claggart seems to be an aristocrat with a criminal record. He is well educated, intellectual, sly, and suspicious. He is also fanatically envious and careful. Whereas Billy is loved, especially in the more natural setting of the merchant ship, Claggart, as the Master-of-Arms or policeman, is hated. As Billy is all sailor, Claggart is basically a landsman who has found his way aboard ship, probably to escape the law. Billy is rosy from his days in the sun. Claggart has a pallor.

According to the narrator, Claggart's meanness comes from his "natural depravity" (325) and such men are usually respectable, highly civilized, proud, but in possession of a deranged heart.

Captain Vere

No work of this controversial author has elicited such radically opposed interpretations. Some, chiefly older, critics have argued that "Billy Budd" is Melville's testament of acceptance—that he has finally come to terms with the order and authority, both human and divine, that he railed against in his youth. Others take a diametrically opposed stance, arguing that "Billy Budd" is Melville's last testament of resistance against human tyranny and divine injustice. The position that any reader takes with regard to acceptance or resistance hinges on his or her interpretation of Captain Vere.

As Melville continued writing about a case of a man accused of mutiny, he turned his focus from Billy to Captain Vere, a man full of contradictions. Vere is a 40-year-old bachelor. As an aristocrat, he is well educated and is known for being "pedantic" (312). While he always considers the best interests of his men, at the same time, he has the reputation for having mastered naval law and for being a stickler for the rules, "never tolerating an infraction of discipline" (309).

Although Vere is an accomplished seaman, he, unlike Billy, is as much at home on land as on sea. "Ashore, in the garb of a civilian, scarce anyone would have taken him for a sailor" (309). There is so much of the landsman in Vere that someone coming aboard ship for the first time might take him for "a civilian aboard the King's ship" (309–10).

Personally, he is aloof, undemonstrative, and without a sense of humor, never falling "into the jocosely familiar" (312). He is also "lacking in the companionable quality."

Politically and philosophically, he is a staunch conservative. He hates the turmoil created by the new climate of revolution, which held up equality and liberty as ideals and threatened to disrupt the age-old class system. He established his point of view long ago and is not likely to change his mind. "His settled convictions were as a dike against those invading waters of novel opinion social, political, and otherwise" (312). Other aristocrats were made irate by revolutionary thought because it threatened their privileged position. Vere coolheadedly objects for that same reason and also argues that the radically new ideas would disrupt traditional institutions and the peace of the world.

After Vere's death, the narrator suggests that the captain of the *Bellipotent* may have been motivated by ambition.

COMPARISON AND CONTRAST AS KEYS TO INTERPRETATION

Subtly situated within the narrative are comparisons that help the reader place Captain Vere in Melville's system of good and evil aboard the *Bellipotent*. First, the narrator sets up definite polarities of good and evil in the persons of Billy and Claggart. Before reading the following list, the class should try its hand at indicating how Claggart and Billy are opposed. The instructor can write responses from the class in two columns on the board. Then position Vere's characteristics as more like Billy or more like Claggart.

The fundamental oppositions between Billy and Claggart can be lined up in the following way:

Claggart	Billy
Embodies evil	Embodies innocence
Basically a landsman	Totally a seaman
Works beneath deck	Positioned aloft
Enforcer of rules	Ignorant of rules
Upper class	Lower-class foundling
Well educated	Illiterate
Sly in his intelligence	Mentally childlike
Suspicious	Trusting
Secretive	Open
Never jovial	Always jovial
Scheming, prudent	Impulsive
Articulate	Stutters
Self-conscious	Un-self-conscious
Self-protective	Impulsive
High level of civilization	Called a barbarian
Compared to snake (Satan)	Compared to Jesus

Now, in this contrast with good and evil, where do Captain Vere's characteristics place him?

Not taken for a sailor
Chiefly on main deck
A stickler for rules ("a martinet" [308])
Aristocratic

Highly educated

Very intellectual

Suspicious (of mutiny)

Prudent

Secretive (in conduct of trial)

No sense of humor

Highly articulate

Self-conscious and proud

Self-protective (against mutiny)

High level of civilization

Thus, in general, Captain Vere would appear to out-Claggart Claggart. Vere and all he represents, namely social conservatism, authoritarianism, the military, and war, seem closer to the evil of Claggart than the good heart of Billy Budd.

Natural Depravity

Another comparison between Vere and Claggart is hidden in what appears to be a description of only Claggart, but upon examination is a perfect illustration of Vere's behavior. This is the topic of natural depravity. The naturally depraved person is described by the narrator as one who, ironically, is never criminal, is never jailed or executed. They have nothing of "the brute in them" (325). Indeed, "[c]ivilization, especially if of the austerer sort, is auspicious to it" and "invariably are dominated by intellectuality." It is marked by "respectability" and "negative virtues." For example, such people never drink too much. Other characteristics of natural depravity, to be discussed later, are pertinent to Vere's behavior subsequent to Claggart's death at Billy's hands.

ADMIRAL NELSON

Another key comparison is made between Captain Vere and Admiral Nelson. The narrator cites Nelson as having the reputation of being "the greatest sailor since our world began" (307). He is poetry transformed into action. Speaking of Nelson's daredevil foolhardiness in battle, the narrator comments, "Personal prudence [meaning protecting one's self] surely is no special virtue in a military man" (307). Yet Vere, secretly terrified of the possibility of mutiny, like that at the Nore, acts repeatedly to protect himself.

The most pointed contrast with Vere appears in the narrator's description of how Nelson, just a few months before Vere's trial of Billy, had himself reacted after the Great Mutiny:

In the same year with this story, Nelson, then Rear Admiral Sir Horatio, being with the fleet off the Spanish coast, was directed by the admiral in command to shift his pennant from the *Captain* to the *Theseus,* and for this reason: that the latter ship having newly arrived on the station from home, where it had taken part in the Great Mutiny, danger was apprehended from the temper of the men; and it was thought that an officer like Nelson was the one, not indeed to terrorize the crew into base subjection, but to win them, by force of his mere presence and heroic personality, back to an allegiance if not as enthusiastic as his own yet as true. (308)

No one, including Vere, really thinks that Billy has fomented mutiny. Yet Vere's reaction is to string up Billy to "terrorize the men into base subjection" (308). By contrast, Nelson has on his ship admitted mutineers who had just participated in disruptions at the Spithead and the Nore. He does not terrorize them, but wins them over by the force of his personality.

A CONFLICT OF LAWS

One of the fundamental issues in "Billy Budd" involves the conflict between moral law, or the law of the heart, and military law. Early in the tale, one finds that Billy, who is all heart, is anathema to military law and "usage" as he stands up in the boat carrying him to the *Bellipotent* and yells, "And good-bye to you too, old *Rights-of-Man*" (297). "[A] terrible breach of naval decorum" (297), the incident is reported to Captain Vere and is later used by Claggart in his attempt to incriminate Billy.

While Billy represents the law of the heart and remains innocent of, and uneasy with, military law, Claggart is an enabler of military law, which it is his job to enforce.

The conflict of laws is mentioned early on in Billy's trial when the narrator, speaking of the Articles of War, writes that while there is a "right and wrong" in such cases, any ship's commander is "not authorized to determine the matter on that primitive basis" (354). In short, the moral law of right and wrong has little to do with military law.

Vere's own words acknowledge the clash between moral and military laws as he interrupts the court considerations to urge the board to find Billy guilty. He tells them that he is aware of their "troubled hesitancy, proceeding, I doubt not, from the clash of military duty with moral scruple" and that Billy's fate must be dealt with "under martial law" (362). Vere admits that Billy is "innocent before God, and whom we feel to be so" (361). Nevertheless, he reminds the members of the board that their allegiance is to the King. He tells them to look at condemning an innocent man in a different way: they themselves, including Vere, are not executing Billy directly; rather it is "martial law operating through us. For that law and the rigor of it, we are not responsible. Our vowed responsibility is in this: That however pitilessly that law may operate in any instance, we nevertheless adhere to it and administer it" (362). Vere goes on to say that military law even supersedes conscience.

On the matter of moral versus military law, the narrator actually speaks his mind unmistakably in one scene in the novel. Here he clearly and unmistakably condemns agents of war, military law, the Articles of War, and the conduct of Billy's trial. This is found in Billy's encounter with the ship's chaplain. As he approaches Billy, the chaplain is described as "the minister of Christ though receiving his stipend from Mars," the god of war (372). Even for the chaplain, the ethos of war supersedes every human instinct, every lesson of compassion. As the chaplain takes his leave of Billy, he stoops to kiss the condemned man's cheek, an act that some critics have compared to the kiss of Judas, the betrayer of Jesus. The narrator's summation of the omnipotence of war over morality and the heart is found in the last paragraph in the section on the chaplain. The chaplain, he declares, is a contradiction on a warship. His job is to lend the appearance of godliness to an institution devoted to slaughter:

> Marvel not that having been made acquainted with the young sailor's essential innocence the worthy man lifted not a finger to avert the doom of such a martyr to martial discipline. So to do would not only have been as idle as invoking the desert, but would also have been an audacious transgression of the bounds of his function, one as exactly prescribed to him by military law as that of the boatswain or any other naval officer. Bluntly put, a chaplain is the minister of the Prince of Peace serving in the host of the God of War—Mars. As such, he is as incongruous as a musket would be on the altar at Christmas. Why, then, is he there? Because he indirectly subserves the purpose attested by the cannon; because too he lends the sanction of the religion of the meek to that which practically is the abrogation of everything but brute Force. (373–74)

On the morning after Billy's execution, there is a final comment on the emptiness of a religion that has as its only function the sanctifying of war. The narrator speaks of "the music and religious rites subserving the discipline and purposes of war" (380).

BREAKING MILITARY LAW

The argument is often presented in Vere's defense that, as captain of a warship, he had no other choice but to uphold the rules of military law. But the truth is that Captain Vere, who won't tolerate an infraction of naval discipline, violates naval law and usage repeatedly at every turn to insure that Billy will be executed hastily. The strange turn of events is verified by the opinions of the narrator, other ship's officers, members of the drumhead court, and the ship's surgeon. Consider first a brief summary of Vere's infractions of law:

1. He calls for a drumhead court, refusing to take the case to the Admiralty.

2. He appoints to the drumhead court men who know nothing of naval law and whom he can easily manipulate.

3. He insists on complete secrecy.

4. He refuses to allow witnesses other than himself.

5. He himself is the only witness allowed, and in giving testimony, he subtly refuses to "sink his rank" (356).

6. He allows Billy, an intellectual child, no representation nor any opportunity for appeal.

7. He interjects himself into the middle of the drumhead court's deliberations, telling them what they must do.

8. He forbids the court to consider mitigating circumstances.

9. As a consequence, Vere is the accuser, sole witness, judge, and jury.

10. He makes clear to the court before they have come to a verdict that he has already prejudged the case.

11. He demands that Billy be executed at dawn, instead of waiting to get to shore.

The first indication that Vere is ignoring military usage comes from the surgeon, who bases his suspicion that Vere is "unhinged" not only on his agitated state but on Vere's insistence on a drumhead court:

> As to the drumhead court, it struck the surgeon as impolitic, if nothing more. The thing to do, he thought, was to place Billy Budd in confinement, and in a way dictated by usage, and postpone further action in so extraordinary a case to such time as they should rejoin the squadron, and then refer it to the admiral. (352)

The surgeon's dismay is shared by the junior lieutenant, the sailing master, and the captain of the marines appointed to the court:

> They fully shared his own surprise and concern. Like him too, they seemed to think that such a matter should be referred to the admiral. (353)

When report of the trial was broadcast, captains and officers on other warships condemned Vere for his insistence on secrecy. The narrator, so measured and careful in his comments, always seeming to give Captain Vere the benefit of a doubt, says that Vere's secrecy was no different from the tyranny of the Russian tsars, known in the nineteenth century for their reigns of terror:

> [H]e deemed it advisable ... to guard as much as possible against publicity. Here he may or may not have erred. Certain it is, however, that subsequently in the confidential talk of more than one or two gun rooms and cabins he was not a little criticized by some officers, a fact imputed by his friends and vehemently by his cousin Jack Denton to professional jealousy of Starry Vere. Some imaginative ground for invidious comment there was. The maintenance of secrecy in the matter, the confining all knowledge of it for a time to the place where the homicide occurred, the quarter-deck cabin; in these particulars lurked some resemblance to the policy adopted in those tragedies of the palace which have occurred more than once in the capital founded by Peter the Barbarian. (354)

His choices for Billy's drumhead court also demonstrate his refusal to follow custom and proper procedure. The narrator makes this clear in his timid, qualified statement: "In associating an officer of marines ... in a case having to do with a sailor, the commander perhaps deviated from general custom" (355). One would automatically suspect that a sailor would not get a fair hearing from a marine because marines, not being subject to discipline by the ships' captains, were hated by the sailors aboard ship, who viewed them as spies and stooges for the officers. Earlier in the tale, we are told that the marines had helped the military officers put down the mutiny at the Nore. Even the polite narrator speculates that he would have thought that the captain of the marines "might not prove altogether reliable in a moral dilemma involving aught of the tragic" (356). The sailing master appointed to the court is so intimidated that he speaks only once, and then "falteringly" (363).

The narrator also finds Vere's choices of the lieutenant and sailing master puzzling because they are fighters, not men of education and intelligence, nor knowledgeable about military trials. "[T]heir intelligence was mostly confined to the matter of active seamanship and the fighting demands of their profession" (356).

Vere's motive seems to have been to choose men he could intimidate. And that is exactly what he accomplishes. The captain of the marines, unsure of himself, is described as speaking fairly late in the examination of Billy (358). When he speaks again, it is with "dubiety" (359). Vere easily shuts him up: "[T]he marine soldier, knowing not how aptly to reply, sadly abstained from saying aught" (359). The first lieutenant is completely ruled by Vere. It is said that he is "overrulingly instructed by a glance from Captain Vere, a glance more effective than words" (359).

Vere's skirting of the rules of fair play are also shown in his behavior as sole witness. Ordinarily a courtroom witness has a role entirely separate from judge and jury/board. A witness is required to merely report on the facts that he has seen. It is the duty of the board to determine if the witness is to be believed. Thus, someone like Captain Vere is expected to "sink his rank" (356) as witness, rather than appear before the jury/board as supreme captain of the ship. Instead of sinking his rank, however, Vere chooses to give his testimony from the side of the ship that elevates him above the three men on the drumhead court, subtly reminding them that he is the god of the ship and what he says is to be believed without question.

In one of Vere's long speeches to the three-man court, he insists that, in striking a superior, Billy had committed a capital crime. The once reluctant officer of the marines interrupts him to object that Claggart's death was an accident: "Ay, sir," emotionally broke in the officer of marines, "in one sense it was. But surely Budd proposed neither mutiny nor homicide" (363). Vere acknowledges the truth of the marine's statement, even conceding that "before a court less arbitrary and more merciful than a martial one, that plea would largely extenuate" (363). But he reminds them that the Articles of War and the Mutiny Act have overridden traditional law, and "Budd's intent or nonintent is nothing to the purpose" (363). So Billy's accidental, provoked striking of Claggart is treated in the same way as a cunningly planned homicide and masterminded mutiny would be.

Shortly after his and Billy's testimony, Captain Vere makes it clear that he has already made up his mind about the guilt or innocence of Billy Budd by announcing, for the first time, that no mitigating circumstances should be taken into account, only "the striker's deed" (358). Billy is too childlike to realize that Vere has already condemned him. But the court decides Vere must be crazy, so stunned are they by the Captain's unabashed admission that he has already decided Billy's guilt:

> Nor was the same utterance without marked effect upon the three officers, more especially the soldier. Couched in it seemed to them a meaning unanticipated, involving a prejudgment on the speaker's part. It served to augment a mental disturbance previously evident enough. (359)

In his maintenance of total secrecy, Vere refuses to allow other witnesses, like old Dansker, to testify in Billy's behalf. Many aboard ship know that Claggart has been sabotaging Billy and that Claggart's charges were lies. Even the captain of the marines realizes that forbidding other witnesses is a breach of law, not to mention fairness:

> The soldier once more spoke, in a tone of suggestive dubiety addressing at once his associates and Captain Vere: "Nobody is present—none of the ship's com-

pany, I mean—who might shed lateral light, if any is to be had, upon what remains mysterious in this matter." (359)

Vere, in what seems to be a completely incomprehensible, insane response, positively cuts off any prospect of allowing other witnesses. In answer to the soldier of marines' question, he says,

> That is thoughtfully put...I see your drift. Ah, there is a mystery; but, to use a scriptural phrase, it is a "mystery of iniquity," a matter for psychologic theologians to discuss. (359)

Vere's insistent conduct of the case refuses Billy—an uneducated, intellectually slow boy—any representation or appeal. Even the timid sailing master who speaks "falteringly" only once during the trial, is moved to ask why they cannot convict yet delay "the penalty" (363). Obviously, like the other two members of the board, he thinks the only way to save Billy would be to proceed according to tradition and the law in this one practice, to delay the hanging until they reach the Admiralty. Vere strangely responds that even though such a delay might be lawful, "under the circumstances" the only practical thing to do is to string Billy up at dawn (364). In essence, then, Billy would have absolutely no opportunity to appeal his case. When Vere speaks of the law, he is not referring to long-standing naval regulations that protect the rights of the accused, but to the Articles of War, that extraordinary battle exception that allows the military to break the law in time of war. Vere describes the conduct of Billy's trial as "a lawful rigor *singularly demanded at this juncture*" (364; italics mine).

As far as Vere is concerned, in this instance, the enemy is his own men. In arguing for an immediate execution of Billy, he makes clear that the men, "most of them familiar with our naval usage and tradition," would become dangerous if they had time to "ruminate" on the way Billy's trial was conducted (364). So, rather than leading his men with the force of his character (as Nelson had done), he decides to "terrorize the crew into base subjection" (308) with a quick execution.

Vere's final breaking of naval decorum in the case of Billy Budd comes minutes after Billy's execution, when the captain, after hearing the murmuring of the men, sends them to their quarters an hour early. Note that the wishy-washy narrator justifies and damns Vere in a single sentence:

> That such variance from usage was authorized by an officer like Captain Vere, a martinet as some deemed him, was evidence of the necessity for unusual action implied in what he deemed to be the mood of his men. (380)

Vere's breaking and abuse of the very military law he claims to live by, as C. B. Ives has so graphically argued, becomes abundantly clear when one examines the Articles of War and the Mutiny Act, both of which Vere mentions, claiming that he is bound by both to try, convict, and execute Billy Budd aboard ship within a few hours of the crime. In the coercive speech he gives to the board, Vere indicates that the Articles of War and the Mutiny Act compel them to the decision he insists upon:

> In wartime at sea a man-of-war's man strikes his superior in grade, and the blow kills. Apart from its effect the blow itself is, according to the Articles of War, a capital crime....
> We proceed under the law of the Mutiny Act. (363)

But, as will be examined more closely in the contextual discussion of military law, the Mutiny Act did not apply to sailors, only to the army. Furthermore, the Articles of War dictated that a sailor who strikes a superior must be tried and convicted by a court-martial board called by the Admiralty, not a drumhead court called by the captain. Mutineers could be hanged aboard ship if it was decided by the captain, in consultation with his officers, that they posed an immediate threat. But a mutiny was formally defined as a conspiracy of two or more persons, and Billy was in no way a mutineer.

Critics have sought a clue to Captain Vere's character in Melville's choice of "Vere" for his name. Those on one side of the argument claim that Vere stands for *veritas,* or Truth. But two things seem to work against Vere as the embodiment of Truth: his secretiveness at trial and his using Billy as a scapegoat when he knows Billy is not a part of a mutiny nor meant to kill Claggart. Moreover, one has to speculate on how the naval chronicle got its scurrilous story about Claggart's death and Billy's execution. If the source was Vere, he is the opposite of, rather than the embodiment, of Truth.

Other critics have pointed out that "Vere" was often used in obscure nineteenth-century gothic novels as a name for villains.

THE MIND OF CAPTAIN VERE

The profound disagreements about Vere's conduct of Billy Budd's trial, suggested in the words and actions of the narrator, the surgeon, other ships' officers, and the drumhead court itself, lead one to ponder Captain Vere's motives in insisting on such an extralegal, unpopular, and unjustifiable action.

The answer appears to lie in his fanatical terror of the social changes spreading throughout the Western world. For a man convinced that "[w]ith mankind...forms, measured forms, are everything" (380), any ideas that challenge and upset the old way of thinking are fundamentally distasteful. What has issued from this philosophical iconoclasm is a challenge to the old, honored class structure and systems of power—in which Vere has enjoyed an advantage. The captain of a warship is an absolute monarch, a god of his little world isolated at sea. And Vere sees his own dominion under attack by new religious thought and the adoption of liberty, fraternity, and equality as the supreme ideals. All this philosophical and social turmoil, apparent in "the disruption of forms going on across the Channel," is embodied in the recent mutinies at the Spithead and the Nore.

In charging Billy Budd with fomenting mutiny, Claggart's reminder of the Nore, where a chief officer had been held by the mutinous mob, fans the embers of Vere's fear into a roaring fire. As the trial proceeds, Vere himself makes reference to social revolution, insinuating that if the court doesn't act quickly and secretly, the men on the *Bellipotent* will revolt and seize control: "Will they not revert to the recent outbreak at the Nore? Ay. They know the well-founded alarm—the panic it struck throughout England" (364). So Vere's apprehension might explain his secrecy, his interference in the trial, and his abrogation of Billy's basic rights at trial, were it not for the testimony of others that his tactics were unwarranted.

One answer, strongly supported by the text, is that Vere's own fanatical fear of disruption aboard his ship has brought him to the brink of insanity. Even before Billy's trial, Vere is known for his fits of abstraction: "He would absently gaze off at the blank sea" (310), and momentarily become disturbed if someone interrupted him to attend to some business. This habit of his was what, in part, gave him the nickname of "Starry Vere."

The first suspicion that Vere might be insane comes not from an ordinary seamen or officer, but from the ship's surgeon. In the cabin, where the surgeon has gone to examine Claggart's body, Vere grabs the surgeon's arm "convulsively" and, to the amazement of the surgeon, pointing to the dead Claggart, blurts out, "It is the divine judgment on Ananias! Look!" (351). He then declares, "Struck dead by an angel of God! Yet the angel must hang!" (352).

Even after he has heard the story from the captain, the surgeon suspects Vere's sanity:

> Full of disquietude and misgiving, the surgeon left the cabin. Was Captain Vere suddenly affected in his mind, or was it but a transient excitement, brought about by so strange and extraordinary a tragedy?... He recalled the unwonted agitation of Captain Vere and his excited exclamations, so at variance with his normal manner. Was he unhinged? (352)

Secretly the surgeon realizes that if Captain Vere is "unhinged," there is virtually nothing he or anyone else can do about it, because a ship is an isolated world, and any captain is the god of that world.

> No more trying situation is conceivable than that of an officer subordinate under a captain whom he suspects to be not mad, indeed, but yet not quite unaffected in his intellects. To argue his order to him would be insolence. To resist him would be mutiny. (353)

The narrator goes on to reflect on how difficult it is in marginal cases to determine insanity from sanity.

Vere's testimony as the sole witness "served to augment a mental disturbance previously evident enough" (359). During the trial, after the testimony and Vere's explanation of the court's charge, Vere is described as standing with his back to them, "apparently in one of his absent fits" (360).

The suspicion that Vere is insane leads the reader back to other lines about madness in Melville's story—the section on natural depravity. Here the narrator claims that the naturally depraved man is able to hide his madness, and that he uses reason to commit an unreasonable action:

> But the thing which in eminent instances signalizes so exceptional a nature is this: Though the man's even temper and discreet bearing would seem to intimate a mind peculiarly subject to the law of reason, not the less in heart he would seem to riot in complete exemption from that law, having apparently little to do with reason further than to employ it as an ambidexter implement for effecting the irrational. That is to say: Toward the accomplishment of an aim which in wantonness of atrocity would seem to partake of the insane, he will direct a cool judgment sagacious and sound. These men are true madmen, and of the most dangerous sort, for their lunacy is not continuous, but occasional, evoked by some special object; it is self-contained, so that when, moreover, most active it is to the average mind not distinguishable from sanity, and for the reason above suggested: that whatever its aims may be—and the aim is never declared—the method and the outward proceeding are always perfectly rational. (326)

AN INSIDE MUTINY

Another meaning of Melville's subtitle, "An Inside Narrative," is, as William Dillingham so brilliantly argues in *Melville's Later Novels,* Vere's fear of the possibility of his own inner mutiny against the staunch ideas he has clung to for most of his life. As Dillingham says:

Vere is overtly concerned with mutiny in the British navy and with preventing it aboard the *Bellipotent,* but his great underlying anxiety is that mutiny will occur within him and that all those things he has sworn allegiance to will be overturned. (398)

Vere forms an immediate emotional attachment to Billy. He knows who Billy is even before Claggart brings Billy to his attention, and his impression has been immensely favorable. Admiring him for his spirit, his popularity with many of his fellow sailors, and his natural ability as a sailor, he is contemplating promoting Billy to captain of the mizzentop. After witnessing Billy administer a killing blow to Claggart, he calls him "an angel of God" (352). He presents himself as a fatherly figure to Billy, and says to him, " 'I believe you, my man' . . . his voice indicating a suppressed emotion not otherwise betrayed" (357). When he leaves Billy, after having told him of the court's verdict, "his face had the look of agony" (367). And, curiously enough, Vere's dying words are "Billy Budd, Billy Budd," but uttered without remorse.

So Billy is presented as a test to Captain Vere. He calls forth the heart, the emotions, the sympathies, the private conscience. Captain Vere is terrified that he will respond, thus disregarding his seemingly intellectual, regimented side devoted to tradition, rules, and order.

Vere fears revolution and mutiny because they disturb, he thinks, the peace of the world. And following his private conscience and heart in the matter of Billy Budd will be an inner mutiny that disrupts his private peace. He is terrified of losing control.

SOCIAL IMPLICATIONS: A WAR-SUPPORTED SOCIETY

In 1850 a young Herman Melville published *White Jacket,* a novel drawn from his own experiences aboard a warship in 1843 and 1844. *White Jacket* was an indictment of the abuses aboard military vessels, including the brutal and capricious Articles of War, which took away all rights from common sailors and was enforced even in peacetime. Some literary critics have argued that "Billy Budd" is a mature Melville's departure from his radical young self, that it is a novel of reconciliation with authority and social order, including war and systems that thrive upon and are shaped by war.

However, there is ample evidence in "Billy Budd" to support the opposite interpretation—that, far from being a testament of reconciliation, this last work of Melville's is his continuing testament of resistance against war, military values, and the despotism they support. The first suggestion that resistance rather than reconciliation is Melville's aim lies in his dedication. Jack Chase, to whom "Billy Budd" is dedicated, is one of the important characters in *White Jacket.* He was a common sailor, extraordinary in this sense: he was a social revolutionary who on occasion jumped ship to help resurgents on land battle corruption and injustice. Another clue lies near the end of the novel, when the narrator declares that the *Atheist* is the most apt name for a warship. Throughout the text, as in the scene with the ship's chaplain, war is opposed to the *spirit* of Christianity, the Prince of Peace, and the heart. War is, the narrator writes, "the abrogation of everything but brute Force" (374).

The most effective indictment of war, and the society that depends upon and is shaped by war, is found in an allegory within the story of Billy Budd—an allegory in which the two main ships, the *Rights-of-Man* and the *Bellipotent,* assume symbolic force as social structures. The *Rights-of-Man,* a merchant ship, was named for an essay by Thomas Paine, who participated in the American and French Revolutions to overthrow royal totalitarianism. As such, the *Rights-of-Man* represents the kind of democratic republic that Paine had envisioned. Captain Graveling is benevolent and runs a loose ship with few rules and regulations and less decorum. He is not in any sense autocratic. Although Red Whiskers is a disruptive element aboard this democracy, at least there is no intrigue and no flogging.

Billy, for all his imperfections, is the epitome of the Handsome Sailor, with a merry heart, physical beauty and strength, and a sweet moral nature. His good-heartedness leads Captain Graveling to see him as embodying the best in human nature. Reference to Billy's being a peacemaker, a lamb, and a martyr also implies a Christlike goodness. So, to carry through with the allegory, the best in human nature flourishes aboard the "democracy" as Billy slams the disruptive Red Whiskers and even makes him a friend.

But Billy is forced out of the democracy. His shout as the boat takes him to the *Bellipotent* is layered with meaning: "And good-bye to you too, old *Rights-of-Man.*" For Billy is not only saying good-bye to his friends and a ship he loved; he is saying good-bye to the fundamental rights guaranteed by a democracy.

The *Bellipotent,* translated as "War Almighty," is representative of a totalitarian, militaristic monarchy. Captain Vere, a representative of the king of England, holds absolute power aboard a ship whose very structure was a military hierarchy. Strict rules, usages, and decorum direct every working minute of the people aboard ship. And the extraordinary Articles of War leave them with no fundamental rights. Here Billy encounters, for the first time, secrecy, intrigue, and brutal punishments—common aboard a warship, but not the merchant ship.

Finally, while the best in human nature flourishes aboard the democracy, it is annihilated aboard the totalitarian state.

The concept of peace takes on a sociopolitical meaning in "Billy Budd." In one sense, Billy's behavior aboard the *Rights-of-Man* illustrates that true peace can sometimes come through violence. Red Whiskers disrupts the ship until Billy beats him up. Even so, centuries of the tyranny of French kings only comes to an end as a result of violent revolution.

Vere abhors revolutionary challenges to royal authority because he believes it disrupts the "peace of the world" (312). But the peace that Vere cherishes necessarily allows the injustices of centuries to continue. It is the serenity of the upper classes, who can continue to live lives undisturbed by the discord and rebellion of the miserable—on whose backs their lives of privilege have been built.

BIBLICAL PARABLES

Other symbolism in "Billy Budd" takes us beyond the social message to another layer of cosmic meaning. The simplest and most obvious is the parable of good and evil, represented by Billy on one hand and Claggart on the other. Claggart is naturally depraved, lies, conspires, and is compared to a snake or Satan. Good appears to triumph over evil as Claggart is unintentionally killed by Billy. Biblical reference also associates Billy with Adam before the Fall; with Isaac, almost sacrificed by his father, Abraham, on God's orders; and with Jesus. He is fundamentally innocent (meaning both blameless and without knowledge), like the first man in the Garden of Eden. As such, he has not been corrupted by civilization. He is natural man.

When Captain Vere informs Billy in private of the findings of the drumhead court, they are spoken of as father and son. Billy is the young Isaac. Vere is his father, Abraham, who is on the brink of killing his son as a sacrifice on God's orders just before God stops his hand. Just so, Vere is sacrificing Billy, on the basis, he claims, of a higher power, in this case the king's navy.

Finally, Billy is compared to Jesus of Nazareth. He is a "martyr," (376) and a "Lamb of God" (373). His final words, "God bless Captain Vere," (375) resonate with the sentiments of Jesus, who forgives his persecutors on his death bed. While Jesus was said to have risen from his grave, so a supernatural element seems to touch the death of Billy Budd:

At the same moment it chanced that the vapory fleece hanging low in the East was shot through with a soft glory as of the fleece of the Lamb of God seen in mystical vision, and simultaneously therewith, watched by the wedged mass of

upturned faces, Billy ascended; and, ascending, took the full rose of the dawn.
(376)

But even more phenomenal than the strange light was the fact that Billy's body is perfectly still, evincing no muscular spasms that are "invariable in these cases" (376).

In addition, after Billy's death, he is deified by the common sailors, who treat the spar from which Billy was hung as a religious relic. "To them a chip of it was as a piece of the Cross" (383).

Captain Vere often seems to be the father figure, even a Jehovah figure. There are no checks on his power aboard his ship. He is God.

But "Billy Budd" is scriptural allegory turned upside-down. In the matter of Billy, John W. Rathburn argues the following:

> As the novel progresses, Billy takes on in turn the characters of the Pre-Fall Adam, Isaac, and Christ, but with the results radically different from the original Biblical versions. Billy becomes the Adam who does not fall, the Isaac who is not saved, the Christ who does not redeem. ("*Billy Budd* and the Limits of Perception," 98–99)

In the struggle between good and evil, good at first appears to triumph over evil when Billy strikes Claggart dead. But immediately good is sacrificed and the reputation of evil is purified as in the naval journal's account.

Vere may well be an all-powerful Jehovah figure, but he is a base and mindless Jehovah who is determined to destroy justice and goodness in the figure of Billy.

Is this Melville's testament of reconciliation with God? It would not appear so. "Billy Budd" is no less a powerful argument against social injustice than was *White Jacket*, which uncovered the abuses of the military navy and contributed to the outlawing of flogging aboard naval vessels. And this, his last novel, is scarcely a departure from his view in *Moby Dick* of a mad, mindless power in control of the fate and hearts of mankind.

QUESTIONS AND PROJECTS

1. The two main projects on "Billy Budd" are incorporated in the text of this chapter: the debate on Captain Vere's actions and the listing and comparison of Billy's, Claggart's, and Vere's characteristics.

2. Using hints from the text, imagine a description of the narrator. How old is he? What is his rank? What does he look like? What is his background and schooling? Who does he associate with? What is his personality?

3. Construct a dictionary of the nautical terms used in "Billy Budd."

4. Why do you suppose Melville made a point of Vere's being a bachelor?

5. Research Billy's speech impediment. Do you find anything of interest to explain Billy? Write an essay on how his stutter functions in the story.

6. Melville provides us with further names for merchant ships and warships. Locate these names and write an essay on how these names function in the tale.

7. Pretend you are the soldier of marines. Write an anonymous letter to the editor of the naval chronicle correcting details in their news story about the case of Billy Budd.

8. The ballad "Billy in the Darbies" is as fanciful as the official naval report, but contains more of the spirit of truth than the official story. Write on who may have written each and contrast the effects of each on our reading of Melville's story of Billy Budd.

9. Captain Vere's dying words remain an enigma. Make your own argument for what they mean.

10. Have a debate on the position of a chaplain in any military organization.

11. Have a debate on the following statement: "Violence is sometimes necessary."

12. Have a debate on the following statement: "War is inconsistent with Christianity."

FURTHER READING

Dillingham, William B. *Melville's Later Novels*. Athens: University of Georgia Press, 1986.

Dryden, Edgar A. *Melville's Thematics of Form: The Great Art of Telling the Truth*. Baltimore: Johns Hopkins University Press, 1968.

Duban, James. *Melville's Major Fiction: Politics, Theology, and Imagination*. Dekalb: Northern Illinois University, 1983.

Ives, C. B. "*Billy Budd* and the Articles of War." In *Critical Essays on Melville's Billy Budd, Sailor,* ed. Robert Milder. Boston: G. K. Hall and Co., 1989.

Melville, Herman. *Billy Budd and Other Stories*. New York: Penguin Books, 1986.

Miller, Haviland. *Melville*. New York: George Braziller, 1975.

Parker, Hershel. *Reading Billy Budd*. Evanston, Ill.: Northwestern University Press, 1990.

Rathbun, John W. "*Billy Budd* and the Limits of Perception." In *Critical Essays on Melville's Billy Budd, Sailor,* ed. Robert Milder. Boston: G. K. Hall and Co., 1989.

Sealts, Merton M., Jr. *Innocence and Infamy: Resources for Discussing Herman Melville's Billy Budd, Sailor*. Madison: Wisconsin Humanities Committee, 1983.

Springer, Haskell, ed. *The Merrill Studies in Billy Budd*. Columbus, Ohio: Charles E. Merrill, 1970.

Thompson, Lawrance. *Melville's Quarrel with God*. Princeton, N.J.: Princeton University Press, 1952.

Yannella, Donald. *New Essays on Billy Budd*. Cambridge: Cambridge University Press, 2002.

9

The French Revolution

The hardheaded Dundee owner was a staunch admirer of Thomas Paine, whose book in rejoinder to Burke's arraignment of the French Revolution had then been published for some time and had gone everywhere. (297)

The historical spine of "Billy Budd" is the French Revolution, which culminated in 1789 with the fall of the Bastille, the notorious prison in Paris—by that time primarily an arsenal. Even as the Bastille fell, the concepts of the revolution were sweeping across Europe like wildfire to challenge old ideas and old systems based on aristocratic privilege. The first reference to the French Revolution in "Billy Budd" occurs in the first three paragraphs about "the Handsome Sailor," who collects around him an international group, representative of the human race, reflecting the ideals of the revolution.

The ship from which Billy is impressed, the *Rights-of-Man,* is named for Thomas Paine's pamphlet written in defense of the French Revolution. The narrator cites other ships named for philosophers who prepared the way for the revolution: Diderot and Voltaire. In part 3, the narrator warns of French Revolutionary ideas and their unwelcome influence on England—"cinders blown across the Channel from France in flames" (303).

As the French Revolution is linked with Billy, so there is a comment on its impact on Vere and Claggart. Vere's staunch, unchangeable convictions keep him from being seduced by the revolutionary ideas from France. The presence aboard ship of Claggart, strongly suspected of being a criminal, is explained by the narrator in terms of the French Revolution: in straitened times of wars, "which like a flight of harpies rose shrieking from the din and dust of the fallen Bastille" (316), England had to raid prisons to get its quota of fighting men. Ideas from France threatened to disrupt many countries, America included, where some citizens who had fought at Bunker Hill hoped for a greater revolution (than the American one) would cross the Atlantic Ocean.

Thomas Paine, political writer, who is often regarded as the moving force behind revolutions in America, France, and England. Print and Picture Collection, The Free Library of Philadelphia.

Toward the end of the story, the narrator indicates that Vere, who cherishes "forms, measured forms" (380) that hold mankind together, referred to the French Revolution as a time when forms failed and people became destructive.

More than just providing historical background, however, "Billy Budd" is a parable of the clash of values: those of the old regime, represented by the *Bellipotent,* and those of the French Revolutionaries seeking reform, represented by the *Rights-of-Man.*

CONDITIONS

Conditions in France made it ripe for revolution. The old order was based on an unequal social hierarchy with the king at its head, a monarch who was upheld by the church, which insisted that the king was ordained by God: church, government, and tradition taught that a few people were chosen by God—*born*—to rule. Most others were born to serve, to labor, to remain quietly in their places. A poor person's aspiration to a life or calling, other than the lowly squalor into which he or she was born, was sacrilegious, a slap in the face of God.

The structure of French society, at the head of which sat the king, included three estates. The first order was an immensely wealthy church that exercised control over the daily lives and the minds of French citizens. In the pursuit of wealth, the church levied annual taxes on all citizens and charged exorbitant fees for conducting marriages, funerals, and baptisms, excluding many of the poor from these rites. Moreover, the church controlled education and poor relief with an iron hand. In exchange for royal privileges that allowed the church to amass large areas of land and revenue, the church lent the sanctity of religion to its support of the divine right of kings, inherited privilege, and such concepts as blind obedience and acquiescence to authority.

Following the church as first estate was the second estate, comprised of the landed aristocracy. Members of the second order had legal privileges and rights from which all others were excluded. They alone received educations. They alone were able to secure positions as officers in the military, naval, and diplomatic services and as high-ranking officials in the civil service and church. Especially infuriating to the majority of France's citizens was the aristocratic right to be tried in special courts, their exemption from onerous taxes, and particular policies governing land that made farming difficult for the serfs. For example, laws were made forbidding the control of animals and birds reserved for hunting by aristocrats. As a result, uncontrolled deer and bird populations devoured seeds and plants from which poor farmers made their livings.

Ninety-six percent of France's population belonged to the third estate, which was itself stratified, with upper-middle-class professionals and business owners making up the upper level. At the bottom of France's social hierarchy was the immense population of common laborers and the many peasants who struggled and lived marginally. France was overwhelmingly rural, and one out of four farmers had no land of his own. Those farmers who did own land had portions too small to sustain themselves, so in reality all rural peasants were compelled to work for aristocratic landowners. Members of the lower classes had no voice in how the government was run. During wars waged by kings for more power, they were simply cannon fodder. Contributing to the social unrest were huge populations of beggars who ranged throughout the countryside and lived in the streets of cities.

The members of the third estate were taught to obey and accept without question what their betters handed them, whether it be discriminatory laws, lack of representation, poverty, or intolerance.

THE AGE OF REASON

What unquestionably paved the way for the overthrow of entrenched traditions of injustice in France were not so much the radical politicians and the mobs who eventually carried out the revolution, but the philosophers who well before the revolution challenged the ideas upon which France's social system was based. Most prominent among these philosophers were Jean-Jacques Rousseau, Montesquieu, Voltaire, Helvétius, Frederick Grimm, Raynal, D'Alembert, Diderot, and Condorcet.

The old regime had been sustained by religious revelation as taught by the church, superstition, orthodoxy, and blind adherence to tradition. But the great scientific advances of the seventeenth and eighteenth centuries had led thinkers to place more emphasis on facts that can be proved empirically. They contended that a person's individual reason was his or her highest, God-given faculty, and that to reach truth one must use reason to question what was once blindly accepted as truth from the church and the government. So the first declarations of independence were not so much national as personal and individual. Deism, the religion adopted by several of the philosophers, was based on these concepts. Deists also declined to endorse organized religion and avowed a belief in one God, rejecting the Christian belief in the Holy Ghost and the divinity of Jesus. By the 1770s in the American colonies, deists like Benjamin Franklin, Thomas Jefferson, and George Washington had begun to prepare for the American Revolution.

It was initially the philosophical attacks on religious ideas in France that began to undermine not only the first estate, but the monarchy and the second estate. The liberation of the mind led to the liberation of the body.

THE SEQUENCE OF EVENTS

From about 1776 forward: Economic conditions brought about higher rents, higher taxes to be paid to the church, food shortages, inflation that put the price of bread out of the reach of working families, and low wages, all leading to widespread starvation and riots.

March 1789: Rural unrest increases. Elections take place.

April 1789: Riots in the city of Paris continue into July to protest food shortages and low wages.

June 20, 1789: The representatives of the third estate, which has become known as the National Assembly, is ignored and then locked out by the rest of *Parlement.* They meet on the Tennis Court to take an oath of their intentions.

June 23, 1789: Troops loyal to the king surround the meeting hall, and conciliatory demands for reform of the estates and representation are found doomed to failure as the king asserts that he is now in charge of policies. He marches out of the hall, taking deputies of the privileged orders with him, while the National Assembly remains, strongly asserting their demands.

June 24–26, 1789: Some representatives of the first and second estate join those of the third estate.

June 27, 1789: A mob of 30,000 Parisians announce they are ready to march on King Louis's palace at Versailles unless representatives of the first and second estate join those of the third estate as a single governing body. In fear, Louis gives in to the demands of the third estate or National Assembly, ordering deputies of the first and second estates to return to *Parlement.*

Early July 1789: The king surrounds his castle with 6 regiments of military troops and orders 10 regiments of foreign mercenaries into Paris.

July 11, 1789: Prompted by the fear that the military had been sent to suppress the common people and to dissolve the assembly by force, and by displeasure over dismissal of the conciliatory minister of finance, further riots ensue.

July 14, 1789: A crowd of guildmasters, workers, and vagrants joined by sympathetic members of the French Guard march on the Bastille, which is said to hold ammunition and arms. Their capture of the Bastille is ever after symbolic of the fall of an old regime of despotism.

In the wake of the fall of the Bastille, the full assembly of representatives is saved, the troops withdrawn, a people's militia established, and the old local governments run by the first two estates replaced by people's communes. In the countryside, peasantry attack the houses of the aristocracy, many of whom flee. The old courts and old systems of law are suspended.

August 4, 1789: The deputies meet to abolish all rights and privileges of the first and second estates, including forced church tithes, hunting and fishing rights, exclusive courts for the aristocracy, and exclusive rights to public office. It is decided that the whole aristocratic hierarchy will be disbanded. In this, the end the Old Regime, every person is equal before the law.

August 26, 1789: "The Declaration of the Rights of Man and the Citizen" is passed, declaring equality before the law, equality of taxation; and equal rights to employment. Religious tolerance and freedom of thought and speech are also established.

November 2, 1789: The new Assembly appropriates church lands.

January 21, 1793: Louis XVI is executed.

...

The following excerpts document the ideas that guided the French Revolutionaries, the reforms they proposed, and the responses they elicited in England and America. The first is a 1757 essay written by Voltaire on government.
The second is a declaration of grievances given to their representatives by members of a village in France. The third is an excerpt from *Rights of Man* (1789).
The fourth is from Edmund Burke's "Reflections on the Revolution in France"
(1790), and the last is from Thomas Paine's answer to Burke: *Rights of Man*
(1791).

VOLTAIRE, THE FATHER OF THE REVOLUTION

In part 1 of "Billy Budd," the narrator makes reference to ship owners in sympathy with the French Revolution who name their ships for "liberal philosophers" (297). Prominent among them was Philadelphian Stephen Girard, who named his ships "after Voltaire, Diderot, and so forth" (297).

French philosophers laid the groundwork for revolution, though, ironically enough, none of the prominent ones advocated the overthrow of the French monarchy. However, they argued against kingship in general, especially the divine right of kings, church authority, and special class privileges. Alexis de Tocqueville and others observed that what prepared for the French Revolution was the philosophers' attacks on religious belief.

Denis Diderot, one of the philosophers mentioned in "Billy Budd," began in 1751 the *Encyclopedie,* a compendium of all knowledge, belief, and opinion consistently critical of existing institutions. The *Encyclopedie,* edited by Diderot and D'Alembert, was often called the centerpiece of the Enlightenment in its antireligious, humanistic views put forward in essays by Voltaire, Rousseau, and Montesquieu.

Voltaire (1694–1778), considered the most important figure of the French Enlightenment, is best known for his philosophic essays and satiric fiction titled *Candide.* Will and Ariel Durant sum up his importance in volume 9 of *The History of Civilization in Western Europe,* titled *The Age of Voltaire:*

> To the eighteenth-century thinkers...we owe the relative freedom that we enjoy in our thought and speech and creeds...we owe a hundred humane reforms in law and government, in the treatment of crime, sickness, and insanity.... Because of those men we, here and now, can write without fear, though not without reproach. When we cease to honor Voltaire we shall be unworthy of freedom. (786)

The subjects of the following excerpts from Voltaire's "On States. Government" are systems of laws, taxes, liberty of the press, torture, and tolerance. He compares the laws of a monarchy to a chicken yard; shows that, while taxation is necessary, in a monarchy taxation is levied without representation; illustrates that no government was ever destroyed by a book; reveals that the France of his own day resorts to torture to suppress dissent; and points to America as a place of tolerance.

FROM VOLTAIRE, "ON STATE GOVERNMENT," QUOTED IN NORMAN L. TORREY, *VOLTAIRE AND THE ENLIGHTENMENT* (NEW YORK: F. S. CROFTS, 1931)

Sheep live together in society very agreeably; we consider them very meek in character because we do not see the prodigious quantity of animals that they devour. We may believe that they eat them innocently, and without knowing it, just as when we eat a Sassenage cheese. The republic of sheep is the faithful image of the Golden Age.

A poultry-yard is plainly the most perfect monarchy. There is no king comparable to a cock. If he marches proudly in the midst of his people, it is not through vanity. If the enemy approaches, he does not order his subjects to go and be killed for him by virtue of his certain knowledge and plenary powers; he goes himself, lines up his hens behind him and fights to the death. If he is victorious, it is he who sings the *Te Deum*. In civil life, there is no one so gallant, so honest, so unselfish. He possesses all virtues. If he holds in his royal beak a grain of wheat or a worm, he gives it to the first of his subjects to present herself. Solomon in all his harem was not to be compared to a barn-yard cock.

Liberty of the Press

In general, we have the natural right to use our pens like our tongues, at our own risk and peril. I know of many books which have been boring, but I know of none that has done any real harm. Theologians, or self-styled politicians, cry out:

Religion is destroyed, the government is ruined, if you print certain truths or certain paradoxes. Never take it into your head to think until you have asked the permission of some monk or of some bureaucrat. It is contrary to good order for a man to think for himself.

. . .

One cannot reason more justly, my friends; but let's see, pray, what state has been ruined by a book.

You fear books as certain small towns have feared violins. Let people read and let them dance; these two amusements will never do the world any harm.

. . .

Let us remember that in all English America, which includes nearly a fourth of the known world, entire liberty of conscience is established; and provided that one believes in a God, every religion is well received, and as a result commerce is flourishing and population is increasing.

Taxes

In republics and in states called kingdoms but which are republics in fact, each individual is taxed according to his powers and the needs of the state.

In despotic kingdoms, or to speak more politely, in monarchical states, it is not quite the same. The nation is taxed without being consulted. An agriculturist who has twelve hundred francs income is very much astonished when four hundred are demanded of him. There are several even who are obliged to pay more than half of what they take in.

For what is all this money used? The most honest use one can make of it is to give it to other citizens.

The cultivator asks why half of his goods are taken from him to pay soldiers, when the hundredth part would be enough: he is told that besides the soldiers, arts and luxuries must be paid for, that nothing is lost, that among the Persians the queen is assigned towns and villages to pay for her belt, her slippers, and her pins.

. . .

Torture

Although there are few articles of jurisprudence in these honest alphabetical reflections, a word must be said concerning torture, otherwise called the *question*. It is a strange manner of questioning men. It was not invented, however, out of idle curiosity; there is every likelihood that this part of our legislation owes its origin to a highway robber. Most of these gentlemen still are accustomed to squeeze thumbs, burn feet and question by other torments those who refuse to tell them where they have put their money.

When conquerors had succeeded these thieves, they found the invention very useful to their interests: they put it to use when they suspected that anyone opposed them with certain evil designs, such, for instance, as the desire to be free; that was a crime of high treason against God and man. They wanted to know the accomplices; and to accomplish this, they subjected to the suffering of a thousand deaths those whom they suspected, because according to the jurisprudence of these early heroes, whoever was suspected merely of entertaining against them any slightly disrespectful thought was worthy of death. The moment that anyone has thus merited death, it matters little that terrible torments are added for several days, and even for several weeks a practice which smacks somewhat of the Divinity.

COMPLAINTS AND GRIEVANCES

The narrator connects the grievances of French peasants to those of the sailors in "Billy Budd": "Reasonable discontent growing out of practical grievances in the fleet had been ignited into irrational combustion as by live cinders blown across the Channel from France in flames" (303).

In 1789, elections were held to choose deputies from the three estates to the Estates-General, and each rural parish would hold assemblies to draw up a list of grievances to be submitted to their representatives for consideration. These lists of grievances, coming from throughout the country and retained in government files, are some of the most historically revealing documents available detailing the lives of the lower classes.

Excerpts from the "List of Grievances for the Royal Academy of Sciences, Arts, and Letters of Orleans" emphasize the need for fundamental civil rights and changes in government. Excerpts from the "List of Grievances, Complaints, and Remonstrances of the Inhabitants of the Parish of Pithiviers-le-Vieil" present grievances of a more practical nature regarding impediments to farming and the need for church tithes to be kept within the parish church rather than going into the pockets of bishops and cardinals.

FROM "LIST OF GRIEVANCES FOR THE ROYAL ACADEMY
OF SCIENCES, ARTS, AND LETTERS OF ORLEANS" AND
"LIST OF GRIEVANCES, COMPLAINTS, AND
REMONSTRANCES OF THE INHABITANTS OF THE PARISH
OF PITHIVIERS-LE-VIEIL," QUOTED IN PHILIP DAWSON,
THE FRENCH REVOLUTION (ENGLEWOOD CLIFFS, N.J.:
PRENTICE-HALL, 1967)

"List of Grievances for the Royal Academy of Sciences, Arts, and Letter of Orleans" (21–22).

. . .

1. To vote in the Estates-General only as three Order jointly, with the votes counted by head.... Voting by head... putting an end to the vicious distinction between the Orders, would turn all minds toward the public good, which in a well constituted state will always be that of the greatest number.

2. To concern themselves next with the means of establishing on solid foundations a constitution which, regulating the respective rights of Sovereign and of the Nation, assures for each of them the greatest possible degree of strength, authority and well-being.

. . .

4.   To assure individual liberty and security to all citizens.

· · ·

10.   To ask for the reform of the laws and the courts, so that justice is rendered equally to all at the least possible cost and is located nearer the litigants.

"List of Grievances, Complaints, and Remonstrances of the Inhabitants of the Parish of Pithiviers-le-Vieil" (28–29).

· · ·

12.   The right of hunting is devastating our countrysides. We do not ask that it be abolished, but that our grain be protected by law from all the wrongs and damage suffered by cultivators from the gamekeepers and the excessive quantity of game and that hunting be prohibited when our grain is on the stalks. Nothing causes more ravages than the hare. It takes away the cultivator's hope for a harvest, leaving him unable to obtain compensation except by paying fees which make the lawsuit more costly than profitable for him.

13.   The dovecotes are too numerous; the seigneurs of simple fiefs…claim to have the right to them, and the multitude of pigeons work frightful destruction on the grain, especially on the early shoots; in order to oblige the seigneurs to feed their pigeons, at least let individuals be permitted to kill them when they find them devastating their fields.

· · ·

15.   That the militia be abolished. It depopulates our countryside. The young men who are required to draw lots are nearly all from the most indigent class of citizens.

· · ·

18.   That if the casual fees, which the parish priests customarily collect, are abolished, the income of the living of Pithiviers-le-Vieil would be too small for so demanding a parish, composed of 160 households in 14 localities…; that this income can be increased by giving the parish priest all the tithes which, although mere alms, are in the hands of ecclesiastical superiors.

"RIGHTS OF MAN"

On the ship from which Billy is impressed, the *Rights-of-Man,* he flourishes and positively contributes to life aboard ship. In his farewell words, "'And good-bye to you too, old *Rights-of-Man.*'" (297) Lieutenant Ratcliff, who is forcing him from the merchant ship onto a warship, detects a double meaning that Billy is incapable of intending: "This he [Ratcliff] took as meant to convey a covert sally on the new recruits part, a sly slur at impressment in general, and that of himself especial" (298). And in light of Billy's fate, the reader is aware that Billy is, unintentionally, saying good-bye to his rights as a human being. The American revolutionaries had used the phrase "The Bill of Rights," to establish fundamental freedoms in the new government that had liberated itself from the English king. The ideas captured in the much-repeated phrase "the rights of man" was the foundation of the French Revolution and the government that followed it. It was a rallying cry for lowly members of the third estate, who were victims of poverty, discrimination, and intolerance.

On August 26, 1789, after the fall of the Bastille the month before, the representatives of the various estates met to lay down the basic rights for every French citizen. Its full title was "The Declaration of the Rights of Man and the Citizen," usually written simply as "Rights of Man." It has long been considered the foundation of the new government that is no longer based on inherited privileges.

In this excerpt, one sees all those rights that Billy no longer enjoys on the *Bellipotent:* equality before the law and the government; freedom from social stratification; liberty; rights to property, representation, justice, and security; freedom from oppression; freedom of speech; and freedom of the press.

FROM "RIGHTS OF MAN," QUOTED IN LEO GERSHOY, *THE ERA OF THE FRENCH REVOLUTION, 1789–1799* (NEW YORK: D. VAN NOSTRAND, 1957), 129–31

The representatives of the French people, organized in National Assembly, considering that ignorance, forgetfulness or contempt of the rights of man are the sole causes of the public miseries and of the corruption of governments, have resolved to set forth in a solemn declaration the natural, inalienable, and sacred rights of man, in order that this declaration, being ever present to all the members of the social body, may unceasingly remind them of their rights and their duties: in order that the acts of the legislative power and those of the executive power may be each moment compared with the aim of every political institution and thereby may be more respected: and in order that the demands of the citizens, grounded henceforth upon simple and incontestable principles, may always take the direction of maintaining the constitution and the welfare of all.

In consequence, the National Assembly recognizes and declares, in the presence and under the auspices of the Supreme Being, the following rights of man and citizen.

1. Men are born and remain free and equal in rights. Social distinctions can be based only upon public utility.

2. The aim of every political association is the preservation of the natural and imprescriptible rights of man. These rights are liberty, property, security, and resistance to oppression.

3. The source of all sovereignty is essentially in the nation; no body, no individual can exercise authority that does not proceed from it in plain terms.

4. Liberty consists in the power to do anything that does not injure others; accordingly, the exercise of the natural rights of each man has for its only limits those that secure to the other members of society the enjoyment of these same rights. These limits can be determined only by law.

5. The law has the right to forbid only such actions as are injurious to society. Nothing can be forbidden that is not interdicted by the law and no one can be constrained to do that which it does not order.

6. Law is the expression of the general will. All citizens have the right to take part personally or by their representatives in its formation. It must be the same for all, whether it protects or punishes. All citizens being equal in its eyes are equally eligible to all public dignities, places, and employments, according to their capacities, and without other distinction than that of their virtues and their talents.

7. No man can be accused, arrested, or detained except in the cases determined by the law and according to the forms that it has prescribed. Those who procure, expedite, execute, or cause to be executed arbitrary orders ought to he punished; but every citizen summoned or seized in virtue of the law ought to render instant obedience; he makes himself guilty by resistance.

8. The law ought to establish only penalties that are strictly and obviously necessary and no one can be punished except in virtue of a law established and promulgated prior to the offence and legally applied.

9. Every man being presumed innocent until he has been pronounced guilty, if it is thought indispensable to arrest him, all severity that may not be necessary to secure his person ought to be strictly suppressed by law.

10. No one ought to be disturbed on account of his opinions, even religious, provided their manifestation does not derange the public order established by law.

11. The free communication of ideas and opinions is one of the most precious of the rights of man; every citizen then can freely speak, write, and print, subject to responsibility for the abuse of this freedom in the cases determined by law.

12. The guarantee of the rights of man and citizen requires a public force; this force then is instituted for the advantage of all and not for the personal benefit of those to whom it is entrusted.

13. For the maintenance of the public force and for the expenses of administration the general tax is indispensable; it ought to be equally apportioned among all the citizens according to their means.

14. All the citizens have the right to ascertain, by themselves or by their representatives, the necessity of the public tax, to consent to it freely, to follow the employment of it, and to determine the quota, the assessment, the collection, and the duration of it.

15. Society has the right to call for an account from every public agent of its administration.

16. Any society in which the guarantee of the rights is not secured or the separation of powers not determined has no constitution at all.

17. Property being a sacred and inviolable right, no one can be deprived of it unless a legally established public necessity evidently demands it, under the condition of a just and prior indemnity.

REFLECTIONS ON THE REVOLUTION IN FRANCE

In explaining the naming of ships to express political beliefs, the narrator explains that Thomas Paine's *Rights of Man,* for whom Billy's merchant ship was named, was written in response to Edmund Burke's *Reflections on the Revolution in France.* In his novel *White Jacket,* about life aboard a warship, Melville describes Jack Chase, to whom "Billy Budd" is dedicated, as a "stickler for the Rights of Man, and the liberties of the world" (Dedication Page). And, as one studies the conservatism of Captain Vere and the narrator, especially seeing Vere's fear of dramatic reforms that would provide the lower classes with rights and, therefore, upset the hallowed forms that are the foundation of his belief, it becomes apparent that Vere's mind is an echo of Burke's, the renowned British parliamentarian whose attack on the French Revolution was his most famous work. Of Vere, the narrator writes, "With mankind," he would say, "forms, measured forms, are everything; and this is the import couched in the story of Orpheus and his lyre spellbinding the wild denizens of the wood" (380). And this he once applied to the disruption of forms going on across the Channel and the consequences thereof.

Moreover, Vere, like Burke, claims to deplore the French Revolution, not only because it is an attack on the "privileged classes," but because "it is at war with the peace of the world" (312), as the privileged classes defined "peace," a point that Burke also makes repeatedly.

Edmund Burke (1729–97), who entered the British House of Commons in Parliament in 1765, began his political career as a liberal, making a name for himself as a writer of philosophy and political commentary, and actually supporting the Americans in their cause for independence. However, he slowly became more and more conservative, opposing reform of Parliament and the reform of special advantages given to the Anglican Church by the British government. During the last years of his career, he secured his conservative reputation with the publication of his attack on the French Revolutionaries, raising the ire of liberal thinkers throughout the Western world, who were convinced of the necessity for reform.

Burke's *Reflections* was conceived as a letter to a young Parisian, identified as Chames-Jean-Francois de Pont. In fact he had already written a letter to de Pont in which he proclaimed the virtues so valued by Vere: "Prudence (in all things a Virtue, in Politicks the first of Virtues)" (quoted in Conor Cruise O'Brien's introduction to *Reflections,* 15). Burke argues in the more substantial essay for an inherited monarchy, an inherited peerage and authority vested in the Anglican Church. He rails against the usurpation and imprisonment of the French king and queen, the usurpation of the church, and what he sees as an inept and contrived equality in the new French government. In the following excerpts one sees Burke's alarm that peace and order have been disrupted, that "unqualified" men are "meddling" with government structure in the name of civil rights, and the treasonous teaching that rulers should be chosen by the people. He chooses inherited orders and the succession of kings because they promote unity, peace, and tranquility. He deplores the disrespect given to ancient institutions and despairs of France's reorganization of property and political power. His views of the French Revolution, he makes clear, are based on his supreme values of reason, order, peace, and virtue. The final excerpt attests to the depths of his conservative hatred of the ideals of the French Revolution.

FROM EDMUND BURKE, *REFLECTIONS ON THE REVOLUTION IN FRANCE* (1790; REPRINT, LONDON: PENGUIN BOOKS, 1968)

I should...suspend my congratulations on the new liberty of France, until I was informed how it had been combined with government: with public force; with the discipline and obedience of armies; with the collection of an effective and well-distributed revenue; with morality and religion; with the solidity of property; with peace and order: with civil and social manners...Prudence would dictate this in the case of separate insulated private men; but liberty, when men act in bodies, is *power*. Considerate people, before they declare themselves, will observe the use which is made of *power*; particularly of so trying a thing as *new* power in *new* persons, of whose principles, tempers, and dispositions, they have little or no experience, and in situations where those who appear the most stirring in the scene may possibly not be the real movers. (91)

...

[The necessity of] "preserving 'a certainty in the SUCCESSION thereof, the unity, peace, and tranquillity of this nation doth, under God, wholly depend.'" (103)

...

We fear God; we look up with awe to kings; with affection to parliaments; with duty to magistrates; with reverence to priests; and with respect to nobility. Why? Because when such ideas are brought before our minds, it is *natural* to be affected; because all other feelings are false and spurious, and tend to corrupt our minds, to vitiate our primary morals, to render us unfit for rational liberty; and by teaching us a servile, licentious, and abandoned insolence, to be our low sport for a few holidays.... (183)

...

... [I]f that which is only submission to necessity should be made the object of choice, the law is broken, nature is disobeyed, and the rebellious are outlawed, cast forth, and exiled, from this world of reason, and order, and peace, and virtue, and fruitful penitence, into the antagonistic world of madness, discord, vice, confusion, and unavailing sorrow. (195)

· · ·

Good order is the foundation of time and in arrangement. Good order is the foundation of all good things. To be enabled to acquire, the people, without being servile, must be tractable and obedient. The magistrate must have his reverence, the laws their authority. The body of the people must not find the principles of natural subordination by art rooted out of their minds. They must respect that property of which they cannot partake. They must labour to obtain what by labour can be obtained.... But when men think that these beggarly contrivances [financial concerns] may supply a resource for the evils which result from breaking up the foundations of public order, and from causing or suffering the principles of property to be subverted, they will, in the ruin of their country, leave a melancholy and lasting monument of the effect of preposterous politics, and presumptuous, short-sighted, narrow-minded wisdom. (372, 373)

THOMAS PAINE'S *THE RIGHTS OF MAN: PART TWO*

The narrator informs the reader of the history of the name of the merchant ship upon which Billy prospers:

> The hardheaded Dundee owner was a staunch admirer of Thomas Paine, whose book in rejoinder to Burke's arraignment of the French Revolution had then been published for some time and had gone everywhere. (297)

Thomas Paine, the author of the extraordinarily successful pamphlet *Rights of Man,* was an Englishman who came to think of himself as a "citizen of the world." From England he came to the United States, where he was a key figure in fomenting the American Revolution, rallying discouraged troops, and formulating the country's founding documents. After the revolution, he was wildly celebrated in the United States, but having successfully launched one revolution, he was ready to move on to France and England, where ancient abuses of power had enslaved the majority of the population.

In 1790, he published *Rights of Man,* the most successful of many rejoinders to Edmund Burke's attack on the French Revolution. Burke's *Reflections on the Revolution in France* is believed to have sold 30,000 copies; Paine's *Rights of Man* sold 1,500,000. As Leo Gershoy writes in *The Era of the French Revolution, 1789–1799:*

> No other book was so widely read or so influential in the democratic causes as that emphatic affirmation of the right of the people, not merely once when they made their constitution, but at all times to order their destiny according to the general will. (23)

As a result of Paine's publication of *Rights of Man,* he had to flee to France, after learning that he would be arrested for treason in England. He was tried in absentia anyway and found guilty.

In France, after the revolution, he was elected to the French National Assembly, but, in the reign of terror that followed the revolution, he was arrested for arguing against the execution of King Louis XVI. Paine spent 10 months in prison in France, ignored by the Americans who could have helped in his release. In this 10-month period he faced the probability every day that he would be executed, and on two days would have been carried to the guillotine had not some accidents prevented it. When Paine was released, he returned to an America, whose now conservative government was frightened of Paine's political radicalism and resented his unorthodox religious views. Once celebrated in the United States, he died friendless and in poverty.

In the following excerpts from *Rights of Man,* Paine analyzes Burke's attack on a cleric's statement about the rights of Englishmen and argues that the King is not the government of the country, puts forward the fundamental principles by which he thinks a country should be governed, and declares his time to be an age of revolutions.

FROM THOMAS PAINE, "RIGHTS OF MAN," QUOTED IN
LEO GERSHOY, *THE ERA OF THE FRENCH REVOLUTION,
1789–1799* (NEW YORK: D. VAN NOSTRAND, 1957)

Dr. Price had preached a sermon on the 4th of November, 1789, being the anniversary of what is called in England the Revolution, which took place 1688. Mr. Burke, speaking of this sermon, says, "The political Divine proceeds dogmatically to assert, that by the principles of the Revolution, the people of England have acquired three fundamental rights:

1. To choose their own governors
2. To cashier them for misconduct
3. To frame a government for ourselves."

Dr. Price does not say that the right to do these things in this or in that person, or in this or in that description of persons, but that it exists in the *whole;* that it is a right resident in the nation. Mr. Burke, on the contrary, denies that such a right exists in the nation, either in whole or in part, or that it exists anywhere; and, what is still more strange and marvelous, he says, "that the people of England utterly disclaim such a right, and that they will resist the practical assertion of it with their lives and fortunes." That men should take up arms and spend their lives and fortunes, *not* to maintain their rights, but to maintain they have *not* rights, is an entirely new species of discovery, and suited to the paradoxical genius of Mr. Burke.

The method which Mr. Burke takes to prove that the people of England have no such rights, and that such rights do not now exist in the nation, either in whole or in part, or anywhere at all, is of the same marvelous and monstrous kind with what he has already said; for his arguments are that the persons; or the generation of persons, in whom they did exist are dead, and with them the right is dead also. To prove this, he quotes a declaration made by Parliament about a hundred years ago, to William and Mary, in these words: "The Lords Spiritual and Temporal, and Commons, do, in the name of the people aforesaid [meaning the people of England then living], most humbly and faithfully *submit* themselves, their *heirs* and *posterities,* for EVER...to the end of time." (7, 8)

. . .

Reason and Ignorance, the opposite to each other, influence the great bulk of mankind. If either of these can be rendered sufficiently extensive in a country, the machinery of Government goes easily on. Reason obeys itself; and Ignorance submits to whatever is dictated to it.

The two modes of Government which prevail in the world, are—

First Government by election and representation
Secondly Government by hereditary succession.

The former is generally known by the name of Republic; the latter by that of Monarchy and Aristocracy.

These two distinct and opposite forms erect themselves on the two distinct and opposite bases of Reason and Ignorance.

As the exercise of Government requires talents and abilities, and as talents and abilities cannot have hereditary descent, it is evident that hereditary succession requires a belief from man to which his reason cannot subscribe, and which can only be established upon his ignorance; and the more ignorant any country is, the better it is fitted for this species of Government.

On the contrary, Government, in a well-constituted Republic, requires no belief from man beyond what his reason can give. (100)

. . .

When we survey the wretched condition of Man, under the monarchical and hereditary systems of Government, dragged from his home by one power, or driven by another, and impoverished by taxes more than by enemies, it becomes evident that those systems are bad, and that a general Revolution in the principle and construction of Governments is necessary.

What is Government more than the management of the affairs of a nation? Is not, and from its nature cannot be, the property of any particular man or family, but of the whole community, at whose expense it supported; and through by force and contrivance it has been usurped into an inheritance, the usurpation cannot alter the right of things. (103)

. . .

[W]hat we see not in the world, from the Revolutions of America and France, are a renovation of then natural order of things, a system of principles as universal as truth and the existence of man, and combining moral and political happiness and national prosperity.

    I   Men are born, and always continue free and equal in respect of their rights. Civil distinctions, therefore, can be founded only on public utility.

    II   The end of all political associations is the preservation of the natural and imprescriptible rights of man; and these rights are liberty, property, security, and resistance to oppression.

    III   The nation is essentially the source of all sovereignty; nor can ANY INDIVIDUAL, *or* ANY BODY OF MEN, be entitled to any authority which is not expressly derived from it. (104)

QUESTIONS AND PROJECTS

1. Obtain copies of the U.S. Bill of Rights. Write an essay comparing it with the French Declaration of Rights.

2. Make a photocopy of the U.S. Bill of Rights without its title. Allow room for signatures at the end. In a safe environment like a school function or town meeting, ask people—upon exiting—to sign your "petition." Keep track of how many refuse and any comments you hear.

3. Do research to write an essay on why some Americans thought they needed another revolution more like the French Revolution.

4. Based on research, write and produce a play on an eighteenth-century community's discussion of the French Revolution. Include a variety of points of view and raise a number of questions.

5. Using the full texts of Paine's *Rights of Man* and Burke's *Reflections,* dramatize and stage a debate between Paine and Burke.

6. Assuming that the old regime and the new have different mind-sets, make two columns of their contrasting values. Write two columns contrasting the values of Vere and those recommended by the story of "Billy Budd."

7. In an essay, argue your agreement or disagreement with the following: "God places a person in a certain situation and class from birth; therefore, one should not try to leave one's god-given place."

8. Write a self-analysis. Do you regard yourself as primarily a follower of authority or a questioner of authority? Give examples. Why do you think you are the way you are in this respect?

9. In an essay, describe the classes, distinctions, power, authority, prerogatives, and inequalities that exist in your community. What accounts for the class divisions, if any? Race? Money? Education? Inherited status?

10. People throughout the ages have disagreed about how we know truth. Is it, in your opinion, primarily through instinct, the heart, the head, authorities, revealed religion, your own peers, or something else? Have a class discussion on the question, being prepared beforehand to explain and support your point of view.

11. Do some research on countries whose policies are determined by a particular religion—Iran, for example. Choose one such country to report on.

12. The names of the ships and the flags in "Billy Budd" are political statements. What gestures or symbols are *political* statements in our day? One example is the *V* for victory as used by Churchill in World War II. President Nixon also used it when he left office. What did that mean? And the *V* is also called "the peace sign." Examine others: the raised fist, the dove, the fish, the hammer and sickle, the stars and stripes, and so on.

13. Examine the U.S. Bill of Rights for yourself. Are any of them problematic for you today? Have a class discussion on the topic.

FURTHER READING

Aldridge, Alfred Owen. *Tom Paine's American Ideology.* Philadelphia: Lippincott, 1959.
————. *Voltaire and the Century of Light.* Princeton, N.J.: Princeton University Press, 1975.
Andrews, Wayne. *Voltaire.* New York: New Directions, 1981.
Ayer, Alfred Jules. *Thomas Paine.* New York: Athenaeum, 1988.
Ayling, Stanley. *Edmund Burke: His Life and Opinions.* London: John Murray, 1988.
Bosher, John Francis. *The French Revolution.* New York: W. W. Norton, 1988.
Brewer, Daniel. *The Discourse of Enlightenment in 18th-Century France: Diderot and the Art of Philosophizing.* Oxford: Oxford University Press, 1983.
Durant, Will, and Ariel Durant. *The Age of Voltaire.* Vol. 9 of *The History of Civilization in Western Europe.* New York: MJF Books, 1965.
Forrest, Alan I. *The French Revolution.* Oxford: Oxford University Press, 1995.
France, Peter, *Diderot.* New York: Cambridge University Press, 1993.
Freeman, Michael. *Edmund Burke and the Critique of Political Radicalism.* Oxford: B. Blackwell, 1980.
Fruchtman, Jack. *Thomas Paine and the Religion of Nature.* Baltimore: Johns Hopkins University Press, 1993.
Gay, Peter. *Voltaire's Politics.* Princeton, N.J.: Princeton University Press, 1959.
Gershoy, Leo. *The Era of the French Revolution, 1789–1799.* New York: D. Van Nostrand, 1957.
Gilbert, Adrian. *The French Revolution.* New York: Thomson Learning, 1995.
Hunt, Jocelyn. *The French Revolution.* London: Routledge, 1998.
Keane, John. *Tom Paine.* Boston: Little, Brown, 1995.
Lewis, Joseph. *Thomas Paine, Author of the Declaration of Independence.* New York: Freethought Press, 1947.
McPhee, Peter. *The French Revolution.* Oxford: Oxford University Press, 2002.
Melville, Herman. *White Jacket.* New York: The Modern Library, 2002.
Palmer, R. R. *The World of the French Revolution.* New York: Harper Torchbooks, 1967.
Roberts, John Morris. *The French Revolution.* Oxford: Oxford University Press, 1997.
Rude, George F. E. *The French Revolution.* London: Weidenfeld and Nicolson, 1988.
Schama, Simon. *Citizens: A Chronicle of the French Revolution.* New York: Knopf, 1989.
Topazio, Virgil W. *Voltaire. A Critical Study of His Major Works.* New York: Random House, 1967.

10_____

The Clash of the *Bellipotent* and the *Rights-of-Man:* Mutiny at the Spithead and the Nore

To the British Empire the Nore Mutiny was what a strike in the fire brigade would be to London threatened by general arson. (303)

The assemblies of mutineers in 1797 at two major English ports, the Spithead and the Nore, by all accounts, constituted the first instance of a government that was elected by all its citizens, the first instance of universal suffrage, in England. In the winter of 1797, the age-old clash between "the people" and the inherited ruling class broke through the surface in the form of mutinies within the massive British fleet, centering first at the Spithead, a protected anchorage located near Portsmouth on the southwest shore of England, and then at the larger anchorage, the Nore, located in the North Sea near the mouth of the Thames River. England in 1797 had no form of representative government. For example, in the city of Bath, with a population of 25,000, there were only 31 eligible voters. Yet taxes fell primarily on the poor. Laborers making 18 pounds a year paid 10 pounds a year in tax. And all government taxes collected went to the king, the army, the navy, and the church.

REFERENCES TO THE GREAT MUTINY IN "BILLY BUDD"

The characters of "Billy Budd" are shaped by these mutinies; their actions are provoked and determined by the mutinies, and the fundamental conflicts in political and social philosophies that bear on the plot have been defined and exposed by the mutinies.

As the foundation for the story, Melville, in parts 3 and 4, provides a six-page history of the mutinies of 1797 and their aftermath from the point of view of his upper-class narrator. Still, the enormity of this single event, deriving as it did not only from French philosophy but from very real grievances, is made apparent in Melville's history:

> It was the summer of 1797. In the April of that year had occurred the commotion at Spithead followed in May by a second and yet more serious outbreak, in the fleet at the Nore. The latter is known, and without exaggeration in the epithet, as "the Great Mutiny." It was indeed a demonstration more menacing to England than the contemporary manifestoes and conquering and proselytizing armies of the French Directory. . . . Reasonable discontent growing out of practical grievances in the fleet had been ignited into irrational combustion as by live cinders blown across the Channel from France in flames. (303)

The philosophical stance behind the mutinies are suggested in the name of the peaceable ship, the *Rights-of-Man,* for history teaches us that part 2 of Thomas Paine's *Rights of Man* circulated secretly among English sailors in every fleet, its vision of basic *human* rights an inspiration to sailors who were regarded and treated as little more than animals. The names of the warships, given by Melville in "Billy Budd," suggest the old regime of godless brute force: the *Bellipotent,* the *Atheist,* the *Devastation,* and the *Erebus* (meaning "hell"). In actuality, such names were common in the British fleet in 1796 and 1797, the *Vengeance,* the *Resistance,* the *Formidable,* the *Porcupine,* the *Venerable 74,* the *Leopard,* and the *Inflexible.*

The mutinies at the Spithead and the Nore, which occurred only a few months before the impressment of Billy, are constantly on the minds of the officers, but the impulse among them is to act as if the events never happened and to refrain from speaking of them, "very heedful how they referred to the recent events in the fleet" (343).

At the time that Claggart makes his accusation to Vere, he continues to bring up the Great Mutiny to inspire fear in the mind of Vere. Every naval commander must feel anxious, he says, "in view of extraordinary outbreaks so recent" (343). Vere, while he sees through Claggart's unreasonable attempt to alarm him with his reference to the Great Mutiny, is nevertheless apprehensive:

> "Never mind that!" here peremptorily broke in the superior, his face altering with anger, instinctively divining the ship that the other was about to name, one in which the Nore Mutiny had assumed a singularly tragic character that for a time jeopardized the life of its commander. (343)

Later, as the board is contemplating Billy's fate, Vere successfully appeals to their anxiety with a reference to the Nore, insisting that if the board does not take a hard line with Billy, in short terrorize the crew, the discontented sailors aboard will feel free to mutiny as they did at the Nore:

> "You know what sailors are. Will they not revert to the recent outbreak at the Nore? Ay. They know the well-founded alarm—the panic it struck throughout England." (364)

MOTIVES FOR MUTINY: LIFE ABOARD SHIP

Conditions aboard ship made men ripe for mutiny. First was the matter of pay. The pay for a British sailor had, in 1797, been unchanged for a hundred years. Moreover, some of the sailors on fleets anchored off the Spithead and the Nore had not been paid at all for three or four years. Money owed sailors who had served in naval battles was very seldom forthcoming. Bounties they had been promised for serving were rarely paid.

Second was the matter of provisions. The food aboard ship was never adequate for the crew. Food for any ship's voyage was underweighed by the contractors (mentioned by Melville in "Billy Budd"), who bribed the chief accounting officer aboard ship, called the purser. The purser then reduced further the amount that went to the crew by holding back large quantities of the best food, which he then sold to the officers. The fare aboard ship consisted of salt beef and salt pork, dried biscuits, oatmeal, dried peas, cheese, and cocoa. There was no refrigeration, so often the meat that had been below decks in casks for years was so marble hard that it was inedible. Biscuits were rock hard and teaming with worms. Cheese was made of every kind of kitchen waste but no cream. Peas were still hard as rocks even after hours and hours of soaking and cooking. Water brought aboard for the voyage was spoiled within a week. It was inevitably crawling with vermin and scum. The sick in desperate need of water tried to kill the germs with rum.

Working conditions aboard ship led to illness, injury, and deformity. Ships were designed to accommodate guns, not men. Low ceilings below the open main deck required men to work continually in a stooped position, resulting in permanent back and leg deformities. In the lowest cable decks, men ran around doing their work literally doubled over in the dark. The two lowest decks, which housed troops and prisoners of war, were filled with bilge, the ship's waste, rats, and water from leaks.

The environment aboard ship and the nature of the work was bound to create serious medical ailments. The damp led to joint problems. There was no heat aboard ship except in the galley when meals were cooked. Putrid food and air contributed to disease. Soap was not officially issued to sailors until the nineteenth century. Heavy work tore muscles and damaged joints and backs. Anchors, for instance, were so heavy they required 280 men to raise and lower them. Above decks sailors crawling across the yard arms, to work with their hands, developed abdominal ruptures. There was virtually no medical treatment aboard ship for any of these ailments. And, as Melville pointed out in *White Jacket,* ships' surgeons were often not only incompetent and alcoholic, but sadistic.

One of the crucial complaints of many sailors was the condition of the ships they were compelled to sail on. Many were dangerously rickety, death traps in the high seas. In 1782, *Royal George, 104* had sunk at the Spithead, drowning 800 sailors and 300 women and children who were saying good-bye to the men scheduled to go to sea the next day.

But the situation aboard ship that received most attention during the mutinies and that the Admiralty absolutely refused to address was the presence aboard ships of brutal, cruel officers who, for petty infractions, flogged men to death. If those in charge of the cat-o'-nine-tails appeared less than vigorous, they were flogged as well.

To retain impressed and disgruntled sailors, they were typically not allowed to leave the ship when it went into ports. In 1797, when the Channel Fleet returned to the Spithead for provisions, only the ships' captains and the elite crews were allowed to leave the ship. Some men had not been on land for three years.

IMPRESSMENT, CRIMINALS, AND THE BOUNTY SYSTEM

The impressment of Billy is also pertinent to the mutinies, as this was the main way that the British navy supplied its ships with sailors, creating aboard warships certain kinds of individuals whose resentment of impressment, among other abuses, led directly to the mutinies. This practice Melville mentions as a grievance that was never addressed. The narrator confesses that British warships were often forced to leave port without enough sailors and, therefore, resorted to kidnapping men from other ships. He also makes clear that officers and the Admiralty were well aware of the resentment generated in the men who were impressed. When Billy says goodbye to the *Rights-of-Man,* the officer who has stolen him naturally thinks that it is "a covert sally on the new recruit's part, a sly slur at impressment in general, and of himself especial" (297). Billy's naive cheerfulness is in marked contrast to the other men impressed onto the *Bellipotent,* men who may have had families on shore and who were "apt to fall into a saddish mood which in some partook of sullenness" (298). The lingering danger to the warship from impressed men is revealed in the midnight meeting to which Billy is lured.

"Hist! Billy," said the man, in the same quick cautionary whisper as before. "You were impressed, weren't you? Well, so was I": and he paused, as to mark the effect. But Billy, not knowing exactly what to make of this, said nothing. Then the other: "We are not the only impressed ones, Billy. There's a gang of us.— Couldn't you—help—in a pinch?" (332)

Impressment continues to be a critical issue in "Billy Budd," as it was in the mutinies, when Claggart brings up the topic and the notion that some impressed men aboard ship may be from the ranks of mutineers at the Spithead and the Nore:

[H]e had seen enough to convince him that at least one sailor aboard was a dangerous character in a ship mustering some who not only had taken a guilty part in the late serious troubles, but others also who, like the man in question, had entered His Majesty's service under another form than enlistment. (342)

To which Vere says, "Be direct, man; say *impressed men*" (342).

Vere himself brings up the issue of impressment in his bullying argument to the board he has appointed, assuming that most men impressed aboard naval vessels are especially dangerous as being in sympathy with the French Revolutionary government. As a consequence they have no rights:

"In His Majesty's service—in this ship, indeed—there are Englishmen forced to fight for the King against their will. Against their conscience, for aught we know. Though as their fellow creatures some of us may appreciate their position, yet as navy officers what reck we of it?" (363)

The kind of men who made up the British navy in 1797 made mutiny inevitable. It has been estimated that only one-fifth of the men serving in the British navy, composed of 100,000 men, were volunteers. The abominable conditions aboard warships led very few men to volunteer for service. So in order to get sufficient men to go to war for the king, they were forced into service. Some, as in the case of Billy Budd, were coerced from unarmed merchant ships. The British navy's unashamed habit of impressing sailors from American ships was a major cause of America's 1812 war with England. Amazingly enough, impressment remained legal in England until well into the twentieth century. But, in addition, what were called press gangs were sent ashore to kidnap men from port cities. Press gangs preferred to kidnap men with experience at sea. Prowling the streets, they would follow men whose language, dress, or physical deformities suggested that they had been sailors. (The stereotypical bowleggedness of sailors came from their cramped conditions below deck and, to press gangs, a bowlegged man in a port city was a sure sign that he had

had experience aboard a ship.) Following their prey, often to a tavern, the press gang's usual practice was to hit him over the head with a club, tie him up, throw him in a cellar, and take him aboard ship after dark. Boys as young as 10 were kidnapped to serve as powder monkeys and meal servers aboard ship. Impressed men were often the most uneducated and destitute of men. They were also, not surprisingly, the most bitter men aboard ship.

The king and Admiralty also filled their ships with "quota men" in what was called a bounty system: each county in England was given a quota of men that it had to supply to the British navy. These men, often gleaned from debtors' prison, were frequently well educated and especially well read in reform and revolutionary theories, which gave the promise of alleviating their torturous lives of poverty and discrimination. From these ranks primarily came the men who were able to educate and organize those ripe for mutiny. A 1795 act allowed local judges to consign to warships the idle, the unemployed, and criminals of all sorts, from petty thieves to the most violent and dangerous. Such men continued their crimes aboard ship. Judges handed over to ships orphans, delinquents, and runaways as young as 11.

Another category was made up of hardened criminals and petty thieves who escaped punishment for their crimes on land by escaping to ships, where they were promised bounties of up to 70 pounds. Claggart falls into this category. The nobility found places aboard ship for their sadistic and murderous sons, who on land would embarrass the family.

So many men were taken into ships in the English fleets that it actually impinged on the birth rate of the country.

CHRONOLOGY OF THE GREAT MUTINY

February 1797: Under the influence of Thomas Paine's *Rights of Man,* a group of quota men aboard the HMS *Queen Charlotte* meet to draw up an assertion of grievances to be circulated quietly throughout the fleet. Their final draft focuses on wages only.

March 7: The petition is posted to an admiral considered to be the sailors' friend, Richard Earl Howe, called "Black Dick."

March 22: Howe conveys the petitions to the First Lord of the Admiralty, the Earl of Spencer.

March 31: One of the great Channel Fleets returns to the Spithead for provisions. All but the elite are required to stay aboard ships. Provisions brought to ships in boats include contraband copies of part 2 of *Rights of Man* by Thomas Paine.

First week in April: British intelligence finds clear proof that the Dutch and French intend an invasion, hoping that the English underclass will support them. Longer, more detailed petitions are drawn up. The Admiralty promises to raise the pay of seamen, but when or if the money actually reaches the men is uncertain. Now men have decided to submit further grievances and assert that the money is insufficient. The Admiralty insults the men in public print.

April 2: Second copies of the petition are conveyed to Parliament. The new admiral of the fleet, Bridport, urges them to expand their lists of grievances. Chief among their complaints is the continuing presence on ships of sadistic officers. Bridport asks the lords of the Admiralty to keep his fleet in port until cruel officers are removed.

April 3: One fleet of eight ships is ordered to sail from port, and the sailors refuse, saying their petition had not been addressed. Marines are ordered to fire on ships, but they refuse.

April 13: No response from the Admiralty to the sailors' petition. The widespread anger among the men, who meet in groups aboard ship to talk of refusing to sail if the petition is not acknowledged, gets the attention of the ships' captains, who report the threat of mutiny to the Admiralty. Patterned on the U.S. Congress and the French Assembly, delegates elected by the men from each of the ships in the fleet meet to determine a course of action. It is determined that at the firing of two guns from the *Charlotte,* women and officers will be sent ashore, the red flag will go up the mizzentop, and the mutiny will begin.

April 18: The sailors respond with a more detailed petition, citing the need for better quality and adequate food, more vegetables, care for the sick aboard ship, regular shore leaves, care for the wounded, and the immediate removal of cruel officers. The Admiralty refuses to address these demands but considers pay raises. The men reiterate their demands.

April 19: Many officers on board ships support the men in their demands. The Admiralty agrees only to raises, but the whole matter must be passed by Parliament.

April 20: The Admiralty's response that the men will receive a pardon is conveyed by the officers, but the men insist upon seeing a signed pardon from the king before ending their mutiny. In late afternoon the red flag of defiance is raised over one of the ships, the *Royal George.* All fleet delegates meet and insist that every article of their detailed petition be worked into an act of Parliament.

April 22: The Lord of the Admiralty takes the sailors' letter to Parliament, which agrees to urge a king's pardon. This is formalized and sent to the fleet. The men are pacified by these documents and are at this time willing to go to sea to fight the French, but they are unhappy that their grievances have not been considered.

April 24: Bad weather prevents the Channel Fleet from leaving port. Meanwhile, the captains and admirals receive word from the Admiralty refusing to order changes in weight and quality of food, improve the treatment of the wounded, or expel cruel officers. The officers decide to keep this information secret from the men.

April 26: The Lord of the Admiralty submits the sailors' requests to the privy counsel, which dumps it in committee. Mutiny breaks out at Plymouth. The king's pardon is read at the Spithead, but some ships still refuse to sail. Rumors circulate that unless food demands are met, a whole fleet will take their ships to join the French.

April 30: Men aboard the *Venerable 74* refuse to obey their captain until pay and provisions issues are settled, but the Admiralty insists that securing the money will take time.

May 1: The fleet at Yarmouth is particularly discontented because men on several vessels have not been paid in a year. Men aboard the *Standard 64* train their guns on the officers. The red flag raised again, delegates seize the ships' arms and put captains and abusive officers ashore. On board the *London,* the captain orders officers to fire on men below decks, resulting in several wounded and one killed. On board some ships, officers are taken hostage.

May 10: Admiral Howe arrives in Portsmouth with an act of Parliament on the matter of wages and provisions. An agreement is reached with men on each of the ships. But there is continuing displeasure with the refusal to replace cruel officers.

May 14: Many cruel officers are replaced and an agreement is signed. But a new mutiny begins at the anchorage called the Nore. Their grievances are similar to those at the Spithead, with the addition of a request for shore leave for all the men. Some have not been allowed to leave the ship for two years. The leader of the Nore mutiny is Richard Parker, who had been transferred from debtors' prison to the fleet.

May 15: A king's pardon of Spithead mutineers arrives.

May 25: It is reported to the Admiralty that order has been restored everywhere except at the Nore, where mutineers are in full charge.

May 26: The chief legal officer of the realm reports that the king's pardon offered to men at the Spithead does not apply to men at the Nore. Parker goes through with a plan to block commercial ships from entering or exiting the Thames River. Warships on the Thames, some only 15 miles from London, raise the red flag of mutiny.

May 27: Artisans located along the Thames River are prepared to support the mutineers. Soldiers at the largest artillery base in the British Isles are also threatening to join the mutiny. With the prospect of a larger mutiny and warships sinking each other in an attempt to quell the Nore mutiny, Parliament goes into special session, for the first time giving the mutineers their full attention. Prime Minister Pitt takes a hard line, ordering that the sailors' demands be refused and that land troops be sent to the Nore in anticipation of putting down the mutiny.

May 28: Copies of the king's pardon are taken to the Nore. They are told grievances *might* be considered at a later date, but that they have only one day to sign an agreement.

May 29: On this, the deadline given the men by the Admiralty, the blockade of the Thames grows more intense. There is bickering among the mutineers. Some ships declare themselves loyal to the king. The Admiralty orders that no provisions be allowed aboard mutinous ships, in effect starving them out.

May 30: Many ships in the fleet accept pardons and haul down red flags. Fights break out among men aboard ship.

May 31: Eight ships sail into the Nore to support mutineers. Demands are added to the eight original articles: sailor representation on court-martial boards (introducing the concept of trial by one's peers), raises in pay for marines, payment of prize money to those who'd been promised it for capturing vessels in battles, and immediate payment of bounties for joining the navy. The demands are immediately refused.

June 1: The Admiralty responds with harsh new laws on mutiny, including death without benefit of clergy—even to someone suspected of communicating with a mutineer. Parker and his supporters are outraged.

June 2: The mutineers' blockade of London becomes so tight that British coal, grain, cotton, potato, timber, sugar, and tobacco interests are seriously damaged, and the stock market plummets.

June 3: Parker assures his captain that the delegates have no communication with France and are willing to sail to fight the Dutch. But seamen who agreed to stop the mutiny discover out of port that they are still being shortchanged on food. Some ships sailing against the Dutch have locked the men below deck. There are 100 vessels in mutiny at the Nore, and more sailing into port are joining them.

June 6: The Nore mutiny is a month old. Parker demands better provisions for the men. The mutineers move closer to London. About 15 miles from London, Parker commands 10,000 men, 1,300 guns, 17 large ships, and 23 smaller ones.

June 6–7: The government removes all aid to navigation, including buoys and lights in lighthouses, making it difficult or impossible for the mutineers to move. Public displeasure with the mutineers grows. Volunteers are raised to put down the mutiny. Marines are organized, and the navy takes on groups of pardoned deserters and newly impressed men. Provisions are running out, and there is talk among the mutineers of surrender.

June 9: Parker's delegates talk of breaking up the fleet—some ships joining France, some surrendering, and some planning to sail to Scotland. Many men go ashore and disappear.

June 10: Their deadline has been reached and there is no response from the king, so many men capitulate, dropping all demands except to have unsafe ships repaired and cruel officers removed. They also ask that no one be charged with treason. Loyalists begin recruiting mutineers to retake ships. Ships begin to be taken over. Parker reduces their demands to one: remove abusive officers from all ships.

June 11–15: The Admiralty begins boarding ships looking to arrest mutineers and gather supporting documents and evidence. The government flatly rejects a pardon for the Nore mutineers, flatly rejects removing brutal officers. Parker is captured. The Admiralty is instructed to appoint a court-martial board that has had no connection with the mutiny, but most of the members of the 13-captain board have had connections with Parker and are already strongly biased against him.

June 22: Parker's trial begins. He argues that he and his delegates were never disloyal to the king. Was what was more like a sit-down strike to be classified as treason?

June 26: The judge refuses to allow Parker more time to collect evidence. At 1:30 the board convenes, and at 4:00 they enter with a sentence of guilty, with Parker to be hanged and buried in a penal cemetery, not clerical ground.

June 30: Parker is executed. In all, 24 men were eventually hanged for treason and hundreds were flogged or exiled.

The first excerpt is from part 2 of Thomas Paine's *Rights of Man,* called the Bible of the sailor. The second excerpt is the longer petition of grievances issued by the Spithead delegates on April 18, after having their original petition, asking only for pay, ignored. The third is a letter sent out by Nore mutineers to the public in general stating their case for reform in the strongest possible terms. The fourth section includes anonymous 1797 poems and songs in praise of rebellious sailors.

THOMAS PAINE'S *THE RIGHTS OF MAN,* PART TWO

In the five years since the publication of Part 2 of Thomas Paine's *Rights of Man*, it had gone through hundreds of thousands of copies, many of which were smuggled aboard ships by quota men. It was considered a dangerous book in England, where booksellers who stocked it in their stores were arrested on charges of disseminating treason.

Conditions in England made Paine's argument extremely attractive to the poor and reformers. The so-called Bloody Code dictated the death penalty for over 350 actions, most of them against property. For example, one could be put to death for cutting down a tree on a nobleman's estate, fishing in his pond, or carrying a gun onto his property. Poor children were executed for stealing the property, sometimes a doll, from the aristocracy. The forms of execution included hanging, burning, and drawing and quartering.

Part 2 of *Rights of Man* contained several theoretical chapters on civilization, governments, and constitutions, all recommending the kind of representative government that had been adopted by the Americans. The last chapter in his pamphlet was of a more practical turn, outlining ways in which taxes could be levied more equitably. Paine claimed that the tax the poor paid on their beer was more than the rich man paid on his entire estate. Paine went on to show that such as system could allow reforms that would support all the citizens of a country, not just the wealthy.

The following excerpts disclose Paine's philosophy, which he sees as having been incorporated into law in the United States, and the services these taxes could provide for the massive numbers of poor in England.

FROM THOMAS PAINE, *RIGHTS OF MAN* (HEREFORSHIRE, ENGLAND: WORDSWORTH EDITIONS, 1996)

If, from the more wretched parts of the old world, we look at those which are in an advanced stage of improvement, we still find the greedy hand of Government thrusting itself into every corner and crevice of industry, and grasping the spoil of the multitude. Invention is continually exercised to furnish new pretences for revenue and taxation. It watches prosperity as its prey, aid permits none to escape without a tribute.

As Revolutions have begun (and as the probability is always greater against a thing beginning than of proceeding after it has begun), it is natural to expect that other Revolutions will follow. The amazing and still increasing expenses with which old Governments are conducted, the numerous wars they engage in or provoke, the embarrassments they throw in the way of universal civilisation and commerce, and the oppression and usurpation they practise at home, have wearied out the patience and exhausted the property of the world. In such a situation and with the examples already existing, Revolutions are to be looked for. They are become subjects of universal conversation, and may be considered as the *Order of the Day*.

If systems of Government can be introduced less expensive and more productive of general happiness than those which have existed, all attempts to oppose their progress will in the end be fruitless. Reason, like time, will make its own way, and prejudice will fall in a combat with interest. If universal peace, civilization and commerce are ever to be the happy lot of man, it cannot be accomplished but by a Revolution in the system of Governments. All the monarchical Governments are military. War is their trade, plunder and revenue their objects. While such Governments continue, peace has not the absolute security of a day. What is the history of all monarchical Governments but a disgustful picture of human wretchedness, and the accidental respite of a few years' repose? Wearied with war, and with human butchery, they sat down to rest, and called it peace. This certainly is not the condition that heaven intended for man.

All hereditary Government is in its nature tyranny. An heritable crown, or an heritable throne, or by what other fanciful name such things may be called, have no other significant explanation than that mankind are heritable property. To inherit a Government, is to inherit the people, as if they were flocks and herds.

...

FIRST	Abolition of two million poor-rates.
SECONDLY	Provision for two hundred and fifty-two thousand poor families.
THIRDLY	Education for one million and thirty thousand children.
FOURTHLY	Comfortable provision for one hundred and forty thousand aged persons.
FIFTHLY	Donation of twenty shillings each for fifty thousand births.
SIXTHLY	Donation of twenty shillings each for twenty thousand marriages.
SEVENTHLY	Allowance of twenty thousand pounds for the funeral expenses of persons travelling for work, and dying at a distance from their friends.
EIGHTHLY	Employment, at all times, for the casual poor in the cities of London and Westminster.

PETITION FROM MEN ABOARD THE *QUEEN CHARLOTTE*

The sailors in port at the Spithead sent their first petitions of grievances to be conveyed to the Admiralty on March 7, 1797. Although their real grievances were many, at that time, they thought the best political stance would be to focus on pay issues alone. But as time passed and the Admiralty continued to ignore them, their anger grew, and they had more and more intense conversations throughout the fleet about their experiences and intolerable conditions.

In the second week in April, sympathizers with the Admiralty began putting their views out through broadsides—usually one-page printed flyers—distributed through nearby port towns. One, in particular, inflamed the seamen delegates. It took the sailors to task for their refusal to sail until their petitions were addressed, for meetings of men from ship to ship, and for causing grief to the king and his subjects on land at a critical time when Britain was under attack by the French and the Dutch. It questioned the loyalty of the sailors and charged that they were ungrateful children, bleeding their mother country dry.

In response to this flyer circulating in Portsmouth, the sailors dared the writer to make himself public and try to live for one week on the pay and provisions paid a sailor. At the same time, the Lord of the Admiralty had decided to make some concessions to the sailors, but having no hint of this, the mutineers' rage led them to a longer, more detailed petition demanding attention to a variety of deplorable conditions. The following points to low wages, faulty measure of food, the use of large amounts of flour to complete the weight of food due them rather than including meat and vegetables, the treatment of the sick, the lack of shore leave, and the treatment of the wounded.

The effect of the petition was to harden the Admiralty against the men.

FROM "PETITION FROM THE *QUEEN CHARLOTTE*," 17 APRIL 1797, IN ADMIRALTY DOCUMENTS, PUBLIC RECORDS OFFICE, LONDON

To the Right Honourable the Lords Commissioners of the Admiralty.

My Lords,

We, the seamen of His Majesty's navy, take the liberty of addressing your Lordships in an humble petition, shewing the many hardships and oppressions we have laboured under for many years, and which we hope your Lordships will redress as soon as possible. We flatter ourselves that your Lordships, together with the nation in general, will acknowledge our worth and good services, both in the American War as well as the present; for which good service your Lordships' petitioners do unanimously agree in opinion, that their worth to the nation, and laborious industry in defence of their country, deserve some better encouragement than that we meet with at present, or from any we have experienced. We, your petitioners, do not boast of our good services for any other purpose than that of putting you and the nation in mind of the respect due to us, nor do we ever intend to deviate from our former character; so far from anything of that kind, or than an Englishman or men should turn their coats, we likewise agree in opinion, that we should suffer double the hardships we have hitherto experienced before we would suffer the crown of England to be in the least imposed upon by that of any other power in the world; we therefore beg leave to inform your Lordships of the grievances which we at present labour under.

We, your humble petitioners, relying that your Lordships will take into early consideration the grievances of which we complain, and do not in the least doubt but your Lordships will comply with our desires, which are every way reasonable.

The first grievance we have to complain of is, that our wages are too low, and ought to be raised, that we might be the better able to support our wives and families in a manner comfortable, and whom we are in duty bound to support as far as our wages will allow, which, we trust, will be looked into by your Lordships, and the Honourable House of Commons in Parliament assembled.

We, your petitioners, beg that your Lordships will take into consideration the grievance of which we complain, and now lay before you.

First, That our provisions be raised to the weight of sixteen ounces to the pound, and of a better quality; and that our measures may be the same as those used in the commercial code of this country.

Secondly, That your petitioners request your Honours will be pleased to observe, there should be no flour served while we are in harbour, in any port whatever, under the command of the British flag; and also, that there might be granted a sufficient quantity of vegetables of such kind as may be the most plentiful in the ports to which we go; which we grievously complain and lay under the want of.

Thirdly, That your Lordships will be pleased seriously to look into the state of the sick on board His Majesty's ships, that they may be better attended to, and that they may have the use of such necessaries as are allowed for them in time of sickness; and that these necessaries be not on any account embezzled.

Fourthly, That your Lordships will be so kind as to look into this affair, which is nowise unreasonable; and that we may be looked upon as a number of men standing in defence of our country; and that we may in somewise have grant and opportunity to taste the sweets of liberty on shore, when in any harbour, and when we have completed the duty of our ship, after our return from sea; and that no man may encroach upon his liberty, there shall be a boundary limited, and those trespassing any further, without a written order from the commanding officer, shall be punished according to the rules of the navy; which is a natural request, and congenial to the heart of man, and certainly to us, that you make the boast of being guardians of the land.

Fifthly, That if any man is wounded in action, his pay be continued until he is cured and discharged; and if any ship has any real grievances to complain of, we hope your Lordships will readily redress them, as far as in your power, to prevent any disturbances.

It is also unanimously agreed by the fleet, that, from this day, no grievances shall be received, in order to convince the nation at large that we know when to cease to ask, as well as to begin, and that we ask nothing but what is moderate, and may be granted without detriment to the nation, or injury to the service.

Given on board the *Queen Charlotte,* by the delegates of the Fleet, the 18th day of April 1797.

JUNE 5 BROADSIDE POSTED BY MUTINEERS AT THE NORE

On June 1, the Admiralty decided on a new policy with regard to mutiny. The harshest measure dictated that anyone found guilty of mutiny would be considered treasonous and be hanged and buried without benefit of clergy. Not until June 5 was the proclamation made public, and a group of the sailors responded with a broadside addressed to "their countrymen," which attempts to plead their case to landsmen, many of whom were unaware of the conditions aboard ship and the true nature of the mutinies. Of particular interest here is the sailors' statement that they had once been boys, but, in petitioning for their rights, had become men. Members of the underclasses, whether serfs or slaves or sailors, had been kept in their place by treating them as children who needed to obey and not question their betters. And every effort had been made by ships' officers and the Admiralty to keep sailors as "boys" instead of men. This is the reason often given to explain the peculiar uniform of the sailor, which makes them look more like little boys than adults.

FROM "THE DELEGATES OF THE DIFFERENT SHIPS AT THE NORE ASSEMBLED IN COUNCIL, TO THEIR FELLOW-SUBJECTS," QUOTED IN CONRAD GILL, *NAVAL MUTINIES OF 1797* (MANCHESTER, ENGLAND: UNIVERSITY PRESS, 1913)

The Delegates of the different ships at the Nore assembled in Council to their fellow-Subjects:—COUNTRYMEN,

It is to you particularly that we owe an explanation of our conduct. His Majesty's Ministers too well know our intentions, which are founded on the laws of humanity, honour and national safety,—long since trampled underfoot by those who ought to have been friends to us—the sole protectors of your laws and property. The public prints teem with falsehoods and misrepresentations to induce you to credit things as far from our design as the conduct of those at the helm of national affairs is from honesty or common decorum.

Shall we who have endured the toils of a tedious, disgraceful war, be the victims of tyranny and oppression which vile, gilded, pampered knaves, wallowing in the lap of luxury, choose to load us with? Shall we, who amid the rage of the tempest and the war or jarring elements, undaunted climb the unsteady cordage and totter on the top-mast's dreadful height, suffer ourselves to be treated worse than the dogs of London Streets? Shall we, who in the battle's sanguinary rage, confound, terrify and subdue your proudest foe, guard your coasts from invasion, your children from slaughter, and your lands from pillage—be the footballs and shuttle-cocks of a set of tyrants who derives from us alone their honours, their titles and their fortunes? No, the Age of Reason has at length revolved. Long have we been endeavoring to find ourselves men. We now find ourselves so. We will be treated as such. Far, very far, from us is the idea of subverting the government of our beloved country. We have the highest opinion of our Most Gracious Sovereign, and we hope none of those measures taken to deprive us of the common rights of men have been instigated by him.

You cannot, countrymen, form the most distant idea of the slavery under which we have for many years laboured. Rome had her Neros and Caligulas, but how many characters of their description might we not mention in the British Fleet—men without the least tincture of humanity, without the faintest spark of virtue, education or abilities, exercising the most wanton acts of cruelty over those whom dire misfortune or patriotic zeal may have placed in their power—basking in the sunshine of prosperity, whilst we (need we repeat who we are?) labour under every distress which the breast of inhumanity can suggest. The British Seaman has often with justice been compared to the Lion—gentle, generous and humane—no one would certainly wish to hurt such an animal. Hitherto we have laboured for our sovereign and you. We are now obliged to think for ourselves, for there are many (nay, most of us) in the Fleet who have been prisoners since the commencement of the War, without receiving a single farthing. Have we not a right to complain? Let His Majesty but order us to be paid and the little grievances we have made known redressed, we shall enter with alacrity upon any employment for the defence of our country; but until that is complied with we are determined to stop all commerce and intercept all provisions, for our own subsistence. The military have had their pay augmented, to insult as well as enslave you. Be not appalled. We will adopt the words of a celebrated (Dieu et mon Droit) and defy all attempts to deceive us. We do not wish to adopt the plan of a neighbouring nation, however it may have been suggested; but we [will] sell our lives dearly to maintain what we have demanded. Nay, countrymen, more: We have already discovered the tricks of Government in supplying our enemies with different commodities, and a few days will probably lead to something more. In the meantime,

We remain, Dear Countrymen,
Yours affectionately,
YOUR LOVING BROTHERS
RED FOR EVER!

ANONYMOUS POEMS AND SONGS BY SPITHEAD AND NORE MUTINEERS

Melville wrote his ballad "Billy in the Darbies" before he had conceptualized the story of Billy Budd. As he uses the ballad in his novel, "Billy in the Darbies" was a work probably written by one of Billy's coworkers in the foretop and circulated anonymously among various ships, finally finding its way into print in Portsmouth. The narrator says that some sailors are gifted "with an artless *poetic* temperament" (384).

Poem and songwriting was a frequent form of expression among sailors. Documents, like the slanderous account of Billy in the naval chronicle, issued by the king and the Admiralty through the established press, gave what became the official "truth." But the real truth of the sailors' lives was often constructed as folk literature and circulated throughout the fleet. A few were actually written down.

The first ballad, in praise of the mutineers, was found on the HMS *Repulse,* anchored at the Nore in 1797. The second, also a ballad, is written in praise of the sailor, traditionally called "Jack." The third ballad celebrates the mutinies at the Nore and of the North Fleet, while advising caution and paying homage to the king.

FROM "THE MUSE'S FRIENDLY AID," QUOTED IN JAMES DUGAN, *THE GREAT MUTINY* (NEW YORK: G. P. PUTNAM'S SONS, 1965)

The theme I treat is our royal tars,

Whose godlike spirits rival even Mars,

From their suppineness now their souls are roused

To rod and yoke no longer are exposed.

And all alike, each swears he will be true,

All tyrants ne've their former course renew.

At Spithead first their noble blood was fired;

Each loved his King, but one and all aspired;

To serve each other was their full intent,

And insulted were on mischief bent,

But still their country's cause they would maintain,

Against the rebels or the power of Spain.

FROM "ALL HAIL BROTHER SEAMEN," A FORECASTLE BALLAD, QUOTED IN JAMES DUGAN, *THE GREAT MUTINY* (NEW YORK: G. P. PUTNAM'S SONS, 1965)

All hail, brother seamen, that ploughs on the main,
Likewise to well-wishers of seamen of fame,
May Providence watch over brave British tars,
And guide them with care from the dangers of wars.

Good Providence long looked with pity at last
For to see Honest Jack so shamefully thrashed,
But still held his arm for to let Jack subdue
The pride of those masters whose Hearts were not true.

At Spithead Jack from a long silence was roused,
Which waked other brothers who did not refuse
To assist in the plan that good Providence taught
In the hearts of brave seamen that 'ad long been forgot.

FROM "FORECASTLE BALLAD" (1797)

Old Neptune made haste, to the Nore he did come,
To waken his sons who had slept for too long.
His thundering loud voice made us start with surprise,
To hear his sweet words, and he bid us arise.

"Your brothers," says he, "has all firmly resolved,
To banish all tyrants that long did uphold,
Their crewel intentions to scourge when they please,
Sutch a set of brace villians you must instantly seize.

"So away, tell your brothers, near Yarmouth they lie,
To embark in the cause they will never deny.
Their harts are all good, their like lyons I say,
I've furnished there minds and they all will obey.

"And when they arrive, which I trust they soon will,
Be steady and cautious, let wrangling lay still,
And love one another, my favour you'll keep,
Sucksess to King George and his glorious fleet."

QUESTIONS AND PROJECTS

1.   Do research on either American slaves or British sailors in the nineteenth century to explore how and why both were reportedly treated as children. Form your ideas into an essay.

2.   After research, write an essay on the punishments levied on eighteenth-century sailing ships. What were they and for what reasons were men punished?

3.   After further research on the mutiny at the Nore, have a debate on whether the men were loyal or disloyal to the king.

4.   After some basic research, write a paper answering the following question: Is there any fundamental difference between the mutiny of the sailors and a sit-down strike in the twentieth- or twenty-first-century United States?

5.   Write a paper on why you think Paine's essay was banned and why it was valued by sailors.

6.   Make reports to the class on the life of Horatio Nelson. What was his opinion of the mutinies and the lives of sailors? Do you consider him admirable or not?

7.   There now seems to be disagreement about the character of King George III. Do some research on his reign. What were some of his major decisions?

8.   The relationship between sailors and marines was complex. We see marines refusing to fire on sailors and sailors asking for raises and basic civil rights for marines, yet it is marines who finally help the Admiralty put down the Nore mutiny, and Melville seems to have despised marines on board ship when he was a sailor. Do enough research on this question to draw some conclusions.

9.   See if you can locate a sailor retired from the service (not an officer) and have an interview with him or her about questions of conditions aboard ship and the view of officers and marines.

10.   Read Melville's *White Jacket* and make a report on individual issues included in it: Jack Chase, to whom "Billy Budd" is dedicated; punishments; the marines; ships' surgeons; or other matters.

11.   As a separate issue, comment on how reading *White Jacket* changed or reinforced your interpretation of "Billy Budd."

12.   Flogging was outlawed in the United States navy as it was not in Great Britain. See if you can find in the nineteenth-century *Congressional Record* reports and arguments about the passage of this law. Melville had an influence on its passage.

13.   Another popular book about life at sea in Melville's time was Richard Henry Dana's *Two Years before the Mast*. Read it and make a report on any issues that are pertinent to "Billy Budd."

FURTHER READING

Dugan, James. *The Great Mutiny.* New York: G. P. Putnam's Sons, 1965.
Gill, Conrad. *Merchants and Mariners of the Eighteenth-Century.* London: E. Arnold, 1961.

————. *The Naval Mutinies of 1797.* Manchester, England: University Press, 1913.

Guttridge, Leonard. *Mutiny: A History of Naval Insurrection.* New York: Berkley Books, 1992.

Kelly, Samuel. *Samuel Kelley, an Eighteenth-Century Seaman.* London: J. Caps, 1925.

Lewis, Michael. *A Social History of the Navy.* London: Allen and Unwin, 1960.

Mahan, A. T. *Life of Nelson.* Boston: Little, Brown, 1918.

Manwaring, George Ernest. *The Floating Republic.* New York: Harcourt Brace, 1935.

Quennel, Marjorie. *A History of Everyday Things in England, 4 vols.* New York: G. P. Putnam's Sons, 1957–60.

Thompson, E. P. *The Making of the English Working Class.* New York: Pantheon, 1963.

Trevelyan, George M. *English Social History.* London: Longmans, Green, and Co., 1942.

Williams, Neville. *Life in Georgian England.* London: B. T. Batsford, 1962.

11 _____

"Billy Budd," the *Somers* Affair, and the Articles of War

> Would it be so much we ourselves that would condemn as it would be martial law operating through us? (362)

In "Billy Budd," while the three men appointed by Vere are putting together a verdict, after Captain Vere has broken into their deliberations to insist on the need for execution, the narrator brings up the subject of the *Somers* mutiny, one of the most attention-getting, infamous events in the nineteenth century. Only days from land, the captain of the *Somers,* Alexander Slidell Mackenzie, arrested and put in irons several sailors and a young midshipman on charges of mutiny. Because the captain's evidence was questionable and he saw to it that three of the men, including the midshipman, were executed only days from land, Mackenzie's actions were highly suspect and were reviewed by two court-martial boards. The affair received more publicity than it might ordinarily have gotten because the so-called ringleader was Philip Spencer, son of the then secretary of war. In the following passage, the narrator compares the heavy responsibilities, uncertainties, and anguish with which groups aboard both the *Bellipotent* and the *Somers,* charged with rendering decisions, considered the question of guilt and punishment. Melville's particular interest in the case was intensified because his cousin, Guert Gansevoort, had been the first lieutenant in charge of the board on the *Somers.* In the key passage, he mentions the Articles of War, which he had castigated in his novel *White Jacket;* the urgency felt by both captains to hang the suspects aboard ship on flimsy evidence, even though the ships were not far land; and the "vindication" of the actions by an official military court-martial. There is a world of meaning in the words about the official history passed down by the court-martial board. Note what is subtly implied in Melville's passage with his use of the words "so-called" and "or otherwise."

Philip Spencer, the son of the secretary of war, was hung aboard the *Somers* without trial. Schaffer Library, Union College.

Not unlikely they were brought to something more or less akin to that harassed frame of mind which in the year 1842 actuated the commander of the U.S. brig-of-war *Somers* to resolve, under the so-called Articles of War, Articles modeled upon the English Mutiny Act, to resolve upon the execution at sea of a midshipman and two sailors as mutineers designing the seizure of a brig. Which resolution was carried out though in a time of peace and within not many days' sail of home. An act vindicated by a naval court of inquiry subsequently convened ashore. History, and here cited without comment. True, the circumstances on board the *Somers* were different from those on board the *Bellipotent*. But the urgency felt, well-warranted or otherwise, was much the same. (365)

"Billy Budd" is not a historically exact, fictionalized version of the *Somers* mutiny. The setting is 45 years earlier, in a time of war rather than peace, and on a British rather than an American ship, and the scapegoat is a single man rather than three men. But some of the key issues pertinent to the *Somers* are critical in "Billy Budd": the use of the Articles of War, the fear and ambition of the captains, their reputations for prudence and discipline, the suggestions of insanity, the inadequate evidence of mutiny, the secrecy, the coercion of the board by the captains, and the libelous stories about Billy and Spencer that surfaced immediately afterward.

The prominent place in the *Somers* mutiny occupied by Melville's cousin, Lt. Guert Gansevoort, is pivotal to Melville's fascination with the incident and his composition of "Billy Budd," for Guert was a man who had helped and interested Melville all his life. In 1839, when Melville was 20 years old, his immediate family was in financial difficulty, and his own job search was floundering, it was Guert who secured him a position aboard a merchant ship, the *St. Lawrence.* And again in 1840, after he had returned from service on the *St. Lawrence,* it was Guert who helped him find a position aboard a whaler, the *Acushnet.* Melville's experience on the whaler provided him with material for several works, including his great national epic of the white whale, *Moby Dick.* In the middle of this voyage, Melville ended up in Hawaii, where he stayed for a time before joining the navy in 1843 to return home by sailing on a warship named the *United States.* Sailors at sea had no way of receiving daily in-

This painting of the *Somers* shows men hanging from the yardarm. The Beverly R. Robinson Collection, U.S. Naval Academy Museum, USNA, Annapolis, MD.

formation about the outside world. Only when they met other ships or came into port did they get news. It was while the *United States* was briefly anchored in a Pacific port that Melville learned of a supposed mutiny the year before that had resulted in the hanging at sea of two sailors and a junior officer aboard the *Somers,* the very ship on which Guert was serving as a lieutenant. He also learned that Guert was a major participant in the episode.

The story must have hit Melville hard, creating painful conflicts for him, for he was unable to relinquish his high regard for his cousin, but at the same time, Melville himself was a common sailor and knew only too well the practices on board both merchant and naval vessels that could lead sailors to revolt. He had been especially traumatized by what he had seen on the *United States:* hunger; frequent, brutal floggings for minor infractions; oppressive, dangerous work; and constant humiliation. He himself had jumped ship twice since he had signed aboard the *Acushnet,* and his outrage over the treatment of common sailors would eventually lead him to expose those problems in *White Jacket,* a novel that influenced the U.S. government to outlaw flogging.

In October 1844, when Melville was waiting to be discharged in Boston Harbor, Guert, now on another ship in the same harbor, welcomed him home. No one knows what was said between them, but it is hard to believe that Melville, obsessed with the story of the *Somers* case, did not bring it up, and it is hard to believe, given Guert's reticence and loyalty to Mackenzie, that Guert agreed to confide in him. What Melville knew at the time was that Guert had been cleared of wrongdoing by a court-martial board, and he could observe with his own eyes that Guert had been broken and tortured by the episode, looking, as Guert's mother said at the time, like a man of 70.

Guert, continually haunted by the *Somers,* had a well-recognized drinking problem, and had in 1856 been relieved of his command of the *Decatur* on a charge of drunkenness. But Melville continued to love and admire Guert, and closely and sympathetically followed his career in the Mexican War and the American Civil War. (Guert died in 1868, having retired with the high rank of commodore.) In 1888, Melville published a book of poems, *John Marr and Other Sailors,* in which Guert prominently appears as an admirable figure.

In 1888, the same year Melville saw *John Marr* into print, his lifelong fascination with the *Somers* mutiny was intensified by two articles that appeared in national magazines: one was "The Mutiny on the *Somers*" by Lt. H. D. Smith, and the other was Gail Hamilton's "The Murder of Philip Spencer." Even more significant in the 1880s was a chapter on the *Somers* mutiny in the autobiography of Thurlow Weed, a prominent political figure of the time who had run for president on the Anti-Masonic ticket. Weed's book contained Guert's single, private revelation about the mutiny, confided to his cousin, midshipman Henry Gansevoort, who subsequently told Thurlow Weed.

A CHRONOLOGY OF EVENTS

Spring 1842

Alexander Slidell Mackenzie, an author and experienced captain with a reputation for cruelty, takes command of the *Somers*. At a time before the existence of the naval training academy at Annapolis, the main object of the *Somers* is to train young apprentices to be sailors.

Summer

Throughout the summer apprentices are taken aboard the *Somers*. Three-fourths of the sailors are still in their teens, 45 of them between 13 and 16. There are 12 officers, 2 only 16 years old. Among these is a seasoned young lieutenant, Guert Gansevoort. Designed to carry 90 men, the number of sailors and officers swells to a reported 120 during the summer, making the ship profoundly overcrowded by the time of departure.

July–August

Captain Mackenzie regards his trainees as stupid, lazy, and undisciplined, so he sets out from the first to correct them with beatings. The log shows that in the six weeks before the ship leaves the harbor, Mackenzie harshly punishes 50 members of the crew for desertion and theft, being dirty, fighting, losing a hammock, spitting, spilling tea or tobacco on deck, or, the most frequent offense, not working hard enough. For desertion and theft, very young, often undersized boys are hit a dozen times (the maximum allowed by law) with a cat-o'-nine-tails, a whip with nine strands, usually weighted at the end with metal balls. With each blow, the effect is to lay on nine lashes. For the less serious offenses, a boy stripped to his shirt is whipped 42 times with the colt, a rope with three strands on the end.

August

Nineteen-year-old Philip Spencer, the son of the Secretary of War and a recent college dropout with a record on a previous voyage for fighting and drinking, reports to the *Somers*, which is still in port in Brooklyn. Mackenzie objects to having the troublemaker as a midshipman aboard his ship, and Spencer joins him in requesting a transfer, that is rejected. Spencer has two traits that will determine his fate aboard the *Somers*: he has an obsession with intrigue and romance, especially pirates, mutineers, secret societies, and plots, and he has what is called "walleyes," technically named *strabismus*, an affliction that surgery has not corrected, leaving him with a permanent squint and a look as if he is staring.

September 7

Captain John Wilkes of the *North Carolina* is found guilty by a court-martial board of illegally punishing men in his squadron.

September 13

The overcrowded *Somers* embarks on its training voyage to the coast of Africa. Mackenzie has warned the other officers to avoid Spencer.

September 16

Four sailors, including a 13-year-old boy, are given six lashes with a colt, a thick three-stranded rope.

September 17

Two sailors are given 12 lashes with a cat-o'-nine-tails, the maximum allowed by law.

September 22

Nine sailors are flogged.

September 23

A 14-year-old receives 12 lashes. Between the departure from New York and arrival in the Madeiras, there have been 43 floggings.

October 2

On the first Sunday of every month, the Articles of War are read aloud to the assembled crew and officers. By this time, the captain and other officers aboard ship have been confirmed in their dislike of Spencer for the following reasons: he has chosen what they regard as inappropriate friends—the common sailors aboard ship, with whom he is a great favorite; he laughs and talks with common sailors in a manner unbecoming a gentleman; he amuses the sailors by making music with his jaw; he shares his brandy with the sailors; and he has a funny look about his eyes, as if he is up to something. Spencer has become especially friendly with quartermaster Elisha Small and Carpenter Boatswain's Mate Samuel Cromwell.

October 5

The *Somers* lands at Funchal in the Madeiras. The officers notice changes in the crew, who are not as respectful and hardworking as they had been before. At the same time, Spencer is entertaining his close friends with fantasies about taking over the ship and becoming a pirate.

October 21

The *Somers* arrives in the Cape Verde Islands. Punishments have continued without a break. On this day nine crewmen were flogged (one for using improper language).

November 10

The *Somers* anchors near Cape Mesurado. Spencer ignores the captain's shouted order from the ship to row his boat back to put on a dress uniform before heading to shore. Spencer continues toward shore, openly cursing the captain in front of crew members.

November 23 or 24

Spencer continues behavior that irks the officers. With his love for mystery and romance, he tells the fortunes of the men and has one of them give him tattoos.

November 25

Spencer invites Purser's Steward Wales to go aloft with him, where he shares with him some of his dreams of taking over the ship and becoming a pirate, a fantasy replete with all sorts of romance that includes women, robbery, slave running, and forcing boys to walk the plank. More than anything else, Spencer loves the idea of designing a buccaneers' flag and keeping coded messages and passwords, as he did in his old fraternity at Union College.

November 26

Wales reports the conversation to his boss, who reports it to Guert Gansevoort, who reports it to the captain. Although Mackenzie had no love of Spencer, he declared the report to be monstrous and ridiculous and refused to consider it further.

November 27

A day later, the captain becomes convinced by Wales's earnestness that the plan is, indeed, serious enough to be regarded as dangerous. What persuades him is the look in Spencer's eyes. "I turned my eye towards him and immediately caught his eye, which he kept staring upon me for more than a minute, *with the most infernal expression I have ever seen upon a human face.*

It satisfied me at once of the man's guilt" (*Proceedings of the Court of Inquiry Appointed to Inquire into the Intended Mutiny on Board the United States Brig of War Somers,* 20).

Other "evidence" collected that day includes reports that Spencer has made a drawing of a pirate ship, that he has told a sailor's fortune and predicted that he would die a violent death, that he is seen in whispered conversation with several crew members, and that he has been curious about the ship's location.

The captain and Gansevoort become convinced that it is Spencer's plotting and not the continuous brutal punishments that has made the crew insolent. The captain approaches Spencer with his suspicion that Spencer plans to kill him and take over the *Somers*. Spencer, smiling, denies it and says it was all a joke. Mackenzie tells him his joke may cost him his life and orders Gansevoort to put him in irons. Officers then proceed to search Spencer's belongings and come upon a list made in Greek. One of the officers is able to translate it, finding that it contains three categories. The first is titled "Certain" and contains only three names, the second is "Doubtful," and the third is a list of those who *might* join in once things are underway. Among the "certains" is the name of Elisha Small and a name that no one knows. However, other crewmen aboard ship who have had run-ins with Cromwell insist that he is the most dangerous person aboard ship—even though his name does not appear on Spencer's list.

The *Somers* is three weeks from New York and 1,200 miles from Barbados, where it intends docking. After Sunday services, the top of the mast cracks off and dangles. Cromwell immediately climbs up to rescue a young boy who is near the break. All hands rush up to repair the damage. Mackenzie looks on in amazement that a dissatisfied crew are rising to the occasion so readily. But he finally decides instead that the event confirms his suspicion of a mutiny, that the crew is using the occasion to climb aloft to conspire. Moreover, he has also been watching Spencer, in chains on deck, and decides that the young man's strange look (the eyes again) betray his mutinous motives. "The eye of Spencer traveled continually to the mast-head, and he cast quick and stealthy glances about, as he had not done before" (*Proceedings of the Court of Inquiry,* 10).

The Captain is unwavering in his suspicion of Cromwell, even though he is nowhere on the list that the captain insists confirms that a mutiny is afoot. He orders Gansevoort to arrest Cromwell as soon as he climbs down from the rigging. Cromwell, not knowing what he is being charged with, insists he has done nothing wrong, and Spencer insists to Gansevoort that Cromwell is innocent. Small is also arrested. The captain tells all three that they will be confined and taken home, where they will be tried and acquitted if they are innocent.

After dark has fallen, officer Rodgers orders the men to go aft. At his order, the boys start running aft toward the quarter-deck, where Gansevoort and Mackenzie are standing. Gansevoort goes berserk, points his pistol at them, and says he will blow out the brains of the first sailor who steps on the quarter-deck, and Mackenzie dives into his quarters for arms. Just before Gansevoort fires, Rodgers stops him with the yell that he, Rodgers, has ordered the men aft.

It is clear to the officers that the men have become more insolent and that they are talking angrily about the chaining up of Spencer, Small, and Cromwell.

November 28

At nine o'clock, two especially brutal floggings are carried out. Mackenzie then gathers the crew and tells them how wretched their lot would be if Spencer's plan were carried out. The crew seems pacified at first, and Mackenzie considers the ship safe. They are only a week from St. Thomas. But by the afternoon Mackenzie has changed his mind. He gives as his reasons the plausibility of Wales's report, the belief that Spencer has convinced the men that their punishments have not been justice but persecution, the continuing insolence of the crew, and the continuing strange looks on Spencer's face. Further arrests of suspected mutineers would seriously deplete needed manpower aboard ship and, should they run into a gale, they might not be able to save the ship.

November 29

Wales reports that he has seen signs passing between Spencer and some of the men. There is another brutal flogging of a man whose back is raw from a flogging the day before. The men are not at all cowed. In the night Mackenzie hears rebellious talk throughout the ship.

November 30

Gansevoort interviews Spencer, who tells him that these plots are a dangerous game he plays. That morning four others are arrested. Mackenzie sends letters to the other officers aboard, ordering them to his cabin, with the intention of seeking their "counsel" about the fate of Spencer, Small, and Cromwell. However, he writes to the secretary of the navy that he has already made up his mind about what has to be done (hanging for all three) and will see that it is done, whether or not it is corroborated by the evidence he has ordered the officers to gather. Hanging the three is the only way Mackenzie believes he can bring the rest of the men under control.

So the secret trial of Spencer, Cromwell, and Small begins in the morning without the presence or knowledge of the accused.

Throughout the day, the officers, two of whom are 16 years old, deliberate, taking testimony from the men. It is Gansevoort's private statement confided only to his cousin—never confessed at trial—that the board is reluctant to endorse shipboard hanging, that he twice leaves the room to report this to the captain, and that the captain finally bullies the officers into the verdict he is determined to carry out anyway.

December 1

The officers continue to deliberate in the early hours of the morning. Eventually they report their decision orally and then, at 10:30 that morning, in a letter to the captain they recommend that the three men should be put to death "as an example" to the disaffected aboard ship.

The gruesome preparations for hanging begin immediately, and Mackenzie appears on deck in full dress uniform. One of the crew thinks that they must be meeting another ship. At noon, with all the petty officers on deck and fully armed, Mackenzie approaches Spencer and tells him he is to be hanged immediately, giving him a full 10 minutes to ready himself to die. The same message is given to Cromwell and Small. Spencer, choosing what he thinks are his last words, proclaims to all the ship that Cromwell is innocent. Mackenzie decides to extend the 10 minutes long enough to talk privately with Spencer and to take notes of the conversation. Mackenzie tells Spencer that he is determined to hang him before reaching shore because people of wealth and influence, like Spencer, can avoid punishment in the United States, and Mackenzie is determined that he will be punished. Spencer asks him if he has not formed an exaggerated estimate of the extent of the conspiracy. Are you not going too far, going too fast? Spencer asks him. Does the law justify your actions? When Spencer is asked why he had spoken about taking the captain's life, he replies that it was just a fancy. As they are led to the nooses, Small says to Mackenzie, "You are doing your duty, and I honor you for it. God bless the flag and prosper it!"—the tone of which is echoed in Billy Budd's last words.

With the three men swinging in the breeze, Mackenzie draws the men and officers together to again make his case against Spencer and the other two men and urge them to make different choices. Then he calls for the men to cheer the flag. "I gave the order, 'Stand by to give three hearty cheers for the flag of our country'" (*Proceedings of the Court of Inquiry,* 14).

They are four days from land.

December 5

The *Somers* lands at St. Thomas without shore leave.

December 14

The *Somers* docks in New York.

December 17

The *New York Tribune* publishes a completely inaccurate story about the *Somers* from what it considers to be a reliable source. At the same time, the *New York Express* described a scene in which the mutineers, led by Spencer, had marched on the captain's quarters and Spencer had held a gun to Mackenzie's heart.

Throughout December

There are pro- and anti-Mackenzie accounts, including one in the *New York Herald*, calling attention to the absence of any plot other than one in embryo and the absence of any legally constituted court-martial board. Others question Mackenzie's refusal to allow Spencer to write to his parents before he was put to death.

January 19, 1843

The *New York Herald* publishes an editorial summing up its view of the case: Mackenzie, it charges, "is fired with the idea of being a patriot of the old Roman order, and hence gives about a hundred boys, in a short cruise, two thousand colts, cats, or cowhides, and hangs up three individuals, without trial or evidence, merely to enforce order and preserve discipline. Madness all— madness all."

Mid-January

Francs Gregory, captain of the *North Carolina*, the ship to which the other suspected mutineers have been taken, is outraged at the abominable condition of the prisoners and insists on an inquiry into the treatment of the *Somers's* crew and the punishments ordered by Mackenzie aboard ship: 247 floggings of 2,265 lashes inflicted on what Gregory describes as mere boys.

January 28

A court of inquiry comprised of Mackenzie's contemporaries exonerates him of wrongdoing.

February 1

A second inquiry, this time a court-martial board, begins an investigation into the *Somers* mutiny.

March 27

To the charges against Mackenzie of oppression, illegal punishment, and murder, the board returns a verdict of "not proven," scarcely a ringing declaration of a job well done. It is reported than more than half the members of this board initially believed that the charges had been proved, but finally nine voted to acquit Mackenzie and three to find him guilty.

April 1

Charges are dropped against all the 12 men imprisoned on the *Somers* for suspicion of mutiny.

PARALLELS

Although Billy Budd bears no resemblance to Philip Spencer, it is obvious that many issues in the *Somers* mutiny, which had so obsessed Herman Melville, shaped the story of suspected mutiny aboard the *Bellipotent*.

One important similarity between Billy and Philip Spencer is their great popularity with the common sailors aboard ship, which Claggart and Vere in the novel and Gansevoort and Mackenzie in the *Somers* affair regard as a dire threat to their authority. Another is the role that their "afflictions" play in leading them to their doom. Billy's stutter causes him to strike out physically when he cannot speak, resulting in his arrest and execution. Philip Spencer's walleyes create an expression that both Gansevoort and Mackenzie read as sneaky, suspicious, insubordinate, and, as Gansevoort testified, proof that Spencer was plotting a mutiny.

The report that Melville received of the officers charged with making a recommendation to Mackenzie clearly influenced his portrait of the men charged with judging Billy Budd. Both groups are appointed extralegally to recommend what the captains were determined to enact anyway, regardless of what these officers think right to do. Both groups are naive, not fully acquainted with the law, and regarded by the captains as easily manipulated. Both groups are formed and instructed illegally by the captains. With a couple of exceptions, the *Somers* officers are extremely young and inexperienced—two only 16. Yet both groups serve to undermine the judgment of their captains as they resist handing down guilty verdicts and death sentences. Under pressure, both groups understandably capitulate.

Melville reveals his reliance on the *Somers* mutiny most clearly in the character and actions of the two captains. Both men are known for their courage in military situations and are well regarded by certain influential people on land. But both have an inordinate fear for their reputations as military leaders; both are ambitious; and both are highly suspicious, prudent, and known for their stern discipline. One charge repeatedly leveled against Mackenzie was that he could easily have placed those he suspected of mutiny with law enforcement officers on Barbados if he didn't want to take the prisoners to New York. But Mackenzie was too proud to seek help from a foreign government. Likewise, Vere is afraid he will look weak if he doesn't execute Billy immediately.

After Billy has killed Claggart with a blow, Vere looks back on Billy's breach of naval decorum (in saying good-bye to the *Rights-of-Man*) as suspicious behavior. Likewise, Mackenzie was irked by Spencer's continual breach of naval decorum in singing and joking with "inappropriate" friends, and took this as further proof that Spencer was marshaling the common sailors against him. Both captains act upon what they surmise about the two accused rather than upon certainty.

As the newspapers and independent reports claimed after the *Somers* affair, Mackenzie had inadequate evidence of mutiny. All the men involved denied they were part of a conspiracy. Spencer repeatedly claimed it was all a game. Not one man aboard had actually committed any action that could be interpreted as mutiny. So it is with Captain Vere, whose officers challenge him by saying that Billy intended neither mutiny nor homicide.

The lawless actions of Captain Mackenzie may well have given Melville the idea for Captain Vere's flaunting of the law and custom. Part of this is clear in the abnormal and illegal secrecy of the two captains. As Vere is later criticized for keeping the charges and trial secret from the men, appearing suddenly to tell them they are to witness a hanging, so was Mackenzie. Mackenzie had even gone one step further. He kept the trial secret from the accused. They had no idea they were being tried and thus were not allowed to speak at their own trials. Like Vere, Mackenzie suddenly appeared in full dress uniform the next morning to tell the crew and, in his case, inform the condemned that there will be a hanging in 10 minutes. Obviously, neither Billy nor the three condemned men are provided with a defense.

The assessment of Mackenzie in the *New York Herald* shortly after details of the hangings at sea became known brings up a view of his character and actions that might have remained with Melville when he began to construct the character of Vere. That was the statement that Mackenzie was a slave to order and must have been insane to act as he did.

Finally, immediately after the *Somers* landed in New York, grossly distorted tales that made a monster of Spencer were published in the newspapers, very like the official report published to explain Billy's hanging.

Because of public fascination with the *Somers* case, it is particularly well documented. The first excerpts, from Herman Melville's *White Jacket,* are on the practice of flogging. The second, also from *White Jacket,* are Melville's interpretations of the Articles of War. (Note Melville's oblique but unmistakable reference to the *Somers.*) The third excerpts are from Thurlow Weed's revelations in his autobiography about the opinion of the officers who took testimony from the crew aboard the *Somers.*

FLOGGING IN HERMAN MELVILLE'S *WHITE JACKET*

The record of punishments aboard the *Somers* was appalling to many offi-cers and sailors alike when it was revealed in the ship's log presented at trial. Author and ex-sailor James Fenimore Cooper and others argued that it was not the machinations and influence of Spencer that had caused the crew to become resentful and surly; it was instead the constant, brutal floggings for the most minuscule offense. Mackenzie and his supporters argued that Spencer undermined authority aboard the ship by telling the sailors that the floggings, rather than being necessary discipline, were persecution. But, in response, it was argued that the sailors scarcely needed Spencer to tell them how horrific these punishments were.

In 1849, six years after his voyage aboard the *United States* and six years after the court-martial inquiry into the *Somers* affair, Herman Melville published *White Jacket,* a novel drawn from his experiences aboard the man-of-war. (The American copy appeared in 1850.) It was an exposé of the life of the warship's sailor. Six chapters are devoted to the practice of flogging, a theme that runs throughout the other chapters as well.

The first excerpt from *White Jacket* underscores both the physical and psy-chological devastation of flogging. Not only does flogging ravage the body, it unmans and humiliates the sailor. As Billy had been mortified at the sight of floggings aboard the *Bellipotent,* so is the young character named White Jacket. To underscore the navy's brutality, Melville explains the practice of "flogging through the fleet," which was still permitted by the Articles of War.

In 1850 *White Jacket* was largely responsible for leading the U.S. govern-ment to outlaw flogging.

FROM HERMAN MELVILLE, *WHITE JACKET* (NEW YORK: THE MODERN LIBRARY, 2002), 137–38

Mark, the third prisoner, only cringed and coughed under his punishment. He had some pulmonary complaint. He was off duty for several days after the flogging; but this was partly to be imputed to his extreme mental misery. It was his first scourging, and he felt the insult more than the injury. He became silent and sullen for the rest of the cruise.

The fourth and last was Peter, the mizen-top lad. He had often boasted that he had never been degraded at the gangway. The day before his cheek had worn its usual red, but now no ghost was whiter. As he was being secured to the gratings, and the shudderings and creepings of his dazzlingly white back were revealed, he turned round his head imploringly; but his weeping entreaties and vows of contrition were of no avail. "I would not forgive God Almighty!" cried the captain. The fourth boatswain's mate advanced, and at the first blow the boy, shouting "My God! Oh! my God!" writhed and leaped so as to displace the gratings, and scatter the nine tails of the scourge all over his person. At the next blow he howled, leaped, and raged in unendurable torture.

"What are you stopping for, boatswain's mate?" cried the captain. "Lay on!" and the whole dozen was applied.

"I don't care what happens to me now!" wept Peter, going among the crew, with blood-shot eyes, as he put on his shirt. "I have been flogged once, and they may do it again if they will. Let them look out for me now!"

"Pipe down!" cried the captain; and the crew slowly dispersed.

. . .

THE flogging of an old man like Ushant, most landsmen will probably regard with abhorrence. But though, from peculiar circumstances, his case occasioned a good deal of indignation among the people of the *Neversink*, yet, upon its own proper grounds, they did not denounce it. Man-of-war's men are so habituated to what landsmen would deem excessive cruelties, that they are almost reconciled to inferior severities.

And here, though the subject of punishment in the Navy has been canvassed in previous chapters, and though the thing is every way a most unpleasant and grievous one to enlarge upon, and though I painfully nerve myself to it while I write, a feeling of duty compels me to enter upon a branch of the subject till now undiscussed. I would not be like the man, who, seeing an outcast perishing by the roadside, turned about to his friend, saying, "Let us cross the way; my soul so sickens at this sight that I cannot endure it."

There are certain enormities in this man-of-war world that often secure impunity by their very excessiveness. Some ignorant people will refrain from permanently removing the cause of a deadly malaria, for fear of the temporary spread of its offensiveness. Let us not be of such. The more repugnant and repelling, the greater the evil. Leaving our women and children behind, let us freely enter this Golgotha.

. . .

[T]here still remains another practice which, if anything, is even worse than *keelhauling*. This remnant of the Middle Ages is known in the Navy as *"flogging through the fleet."* It is never inflicted except by authority of a court-martial upon some trespasser deemed guilty of a flagrant offence. Never, that I know of, has it been inflicted by an American man-of-war on the home station. The reason, probably, is, that the officers well know that such a spectacle would raise a mob in any American seaport.

By XLI of the Articles of War, a court-martial shall not, "for any one offence not capital," inflict a punishment beyond one hundred lashes. In cases "not capital" this law may be, and has been, quoted in judicial justification of the infliction of more than one hundred lashes. Indeed, it would cover a thousand. Thus: one act of a sailor may be construed into the commission of ten different transgressions, for each of which he may be legally condemned to a hundred lashes, to be inflicted without intermission. It will be perceived, that in any case deemed "capital," a sailor, under the above Article, may legally be flogged to the death.

But neither by the Articles of War, nor by any other enactment of Congress, is there any direct warrant for the extraordinary cruelty of the mode in which punishment is inflicted, in cases of flogging through the fleet. But as in numerous other instances, the incidental aggravations of this penalty are indirectly covered by other clauses in the Articles of War; one of which authorises the authorities of a ship—in certain indefinite cases—to correct the guilty *"according to the usages of the sea-service."*

One of these "usages" is the following:—

All hands being called "to witness punishment" in the ship to which the culprit belongs, the sentence of the court-martial condemning him is read, when, with the usual solemnities, a portion of the punishment is inflicted. In order that it shall not lose in severity by the slightest exhaustion in the arm of the executioner, a fresh boatswain's mate is called out at every dozen.

As the leading idea is to strike terror into the beholders, the greatest number of lashes is inflicted on board the culprit's own ship, in order to render him the more shocking spectacle to the crews of the other vessels.

The first infliction being concluded, the culprit's shirt is thrown over him; he is put into a boat—the Rogue's March being played meanwhile—and rowed to the next ship of the squadron. All hands of that ship are then called to man the rigging, and another portion of the punishment is inflicted by the boatswain's mates of that ship. The bloody shirt is again thrown over the seaman; and thus he is carried through the fleet or squadron till the whole sentence is inflicted.

In other cases, the launch—the largest of the boats—is rigged with a platform (like a headsman's scaffold), upon which halberds, something like those used in the English army, are erected. They consist of two stout poles, planted upright. Upon the platform stand a lieutenant, a surgeon, a master-at-arms, and the executioners with their "cats." They are rowed through the fleet, stopping at each ship, till the whole sentence is inflicted, as before.

In some cases the attending surgeon has professionally interfered before the last lash has been given, alleging that immediate death must ensue if the remainder should be administered without a respite. But instead of humanely remitting the remaining lashes, in a case like this, the man is generally consigned to his cot for ten or twelve days; and when the surgeon officially reports him capable of undergoing the rest of the sentence, it is forthwith inflicted. Shylock must have his pound of flesh.

To say, that after being flogged through the fleet the prisoner's back is sometimes puffed up like a pillow; or to say that in other cases it looks as if burned black before a roasting fire; or to say that you may track him through the squadron by the blood on the bulwarks of every ship, would only be saying what many seamen have seen.

Several weeks, sometimes whole months, elapse before the sailor is sufficiently recovered to resume his duties. During the greater part of that interval he lies in the sick-bay, groaning out his days and nights; and unless he has the hide and constitution of a rhinoceros, he never is the man he was before, but, broken and shattered to the marrow of his bones, sinks into death before his time. Instances have occurred where he has expired the day after the punishment. No wonder that the Englishman, Dr. Granville—himself once a surgeon in the Navy—declares, in his work on Russia, that the barbarian "knout" itself is not a greater torture to undergo than the Navy cat-o'-nine-tails.

Some years ago a fire broke out near the powder magazine in an American national ship, one of a squadron at anchor in the Bay of Naples. The utmost alarm prevailed. A cry went fore and aft that the ship was about to blow up. One of the seamen sprang overboard in affright. At length the fire was got under, and the man was picked up. He was tried before a court-martial, found guilty of cowardice, and condemned to be flogged through the fleet. In due time the squadron made sail for Algiers, and in that harbour, once haunted by pirates, the punishment was inflicted—the Bay of Naples, though washing the shores of an absolute king, not being deemed a fit place for such an exhibition of American naval law.

While the *Neversink* was in the Pacific, an American sailor, who had deposited a vote for General Harrison for President of the United States, was flogged through the fleet.

. . .

We plant the question, then, on the topmost argument of all. Irrespective of incidental considerations, we assert that flogging in the Navy is opposed to the essential dignity of man, which no legislator has a right to violate; that it is oppressive, and glaringly unequal in its operations; that it is utterly repugnant to the spirit of our democratic institutions; indeed, that it involves a lingering trait of the worst times of a barbarous feudal aristocracy; in a word, we denounce it as religiously, morally, and immutably wrong.

THE ARTICLES OF WAR

Vere is able to coerce the drumhead court into finding Billy guilty of mutiny and condemning him to death by appealing to the Mutiny Act and the Articles of War, but distorting them to serve his own purpose. According to the Articles of War, Vere insists, it does not matter that Billy did not intend to raise a mutiny and did not intend to kill Claggart; the mere act of striking Claggart, his superior, was an act of mutiny.

These articles, in effect, terrorized the crew and abrogated the civil rights of the sailors and soldiers involved. Melville forcefully condemned both in his novel *White Jacket*. As repressive as the Articles of War were in wartime, they were typically enforced on military vessels even in time of peace. Such was the situation aboard the *Somers*.

Mackenzie read the Articles of War aloud to his crew on the first Sunday of every month, making a mockery of the services that followed in praise of the "Prince of Peace."

In the following excerpts, the fictionalized Melville, named White Jacket, points out the lack of justice and impartiality in a totalitarianism state called the man of war.

FROM HERMAN MELVILLE, *WHITE JACKET* (NEW YORK:
THE MODERN LIBRARY, 2002), 143–45, 292–95, 297,
298, 300

Flogging Not Lawful

IT is next to idle, at the present day, merely to denounce an inquity. Be ours, then, a different task.

If there are any three things opposed to the genius of the American Constitution, they are these: irresponsibility in a judge, unlimited discretionary authority in an executive, and the union of an irresponsible judge and an unlimited executive in one person.

Yet by virtue of an enactment of Congress, all the commodores in the American Navy are obnoxious to these three charges, so far as concerns the punishment of the sailor for alleged misdemeanours not particularly set forth in the Articles of War.

Here is the enactment in question.

XXXII. *Of the Articles of War.*—"All crimes committed by persons belonging to the Navy, which are not specified in the foregoing articles, shall be punished according to the laws and customs in such cases at sea."

This is the article that, above all others, puts the scourge into the hands of the captain, calls him to no account for its exercise, and furnishes him with an ample warrant for inflictions of cruelty upon the common sailor hardly credible to landsmen.

By this article the captain is made a legislator, as well as a judge and an executive. So far as it goes, it absolutely leaves to his discretion to decide what things shall be considered crimes, and what shall be the penalty; whether an accused person has been guilty of actions by him declared to be crimes; and how, when, and where the penalty shall be inflicted.

· · ·

It will be seen that the XXth of the Articles of War provides, that if any person in the Navy negligently perform the duties assigned him, he shall suffer such punishment as a court-martial shall adjudge; but if the offender be a private (common sailor), he may, at the discretion of the captain, be put in irons or flogged. It is needless to say, that in cases where an officer commits a trivial violation of this law, a court-martial is seldom or never called to sit upon his trial; but in the sailor's case he is at once condemned to the lash. Thus, one set of sea-citizens is exempted from a law that is hung in terror over others. What would landsmen think, were the State of New York to pass a law against some offence, affixing a fine as a penalty, and then add to that law a section restricting its penal operation to mechanics and day labourers, exempting all gentlemen with an income of one thousand dollars? Yet thus, in the spirit of its practical operation, even thus, stands a good part of the naval laws wherein naval flogging is involved.

· · ·

How is it in an American frigate? Let one example suffice. By the Articles of War, and especially by Article I, an American captain may, and frequently does, inflict a severe and degrading punishment upon a sailor, while he himself is forever removed from the possibility of undergoing the like disgrace; and, in all probability, from undergoing any punishment whatever, even if guilty of the same thing—contention with his equals, for instance—for which he punishes another. Yet both sailor and captain are American citizens.

Monthly Muster Round the Capstan

BESIDES general quarters, and the regular morning and evening quarters for prayers on board the *Neversink*, on the first Sunday of every month we had a grand "muster round the capstan," when we passed in solemn review before the captain and officers, who closely scanned our frocks and trowsers, to see whether they were according to the Navy cut. In some ships, every man is required to bring his bag and hammock along for inspection.

This ceremony acquires its chief solemnity, and, to a novice, is rendered even terrible, by the reading of the Articles of War by the captain's clerk before the assembled ship's company, who, in testimony of their enforced reverence for the code, stand bareheaded till the last sentence is pronounced.

To a mere amateur reader the quiet perusal of these Articles of War would be attended with some nervous emotions. Imagine, then, what *my* feelings must have been, when, with my hat deferentially in my hand, I stood before my lord and master, Captain Claret, and heard these Articles read as the law and gospel, the infallible, unappealable dispensation and code, whereby I lived, and moved, and had my being on board of the United States ship *Neversink*.

Of some twenty offences—made penal—that a sea-man may commit, and which are specified in this code, thirteen are punishable by death.

"Shall suffer death!" This was the burden of nearly every Article read by the captain's clerk; for he seemed to have been instructed to omit the longer Articles, and only present those which were brief and to the point.

"Shall suffer death!" The repeated announcement falls on your ear like the intermitting discharge of artillery. After it has been repeated again and again, you listen to the reader as he deliberately begins a new paragraph; you hear him reciting the involved, but comprehensive and clear arrangement of the sentence, detailing all possible particulars of the offence described, and you breathlessly await, whether *that* clause also is going to be concluded by the discharge of the terrible minute-gun. When, lo! it again booms on your ear—*shall suffer death!* No reservations, no contingencies; not the remotest promise of pardon or reprieve; not a glimpse of commutation of the sentence; all hope and consolation is shut out—*shall suffer death!* that is the simple fact for you to digest; and it is a tougher morsel, believe White Jacket when he says it, than a forty-two-pound cannonball.

But there is a glimmering of an alternative to the sailor who infringes these Articles. Some of them thus terminate: *"Shall suffer death, or such punishment as a court-martial shall adjudge."* But hints this at a penalty still more serious? Perhaps it means *"death, or worse punishment."*

Your honours of the Spanish Inquisition, Loyola and Torquemada! produce, reverend gentlemen, your most secret code, and match these Articles of War, if you can. Jack Ketch, *you* also are experienced in these things!

As, month after month, I would stand bareheaded among my shipmates, and hear this document read, I have thought to myself, Well, well, White Jacket, you are in a sad box, indeed. But prick your ears, there goes another minute-gun. It admonishes you to take all bad usage in good part, and never to join in any public meeting that may be held on the gun-deck for a redress of grievances. Listen:—

Art. XIII. *"If any person in the Navy shall make, or attempt to make, any mutinous assembly, he shall, on conviction thereof by a court-martial, suffer death."*

Bless me, White Jacket, are you a great gun yourself, that you so recoil, to the extremity of your breechings, at that discharge?

But give ear again. Here goes another minute-gun. It indirectly admonishes you to receive the grossest insult, and stand still under it:—

Art. XIV. *"No private in the Navy shall disobey the lawful orders of his superior officer, or strike him, or draw, or offer to draw, or raise any weapon against him, while in the execution of the duties of his office, on pain of death."*

Do not hang back there by the bulwarks, White Jacket; come up to the mark once more; for here goes still another minute-gun, which admonishes you never to be caught napping:—

Part of Art. XX. "If any person in the Navy shall sleep upon his watch, he shall suffer death."

Murderous! But then, in time of peace, they do not enforce these bloodthirsty laws? Do they not, indeed? What happened to those three sailors on board an American armed vessel a few years ago, quite within your memory, White Jacket; yea, while you yourself were yet serving on board this very frigate, the *Neversink?* What happened to those three Americans, White Jacket—those three sailors, even as you, who once were alive, but now are dead? "Shall suffer death!" those were the three words that hung those three sailors.

. . .

Art. XLII. Part of Sec. 3. "In all cases where the crews of the ships or vessels of the United States shall be separated from their vessels by the latter being wrecked, lost, or destroyed, all the command, power, and authority given to the officers of such ships or vessels shall remain, and be in full force, as effectually as if such ship or vessel were not so wrecked, lost, or destroyed."

Hear you that, White Jacket! I tell you there is no escape. Afloat or wrecked, the Martial Law relaxes not its gripe.

The Genealogy of the Articles of War

As the Articles of War form the ark and constitution of the penal laws of the American Navy, in all sobriety and earnestness it may be well to glance at their origin. Whence came they? And how is it that one arm of the national defences of a Republic comes to be ruled by a Turkish code, whose every section almost, like each of the tubes of a revolving pistol, fires nothing short of death into the heart of an offender? How comes it that, by virtue of a law solemnly ratified by a Congress of freemen, the representatives of freemen, thousands of Americans are subjected to the most despotic usages, and, from the dockyards of a Republic, absolute monarchies are launched, with the "glorious Stars and Stripes" for an ensign? By what unparalleled anomaly, by what monstrous grafting of tyranny upon freedom, did these Articles of War ever come to be so much as heard of in the American Navy?

Whence came they? They cannot be the indigenous growth of those political institutions, which are based upon that arch-democrat Thomas Jefferson's Declaration of Independence? No; they are an importation from abroad, even from Britain, whose laws we Americans hurled off as tyrannical, and yet retained the most tyrannical of all.

"HEREIN ARE THE GOOD ORDINANCES OF THE SEA, WHICH WISE MEN, WHO VOYAGED ROUND THE WORLD, GAVE TO OUR ANCESTORS, AND WHICH CONSTITUTE THE BOOKS OF THE SCIENCE OF GOOD CUSTOMS."—*The Consulate of the Sea.*

THE present usages of the American Navy are such that, though there is no government enactment to that effect, yet, in many respects, its commanders seem virtually invested with the power to observe or violate, as seems to them fit, several of the Articles of War.

According to Article XV, "No person in the Navy shall quarrel with any other person in the Navy, nor use provoking or reproachful words, gestures, or menaces, on pain of such punishment as a court-martial shall adjudge."

"Provoking or reproachful words!" Officers of the Navy, answer me! Have you not, many of you, a thousand times violated this law, and addressed to men, whose tongues were tied by this very Article, language which no landsman would ever hearken to, without flying at the throat of his insulter? I know that worse words than you ever used are to be heard addressed by a merchant captain to his crew; but the merchant captain does not live under the XVth Article of War.

GUERT GANSEVOORT'S SECRET

Each of the three men chosen to hear the case of Billy Budd repeatedly make known their grave misgivings about finding him guilty and recommending a hanging at sea. Although Vere instructs them to make a decision before the end of the day, they hesitate and deliberate until Vere intrudes himself into the proceedings to insist on the verdict he wants to hear: that Billy is a danger to the ship and must be strung up as an example to the rest of the crew, to terrorize them into docile behavior.

During Alexander Mackenzie's court-martial, he and the officers aboard the *Somers* stood together in saying that he had appointed them to meet separate from him in hearing testimony regarding Spencer and coming to a decision about what should be done about him. They agreed at the hearings into the captain's behavior aboard the *Somers* that they sent their oral and written decision to Mackenzie recommending, for the safety of the ship, that Spencer, Small, and Cromwell should be hung on the morning of the next day. The impression they gave was that the officers and the captain were in complete accord from the beginning.

But in 1883, 40 years later, the official story presented at the court-martial was called into question for the first time. Thurlow Weed, an important political figure in 1843, had been unable to get anyone in authority to listen to the story that Guert Gansevoort had confided to his cousin just after the *Somers* docked in New York City. So the incident attesting to the officers' serious disagreement with Mackenzie, passed to Weed by Guert's cousin, only became known when Weed's autobiography appeared posthumously.

FROM THURLOW WEED, "THE BRIG *SOMERS*," IN
AUTOBIOGRAPHY OF THURLOW WEED, VOL. 1 (BOSTON:
HOUGHTON MIFFLIN, AND CO., 1883), 515–19

Chapter LI.

1842.

THE BRIG SOMERS.—CAPTAIN MACKENZIE.— PHILIP SPENCER.—
LIEUTENANT GANSEVOORT.

IN 1842 Captain Mackenzie. on his return from the coast of Africa in the United States brig Somers, discovered a mutiny headed by Midshipman Spencer, who with two seamen was arrested and put in irons. A court was immediately organized for their trial, which resulted in their conviction, and their execution immediately followed.

The Somers arrived in New York about the 20th of December. I reached New York on my way to Washington on Sunday morning, the Somers having arrived on Saturday. There was a midshipman on board whose warrant I had obtained, and who was a sort of protégé of mine. Immediately after breakfast I went to the navy yard to see him. Commodore Perry informed me that Captain Mackenzie had gone with his officers to church. but that as soon as they returned he would ask Captain Mackenzie to give Midshipman Tillotson leave to come to the Astor House. As I was leaving the hotel on my way to dinner with my friend Moses H. Grinnell, the young man joined us, and I took him with me to dinner. He was instructed by Captain Mackenzie not to converse on the subject of the mutiny until after the captain's official report had been made. He remarked, however, before he left me, that it required all the officers of the vessel except Captain Mackenzie and himself, the junior midshipman, to constitute a court. He, therefore, was officer of the deck, where Captain Mackenzie remained during the trial. Lieutenant Gansevoort, who presided, came on deck twice during the trial and conferred with Captain Mackenzie. He also stated that the arrest of the accused parties took them all by surprise. Midshipman Spencer was very unpopular with the officers, while Small, one of the sailors who was executed, was greatly liked by officers and crew. After the arrest everything was quiet on board, and there were no signs of insubordination among the crew when their comrades were run up to the yard arm.

On Sunday evening I left New York for Washington, stopping over night at Philadelphia, where I met Passed Midshipman Gansevoort, a cousin of Lieutenant Gansevoort, who was first officer on board the Somers. Both of these officers were from Albany, where I had known them in their boyhood. Of course the Somers affair formed the staple of our conversation. He informed me that his cousin, on his way to Washington with the official dispatch, passed the previous evening with him at that hotel, and at a late hour, and after much hesitation, he had made a revelation to him which he thought proper to make to me as a friend of them and their families. That revelation, as literally as I can remember it. was as follows:—

After the witnesses had all been examined, "I," said Lieutenant Gansevoort to midshipman Gansevoort, "went on deck and informed Captain Mackenzie that the testimony was not as strong as had been represented to him, and that I thought from the indications the court did not attach much importance to it. Captain Mackenzie replied that the witnesses had not been thoroughly examined, and directed me to recall them, and put certain interrogations to them, a copy of which he handed to me. I returned and complied with this request, but elicited nothing more specific than the first examination had brought out. Some general conversation after the conclusion of the testimony satisfied me that the court was not prepared to convict the accused. I again repaired to the deck, and expressed my opinion to Captain Mackenzie, who replied that it was evident these young men had wholly misapprehended the nature of the evidence, if they had not also misapprehended the aggravated character of the offense, and that there would be no security for the lives of officers or protection to commerce if an example was not made in a case so flagrant as this. It was my duty, he urged, to impress these views upon the court. I returned and did, by impressing these considerations, obtain a reluctant conviction of the accused." Passed Midshipman Gansevoort, who gave me this startling narrative, sailed the next day in a United States brig, which, with all on board, was engulfed at sea.

I was greatly disturbed as to the course I ought to pursue in reference to this painful revelation. The father of Midshipman Spencer, Hon. J. C. Spencer, was then Secretary of War. We had been for several years intimately associated in public life, and were warm personal friends. I was to meet him in Washington, and the question with me was whether the above statement ought or ought not to be laid before him. I called at his house, undetermined how to act. The servant, who took my card, returned, saying that Mr. Spencer was engaged. I then asked for Mrs. Spencer, a lady whom I had long esteemed. and from whom it required a strong mental effort to conceal information so important, especially as the conversation turned upon her great bereavement.

It is proper to explain here why Mr. Spencer declined to see me. While Secretary of State of New York, in the preceding month of September, Mr. Spencer received a letter from President John Tyler, inviting him to become his Secretary of War. Mr. Spencer brought the letter directly to me, saying that it was a delicate question, on which he wanted advice. I suggested a consultation with his colleagues in the State administration. to which he assented. I therefore invited Governor Seward and such other Whig State officers as were in the city to dinner that day. Vice-President John Tyler, who had succeeded to the presidency on the death of General Harrison, was in collision with the Whig Congress, and was rapidly incurring the displeasure of the Whig party. Mr. Spencer expressed the hope that he would be able, with a seat in the cabinet, to reconcile these differences, or at least, as he phrased it: "bridge over" the breach between the President and the Whigs of this State. In this Mr. Spencer was perfectly sincere, though with our knowledge of his political eccentricity of character none of us doubted that from the moment he entered Mr. Tyler's cabinet he would zealously espouse and warmly defend Mr. Tyler's views and policy. Knowing that Mr. Spencer could not resist the temptation of a cabinet office, our advice was of course in accordance with his wishes. Mr. Spencer, whose trunk was already packed, started for Washington that evening in the steamer. I accompanied him, at his request, to New York, sitting till a late hour in his state room listening to his programme for the political regeneration at Washington.

In October, 1842, Mr. Spencer appeared unexpectedly at Albany. Summoning me to his apartment, he astonished me with the outline of a speech which he had come to deliver at a Whig meeting in Schoharie County. He was evidently quite as much astonished when I informed him that whilst his speech would be accepted by a Democratic audience, it would be indignantly repudiated by Whigs. Of course we separated, after some further conversation, "agreeing to disagree," and Mr. Spencer's contemplated speech took the form of a letter, and appeared in a Tyler organ. Soon after his return to Washington he requested my friend, Christopher Morgan, then a member of Congress from Cayuga County, to write to me, saying that I had "become so obnoxious to the President that my appearance in Washington would seriously embarrass him (Spencer), and to request me not to come there." But notwithstanding this, I had occasion to visit Washington in December, when Mr. Spencer declined to see me, thus depriving himself of the opportunity of proving at the court of inquiry, subsequently held on Captain Mackenzie, that his son had been unjustly executed.

While the court was holding its sittings at the Brooklyn Navy Yard, a sense of justice involuntarily drew me thither, intending either to offer myself as a witness to Mr. Morris, the son-in-law of Mr. Spencer, who was managing the prosecution, or to suggest questions to be put to other witnesses. But Mr. Morris, whom I had known intimately, understanding, if not sharing in Mr. Spencer's feelings of hostility, declined to recognize me, and I returned again disappointed. In the following summer, at Boston, in visiting the United States seventy-four-gun ship Ohio, I encountered Lieutenant Gansevoort, and invited him to dine with me at the Tremont House. At dinner the sad fate of his kinsman was spoken of, when I remarked that I had passed the evening with him previous to his sailing from Philadelphia, adding that we sat gossiping over our hot whiskey punch into the small hours. The lieutenant, with evident surprise, asked, with emphasis, "Did he tell you that I passed the previous night with him?" I answered in the affirmative. He said, "What else did he tell you?" I replied, with equal emphasis, "He told me all that you said to him about the trial of Spencer." Whereupon he looked thoughtfully a moment, then drank off his champagne, seized or raised the bottle, again filled his glass and emptied it, and, without further remark, left the table.

I did not see him again for seven years,—seven years which had told fearfully upon his health and habits. In the last years of his life, when he was stationed at the Brooklyn Navy Yard, then a sad wreck of his former self, he came frequently to see me, but was always moody, taciturn, and restless. In my conversations with him I never again referred to this affair. Nor do I know that he ever spoke of it to others. But I do know that a bright, intelligent, high principled, and sensitive gentleman, and a most promising officer of the navy, spent the best part of his life a prey to unavailing remorse for an act the responsibility of which belonged to a superior officer.

Public opinion was at the time, and has always remained, much perplexed with regard to the motives which prompted Captain Mackenzie to this unusual act of severity, and, although acquitted by a naval court of inquiry, that lenient judgment was never quite in accordance with popular feeling. It is obvious, from the narrative which I have now given, that there was no necessity for or justice in the execution of the alleged mutineers, one of whom, Small, a great favorite with the crew, exclaimed, "God bless the flag!" at the moment he was run up to the yard-arm. I never coincided in the opinion which attributed the execution to cowardice on the part of Captain Mackenzie. I could not then and cannot now resist the belief that he was influenced by ambition for the *éclat* which would follow the hanging of a son of the Secretary of War as a pirate. Captain Mackenzie was Alexander Slidell, a brother of John Slidell, United States senator from Louisiana. He appended the surname of Mackenzie to his own for the purpose of availing himself of a legacy bequeathed on that consideration by a relative.

QUESTIONS AND PROJECTS

1. Have a committee of no more than five compose a dramatization of the court-martial of Captain Mackenzie. A good source book is *Proceedings of the Court of Inquiry* (Delmar, N.Y.: Scholars Facsimiles and Reprints, 1992), but make dramatic changes where needed. Cast and produce the play.

2. Stage a debate between James Fenimore Cooper and William Sumner over the question of whether Mackenzie was justified in his actions. Do research on how the episode was interpreted by the two men, but use your own arguments.

3. Write an in-depth comparison of Captain Vere and Captain Mackenzie.

4. Have a debate on the following question: Did the men of the *Somers* become surly and dissatisfied because of Spencer or because of the floggings?

5. Each of the students in class should be responsible for one chapter of Melville's *White Jacket* (covering all chapters) and make a report to the class. Answer this question: How is this chapter relevant or helpful in the study of "Billy Budd"?

6. Some critics have argued that Melville was probably sympathetic with Mackenzie. Others claim that evidence points to an opposite view. On the basis of your own reading of "Billy Budd" and what you have read and heard about *White Jacket,* what is your opinion and why?

7. Sailors have created ballads about the *Somers,* just as Melville composed one for Billy Budd. Have a class ballad contest to judge the best ballad composed on the subject.

8. Write an essay on Guert Gansevoort. Do you tend to criticize him for his actions or justify him?

9. Interview someone who knows a lot about history—your parents; your history, English, or American Studies teacher; or anyone else knowledgeable. Ask them for ideas about any prominent person in history who was libeled in the public press, perhaps even persecuted, before the real truth emerged about them. One hint: you will often find such people in the ranks of civil rights or labor leaders. Write up your findings.

FURTHER READING

Brown, Bob. *Not One Shred of Decency.* Kingston, Tenn.: River City Books, 2000.

Franklin, Frederick. *The Captain Called It Mutiny.* New York: Washburn, 1954.

Guttridge, Leonard F. *Mutiny: A History of Naval Insurrection.* New York: Berkley, 1992.

Ives, C. B. *"Billy Budd* and the Articles of War." In *Critical Essays on Melville's Billy Budd, Sailor,* ed. Robert Milder. Boston: G. K. Hall and Co., 1989.

McFarland, Philip. *Sea Dangers.* New York: Schocken Books, 1985.

Melton, Buckner F. *A Hanging Offense.* New York: Free Press, 2003.

Proceedings of the Court of Inquiry Appointed to Inquire into the Intended Mutiny on Board the United States Brig of War Somers. 1843 Reprint, Delmar, New York: Scholars' Fascimiles and Reprints, 1992.

Proceedings of the Naval Court Martial in the Case of Alexander Slidell Mackenzie. 1844. Reprint, Delmar, N.Y.: Scholars' Facsimiles and Reprints, 1999.

Reynolds, Larry J. "*Billy Budd* and American Labor Unrest: A Case for Striking Back." In *New Essays on Billy Budd,* ed. Donald Yannella. Cambridge, England: Cambridge University Press, 2002.

12

The Mutiny Act and the Patriot Act

> War looks but to the frontage, the appearance. And the Mutiny
> Act, War's child, takes after the father. (363)

This chapter, which applies issues in "Billy Budd" to contemporary life, centers on the topic of the government's abrogation of individual civil liberties in threatening times. In the wake of the French Revolution and the mutinies at the Spithead and the Nore, the Mutiny Act, a more severe "child" (as Vere called it) of the Articles of War, was used to deprive Billy Budd of the basic legal rights afforded Englishmen since the signing of the Magna Carta. A similar situation arose in October 2001, when the U.S. Congress passed the Patriot Act in response to the bloody attacks on the World Trade Center and the Pentagon and the crash of a passenger jet in a planned attack on another federal building. The situations are not completely comparable, of course. Nevertheless, they hold certain problems in common. Both the Mutiny Act and the Patriot Act seemed to arise from stark fear rather than from knowledge and wisdom. In "Billy Budd," the perceived terrorists are primarily those foreign to England, especially Europeans and the Irish, who had been inspired by the French Revolution to demand representative government. Although working-class Englishmen also read Thomas Paine and were angry over their situations, it was often claimed that any discontent arose from foreigners. Note that the false story printed about Billy Budd after his death states that he is not really an Englishman:

> [T]hough mustered into the service under an English name, the assassin was no
> Englishman, but one of those aliens adopting English cognomens whom the
> extraordinary necessities of the service have caused to be admitted into it in con-
> siderable numbers. (383)

There were, of course, many native Englishmen who were also involved in the mutinies and were extremely bitter about impressment and conditions aboard warships, but, as often happens in cases of revolt, the authorities insist to the public that the locals—local laborers or local African Americans, for example—are really satisfied with conditions as they are; the trouble, they insist, comes from "outside agitators."

Immediately after the attacks on September 11, 2001, people known to be Arabs or who appeared to be Middle Eastern, whether or not such individuals were actually dangerous, were targets of assaults by citizens in the United States. On the basis of appearance, there was considerable racial profiling and humiliation of Arabs trying to board airplanes, for example, even after it was determined that they were not carrying weapons. The preface of the Patriot Act actually addresses this problem, decrying public retaliation against all Middle Easterners.

Nevertheless, the Patriot Act is frequently regarded as the modern equivalent of the Mutiny Act, so prominent in "Billy Budd," because it calls for the suspension of some of those civil rights so basic to a democracy. In both cases, times regarded as desperate have led to desperate measures. As Vere argues, martial law supersedes natural law, moral law, and the law of the courts. At one extreme in the eighteenth century, martial law resulted in the continual kidnapping of poor men to serve at sea. In the specific case of Billy Budd, the Mutiny Act allows him to be imprisoned without evidence of mutiny, tried in total secrecy by a drumhead court that is ordered not to consider circumstantial evidence, nor to call witnesses, nor to provide him with a defense. The fundamental question is, how does one balance security against basic civil liberties?

Excerpts from the following documents illuminate the similarity between the origin and operation of the Mutiny Act and the Patriot Act. First is an excerpt from the legislation itself; second, excerpts from a review of recent books analyzing the Patriot Act; and, third, an article reporting the use of the Patriot Act against a group of United States citizens demonstrating for peace.

"THE UNITING AND STRENGTHENING AMERICA BY
PROVIDING APPROPRIATE TOOLS REQUIRED TO
INTERCEPT AND OBSTRUCT TERRORISM ACT OF 2001,"
OTHERWISE KNOWN AS THE USA PATRIOT ACT

Although no one, including Vere, believes that Billy Budd is guilty of either murder or mutiny, Vere is still able to convict and execute him on the basis of the Mutiny Act. England is at war with France, and desperate times call for desperate measures. So even though Billy has never intended either mutiny or homicide, he must be sacrificed. Vere makes this clear when he intrudes on the deliberations of the men called upon to make the decision:

> [B]efore a court less arbitrary and more merciful than a martial one, that plea [for his innocence] would largely extenuate. At the Last Assizes [in heaven] it shall acquit. But how here? We proceed under the law of the Mutiny Act. In feature no child can resemble his father more than that Act resembles in spirit the thing from which it derives—War. . . . War looks but to the frontage, the appearance. And the Mutiny Act, War's child, takes after the father. (363)

Vere is explaining that in grave times, natural, moral and courtroom law have to be sacrificed. Most people assumed after 9/11 that measures had to be taken to better protect the country from further attacks. Investigations suggest that the attacks could well have been prevented had the government kept better track of known and admitted terrorists and had foreseen that dangerous weapons should not have been allowed aboard airplanes and in other public buildings. After the attacks, citizens certainly agreed that reasonable and effective measures should be put into place, that airport security should be increased, and that noncitizens would likely come under greater scrutiny.

But the Patriot Act, passed shortly after the attack, went far beyond effective and reasonable measures, and in the process abrogated legal rights and the rights of free speech and assemblage.

A number of political writers in the winter and spring of 2003 found fundamental provisions of the Patriot Act to be not only unconstitutional but seriously dangerous to American society. For instance, the Patriot Act gives power to the president to seize the property of anyone suspected of planning activities hurtful to the United States. Having seized the property of the suspect, the president can use federal agencies that report to him—the FBI and CIA, for instance—to liquidate or sell that confiscated property.

How are these agencies to know which people in this or any other nation are suspect? The Patriot Act gives the government the authority to place cameras wherever it chooses for the purpose of surveillance. These agencies may intercept "wire, oral, and electronic communications," seemingly without evidence that a crime is being committed. Financial institutions must hand over a person's personal financial records and other documents in their possession if there is the least suspicion that that person has voiced complaints about the government. Hypothetically, someone who secretly or openly dislikes you can secretly notify law enforcement that you are a dangerous person and need to be investigated, and it would be done. Note that as in the days of Alexander Mackenzie, just speaking one's mind is sufficient to prompt an investigation.

Educational institutions—technical schools, junior or community colleges, private colleges and universities—are subject to the disclosure policies of the Patriot Act, and, if asked, are required to hand over the personal and academic records of students and faculty. Have you ever complained about some practice of the government? Have you ever joined a protest of any kind? The FBI may demand the written comments of your teachers, counselors, or coaches.

Librarians are required to monitor the reading habits and Web interests of their patrons. The American Library Association has vehemently protested this provision of the Patriot Act, and significant numbers of librarians have vowed they will not cooperate.

The element of secrecy prevails here as it did in the days of Captain Vere and the Mutiny Act. That is, institutions from which information has been demanded are bound by the terms of the act to keep the investigation secret from the person being investigated.

FROM "THE UNITING AND STRENGTHENING AMERICA BY PROVIDING APPROPRIATE TOOLS REQUIRED TO INTERCEPT AND OBSTRUCT TERRORISM ACT OF 2001," OTHERWISE KNOWN AS THE USA PATRIOT ACT, 107TH CONG., 1ST SESS., H. R. 3162, IN THE SENATE OF THE UNITED STATES (24 OCTOBER 2001)

An Act

To deter and punish terrorist acts in the United States and around the world, to enhance law enforcement investigatory tools, and for other purposes. Be it enacted by the Senate and House of Representatives of the United States of America in Congress assembled,

. . .

Presidential Authority . . .

Section 203 of the International Emergency Powers Act (50 U.S.C. 1702) . . . (C) when the United States is engaged in armed hostilities or has been attacked by a foreign country or foreign nationals, [the president may] confiscate any property, subject to the jurisdiction of the United States, of any foreign person, foreign organization, or foreign country that he determines has planned, authorized, aided, or engaged in such hostilities or attacks against the United States; and all right, title, and interest in any property so confiscated shall vest, when, as, and upon the terms directed by the President, in such agency or person as the President may designate from time to time, and upon such terms and conditions as the President may prescribe, such interest or property shall be held, used, administered, liquidated, sold, or otherwise dealt with in the interest of and for the benefit of the United States, and such designated agency or person may perform any and all acts incident to the accomplishment or furtherance of these purposes.

...

Title II—Enhanced Surveillance Procedures

Sec. 201. Authority to intercept wire, oral, and electronic communications relating to terrorism.

Sec. 202. Authority to intercept wire, oral, and electronic communications relating to computer fraud and abuse offenses.

Sec. 203. Authority to share criminal investigative information.

...

SEC. 501. [THE GOVERNMENT IS PROVIDED] ACCESS TO CERTAIN BUSINESS RECORDS FOR FOREIGN INTELLIGENCE AND INTERNATIONAL TERRORISM INVESTIGATIONS.

(a)(1) The Director of the Federal Bureau of Investigation or a designee of the Director (whose rank shall be no lower than Assistant Special Agent in Charge) may make an application for an order requiring the production of any tangible things (including books, records, papers, documents, and other items) for an investigation to protect against international terrorism or clandestine intelligence activities, provided that such investigation of a United States person is not conducted solely upon the basis of activities protected by the first amendment to the Constitution. p. 10

...

(d) No person shall disclose to any other person (other than those persons necessary to produce the tangible things under this section) that the Federal Bureau of Investigation has sought or obtained tangible things under this section. 19

...

SEC. 351. AMENDMENTS RELATING TO REPORTING OF SUSPICIOUS ACTIVITIES.

(a) AMENDMENT RELATING TO CIVIL LIABILITY IMMUNITY FOR DISCLOSURES- Section 5318(g)(3) of title 31, United States Code, is amended to read as follows:

(3) LIABILITY FOR DISCLOSURES-

(A) IN GENERAL- Any financial institution that makes a voluntary disclosure of any possible violation of law or regulation to a Government agency or makes a disclosure pursuant to this subsection or any other authority, and any director, officer, employee, or agent of such institution who makes, or requires another to make any such disclosure, shall not be liable to any person under any law or regulation of the United States, any constitution, law, or regulation of any State or political subdivision of any State, or under any contract or other legally enforceable agreement (including any arbitration agreement), for such disclosure or for any failure to provide notice of such disclosure to the person who is the subject of such disclosure or any other person identified in the disclosure.

. . .

SEC. 411. DEFINITIONS RELATING TO TERRORISM....

(IV) to read as follows: (IV) is a representative...of...

(aa) a foreign terrorist organization, as designated by the Secretary of State under section 219, or

(bb) a political, social or other similar group whose public endorsement of acts of terrorist activity the Secretary of State has determined undermines United States efforts to reduce or eliminate terrorist activities,

. . .

has used the alien's position of prominence within any country to endorse or espouse terrorist activity, or to persuade others to support terrorist activity or a terrorist organization, in a way that the Secretary of State has determined undermines United States efforts to reduce or eliminate terrorist activities, or

(VII) is the spouse or child of an alien who is inadmissible under this section, if the activity causing the alien to be found inadmissible occurred within the last 5 years;

SEC. 507. DISCLOSURE OF EDUCATIONAL RECORDS

(A) collect education records in the possession of the educational agency or institution that are relevant to an authorized investigation or prosecution of an offense listed in section 2332b(g)(5)(B) of title 18 United States Code, or an act of domestic or international terrorism as defined in section 2331 of that title; and (B) for official purposes related to the investigation or prosecution of an offense described in paragraph (1)(A), retain, disseminate, and use (including as evidence at trial or in other administrative or judicial proceedings) such records, consistent with such guidelines as the Attorney General, after consultation with the Secretary, shall issue to protect confidentiality.

'(2) APPLICATION AND APPROVAL-

'(A) IN GENERAL- An application under paragraph (1) shall certify that there are specific and articulable facts giving reason to believe that the education records are likely to contain information described in paragraph (1)(A).

. . .

(3) PROTECTION OF EDUCATIONAL AGENCY OR INSTITUTION- An educational agency or institution that, in good faith, produces education records in accordance with an order issued under this subsection shall not be liable to any person for that production.

. . .

SEC. 355. AUTHORIZATION TO INCLUDE SUSPICIONS OF ILLEGAL ACTIVITY IN WRITTEN EMPLOYMENT REFERENCES.

Section 18 of the Federal Deposit Insurance Act (12 U.S.C. 1828) is amended by adding at the end the following:

'(w) WRITTEN EMPLOYMENT REFERENCES MAY CONTAIN SUSPICIONS OF INVOLVEMENT IN ILLEGAL ACTIVITY-

'(1) AUTHORITY TO DISCLOSE INFORMATION- Notwithstanding any other provision of law, any insured depository institution, and any director, officer, employee, or agent of such institution, may disclose in any written employment reference relating to a current or former institution-affiliated party of such institution which is provided to another insured depository institution in response to a request from such other institution, information concerning the possible involvement of such institution-affiliated party in potentially unlawful activity.

. . .

Passed the House of Representatives October 24, 2001.
Attest:
JEFF TRANDAHL,
Clerk.
END

ETHAN BRONNER, "CIVIL LIBERTIES AND THE WAR ON TERRORISM"

Three elements that arise in Bronner's review of books on the Patriot Act are especially pertinent to "Billy Budd": the opportunity for blanket charges against citizens to be made without legal investigations, the ability of the government to arrest and imprison individuals indefinitely without bringing charges or allowing them a defense, and the abrogation of legal rights by allowing investigations to proceed in secrecy.

In Ethan Bronner's review of books on the Patriot Act, he contends that it should be expected that after the attacks of 9/11, some freedoms and conveniences would have to be sacrificed. But, he writes, the Patriot Act went far beyond measures that most citizenry could agree was necessary or even effective. The act took away basic rights of privacy, freedom of speech, freedom of assembly, trial after arrest, and not being held in prison indefinitely.

Bronner draws attention to the two-and-a-half-year imprisonment in Guantanamo Bay in Cuba of hundreds of prisoners captured during the first year of the war in Afghanistan. Here they have remained without being charged, tried, or legally defended. He also cites the arrests and continuing imprisonment of individuals on minor immigration infractions. There is also the case of Jose Padilla, an American citizen, who has been held for 20 months without being charged.

Bronner also cites provisions in the Patriot Act that allow what seems to be limitless surveillance on ordinary citizens. One's financial records, purchases, educational records, reading habits, use of the Web, and medical records are all subject to scrutiny without one's knowledge.

FROM ETHAN BRONNER, "CIVIL LIBERTIES AND THE WAR ON TERRORISM," *NEW YORK TIMES,* 22 FEBRUARY 2004

Every time we use a cell phone, strike a computer key or do business with a bank, we leave retrievable digital marks.

. . .

If the government is investigating you, the amount of information about your interests, actions and whereabouts it can gather is staggering. In effect, [Christian] Parenti notes, routine digital surveillance is everywhere—credit cards, workplace ID's, gym memberships, health insurance records and internet accounts.

. . .

Of course, keeping terror suspects imprisoned for years without access to lawyers may seem like a more serious problem than on-line companies tracking your purchases... But like the complaints about the muzzling of the media, both smack of Big Brother. And, in the end, that is what ties all these books together—the concern that under the threat of militant Islamic terrorism, we are handing over the keys of our souls to the state and corporations, and we don't even realize it.... The message of all these books can be summed up in five simple words: be worried, be very worried.

. . .

In *Enemy Aliens,* David Cole...focuses on the most egregious outrages of 9/11—the way in which thousands of foreigners have been rounded up, held without charge or on minor immigration violations, and simply forgotten.... I am horrified that the prisoners at Guantanamo have not been charged or given access to some judicial forum to make their case. But it is far from clear to me that they should be treated precisely as American citizens should be. Nevertheless, Cole's indictment of the way we have handled foreign captives is accurate and sears the conscience.

THE ATTACK ON PROTESTERS

Two of the main issues broached in "Billy Budd" are war and patriotism. In the eighteenth-century context, patriotism means one thing only: unquestioning allegiance to the king. In two instances, patriotism is associated in "Billy Budd" with Claggart, the embodiment of evil. An early instance of Claggart's patriotic zeal has irritated Vere. A later reference comes in the "News from the Mediterranean" that cites Claggart's "strong patriotic impulse" (383). The article then refutes the statement of Dr. Samuel Johnson that patriotism is the last refuge of a scoundrel, a statement with which, on the contrary, the author seems to agree.

Perhaps what Dr. Johnson meant was that patriotism, in any era, is likely to become politicized, especially in times of national crisis. At the time of "Billy Budd," those who fight without complaint in the king's wars, to enlarge or secure his royal empire, are considered patriotic. These were private wars that brought no benefit whatsoever to the common people, who merely served as cannon fodder. And patriotism at this time was a complicated business, for so many soldiers and sailors were forced into service. What of their patriotism? Those who willingly gave their lives for the king were loyal. Those who wanted peace were unpatriotic.

War is clearly disparaged by Melville in "Billy Budd" as being anti-Christian (opposite of the Prince of Peace) and even atheistic—the most appropriate name for a warship is the *Atheist.*

The loyalty of those who struggle for peace and denounce war is inevitably questioned by governments that wage war. One of the clearest illustrations of the conflict between the military and workers for peace came in the twentieth century with massive protests against the Vietnam War. The government regarded peaceniks as little more than criminals, and used law enforcement to spy on these groups, undermine them in the press, and arrest them by the hundreds.

On February 5, 2004, a bad dream—one that had haunted those in opposition to the Patriot Act—became a reality. The government's targets were not al-Qaeda-trained, bomb-carrying terrorists. They were peace activists, some of them college students at Drake University in Des Moines, Iowa, who had staged a nonviolent rally the previous November. The government, without revealing any charges against them, ordered them to appear in court and subpoenaed their educational records held by Drake University. The university, cognizant of the provisions of the Patriot Act, agreed to hand over the records, but not without protest. With vigorous objection by civil liberties organizations, the government rescinded its subpoenas on February 11, 2004. The following is an article from *The Des Moines Register,* reporting on the background of the subpoenas and the response to them.

FROM JEFF ECKHOFF AND MARK SEIBERT, "DES MOINES ACTIVISTS ORDERED TO TESTIFY IN US COURT," *THE DES MOINES REGISTER* (IOWA), 5 FEBRUARY 2004

Three Des Moines peace activists have been subpoenaed to appear before a federal grand jury next week as part of an investigation that the activists believe is being conducted by the FBI's Joint Terrorism Task Force. Activists Brian Terrell, Patti McKee and Elton Davis say they have been ordered to testify in federal court Tuesday about something documents describe only as a "possible violation of federal law."

Authorities also have subpoenaed membership and meeting records involving the Drake University chapter of the National Lawyers' Guild, a 65-year-old legal organization that frequently has been involved in social activism and the defense of public protesters. Government Officials won't say what kind of crime the investigation involves. But activists say the subpoenas were delivered by Jeff Warford, a Polk County sheriff's detective, who reports on a day-to-day basis, to the federal terror task force. "We're just speculating on what his MOTIVE may be," Terrell, a member of the Catholic Peace Ministry and frequent war protester, said Wednesday. "I think it's just part of the fact that more and more authorities are seeing dissent as criminal."

A sheriff's department spokesman referred all calls to the U.S. attorney's office. Stephen Patrick O'Meara, U.S. attorney for the Des Moines-based southern district of Iowa, said government rules don't allow him to comment on the subject matter of any grand jury. "We can't acknowledge that a matter is or is not under investigation," O'Meara said. "We can't acknowledge really any subject matter before the grand jury, whether it's in a general description or any specific testimony."

Local peace activists say they worry that the subpoenas are part of an effort to discourage protests against America's actions in Iraq. Sally Frank, a Drake University law professor who several times has defended war protesters in court, said that "one can only assume that (the grand jury) is an attempt to put a chill on the peace movement in Iowa." Heidi Boghosian, a spokeswoman for the New York office of the National Lawyers' Guild, said the subpoenas seek all records that would identify the officers of the Drake chapter in November 2003, the current location of any local offices, "as well as any meeting agenda or annual reports of this organization."

Frank, who is a local contact for the guild, said protesters believe that federal lawyers provided the Polk County attorney's office with a copy of an activist's e-mail intending to announce a series of anti-war events the weekend of Nov. 15–16. On that weekend, protesters from across Iowa came to Des Moines for a conference called "Stop the Occupation! Bring the Iowa Guard Home!" Activists met at Drake that Saturday for workshops, and then about 70 of them protested Sunday outside the Iowa National Guard headquarters in Johnston. A dozen people were arrested, including Davis.

One woman was charged with assault. Terrell was present and was quoted in a newspaper article, although he was not arrested.

Frank acknowledged Wednesday that activists had been concerned for months about official scrutiny of their actions, and are seeking information on any other intercepted e-mail. Copyright © 2004, *The Des Moines Register*

QUESTIONS AND PROJECTS

1.   Write a worst-case scenario of what the Patriot Act could allow to happen to a high school student who expressed an unpopular opinion. Could a disgruntled classmate "get back" at someone by using the Patriot Act?

2.   Secure a complete copy of the Patriot Act and have a well-prepared debate on whether the canceling of civil rights is justified by the need for security.

3.   Write an extensive article comparing Vere's argument in favor of the Mutiny Act and Ashcroft's brief for the Patriot Act.

4.   Read George Orwell's *1984* and write an analysis of it in light of the Patriot Act.

5.   Do a search through the *New York Times* for articles on the controversy surrounding the imprisonment of Jose Padilla.

6.   Create your own class television show by choosing a host and inviting two well-known community members who are familiar with the law (but who have opposite opinions about the Patriot Act) to argue the issue.

FURTHER READING

Brown, Cynthia, ed. *Lost Liberties: Ashcroft and the Assault on Personal Freedom.* New York: New Press, 2004.

Cole, David. *Enemy Aliens: Double Standards and Constitutional Freedoms in the War on Terrorism.* New York: New Press, 2004.

Dodge, David. *Casualty of War: The Bush Administration's Assault on a Free Press.* Amherst, N.Y.: Prometheus Books, 2004.

Hentoff, Nat. *The War on the Bill of Rights.* New York: Seven Stories Press, 2004.

Heymann, Philip B. *Terrorism, Freedom, and Security: Winning without the War.* Cambridge, Mass.: MIT Press, 2004.

Leone, Richard C., and Greg Anrig Jr., eds. *The War on Our Freedoms: Civil Liberties in an Age of Terror.* New York: Century Foundation, 2004.

Parenti, Christian. *The Soft Cage: Surveillance in America from Slavery to the War on Terror.* New York: Basic Books, 2004.

Rosen, Jeffrey. *The Naked Crowd: Reclaiming Security and Freedom in an Anxious Age.* New York: Random House, 2004.

Index

The Greenwood Press "Literature in Context" Series
Student Casebooks to Issues, Sources, and Historical Documents

About the Author

CLAUDIA DURST JOHNSON, former chairperson of English at the University of Alabama, is an independent scholar and freelance writer in Berkeley, California. Her many books include *Youth Gangs in Literature* (2004), *Understanding The Odyssey* (2003), and *Daily Life in Colonial New England* (2002), all available from Greenwood Press.